War Resisters League Organizer's Manual

D1211115

Edited by Ed Hedemann

War Resisters League   **New York, NY**

First Edition, July 1981, 3000 copies
Revised Edition, February 1986, 3000 copies
Published by the War Resisters League, 339 Lafayette
Street, New York, NY 10012

Library of Congress Catalog Card No.: 85-52418

International Standard Book Number: 0-940862-03-4

Design by Susan Pines and Peg Averill
Cover design by Ben Hillman
Typeset and printed by Faculty Press, Brooklyn, NY 11218

Dedication

There is no more fitting person than William Douthard to whom to dedicate this book. He was a tireless organizer from his pre-teen years in Birmingham right through the civil rights movement, the movement against the Indochina War, and the anti-nuclear movement. William wrote the chapter on "Working with Minority Communities" two months before his death, on January 4, 1981. In his last communication with the WRL office he said he planned to participate in the mass civil disobedience, should one be organized, during the 1982 UN Special Session on Disarmament, despite his increasingly-demanding job with the State of New York. William's humor mixed with his outrage at injustice was a most effective combination to disarm those who disagreed with him. His sudden death is a serious loss not only to the War Resisters League, on whose Executive Committee he served, but to the nonviolent movement as a whole.

ACKNOWLEDGMENTS

The chapter on "Conducting a Vigil" was reprinted with permission of Charles Walker. The "Street Meeting" chapter was reprinted with permission of George Lakey, David Richards, and the Friends Peace Committee. About a dozen chapters have been updated and edited from the earlier version of this manual. Ann Davidon proofread some of the chapter manuscripts. Lauri Lowell and Wendy Schwartz aided in proofing of some of the galleys. Elliot Linzer contributed a lot of time in a hurry to put together the index. Thanks to *WIN* Magazine for permission to reprint a number of graphics and photos. All the contributors are to be thanked for their patience with the merciless prodding from the WRL office. Ben Hillman, the cover artist, was provided courtesy of Gallery 345. Susan Pines was indispensable in helping with production such as specifying type, coordinating of typesetting, proofing, and making design suggestions. And finally, Grace Hedemann contributed considerable enthusiasm and skill in research and selection of graphics and photos, often with little notice.

CONTENTS

LITERATURE PRODUCTION

ACTION

WORKING WITH THE ESTABLISHMENT

Introduction

My first effort at organizing was in the fall of 1970 when my wife, Grace, and I began a group called "Direct Action" on the University of Texas campus at Austin. We were trying to mobilize students to oppose the Indochina War through non-payment of the telephone tax, and participation in a 5-mile march from the Southwestern Bell Telephone office to the IRS regional headquarters.

We issued four leaflets, set up a literature table, collected signatures on a petition (which formed the basis of our first mailing list), established an office of sorts, and talked with friends. For our first meeting we reserved a room big enough to hold 50 in the student union, and painfully hand lettered 20 posters with magic markers which were promptly posted around campus the day before the meeting.

Arriving early to put out the literature, we waited nervously for the room to fill. As time wore on, we became crestfallen and embarrassed as only one person stopped by, just long enough to pick up literature and then leave.

In retrospect, it is easy to see our mistakes. Reading the chapters in this manual such as "Leaflets and Posters,"

"Organizing a Local Group," and "Media," would have helped to avoid some of those mistakes.

However, all was not lost. Through persistence, many more mistakes, and then improvements in our organizing techniques, we eventually filled that room of 50.

Organizing runs counter to many common conventions, often reflected by such sayings as "Don't rock the boat" and "You can't fight city hall." Many people feel that it is the job of government and politicians to look after us. Even those who recognize that we must struggle to achieve change, often figure that once something has been won, we don't have to worry about it.

At best, organizing is a radicalizing experience—people seeking to change fundamentally their lives and the conditions in which they live. The best way to learn how to organize, of course, is to do it. But it's surprising how frequently those who wish to organize lack the confidence, or figure another person is better "so why should I bother?" This manual seeks to develop confidence in all who wish to organize. And since there is no single correct way to organize, suggestions or things to keep in mind when writing a press release, organizing a rally, etc., are provided.

The original form of this book, first assembled over seven years ago, was conceived by former WRL staff member Jerry Coffin to be a "working manual." It was assembled in a 3-ring binder so that chapters could be added from time to time. However, this has proven to be very expensive and inefficient in production.

But the idea of a working manual is still appealing. So this book has been designed with a lot of space in the outer column of each page to accomodate notes and updated information.

The Manual is divided into six parts—politics, basic organizing techniques, constituencies, literature production, action, and working with the establishment. The six sections notwithstanding, some chapters could easily have been placed in more than one category. So the divisions are somewhat arbitrary.

Because WRL does not view its organizing in a void, we have included the "Politics" section. Nonviolence as a philosophy unites all WRL members. The visions expressed in the Socialism or Anarchism chapters are those of a large number of WRL activists. And the Feminism chapter reflects the rapidly growing feminist constituency in WRL, and is especially appropriate considering WRL was founded largely through the efforts of three feminists: Jessie Wallace Hughan, Frances Witherspoon, and Tracy Mygatt.

The section on "Basic Organizing Techniques" contains the essential elements of meetings, organizational structure, fundraising, speaking, etc.—things to do and skills to have for any successful organization.

"Constituencies" focuses on the special concerns and needs of particular segments of our society. The chapters stress, especially, the need to be sensitive to cultural differences when organizing with various constituencies.

In the "Literature Production" section, organizers are encouraged to explore the creative possibilities of silk screening and block printing as inexpensive methods to produce posters and T-shirts. Of course, the bulk of this section is concerned with the basics of leaflet design, printing, distribution, etc.

What distinguishes the War Resisters League from most peace groups—most groups, period—is our emphasis on action, in addition to education. The "Action" section of the Manual is an encouragement for organizers to act on their convictions. In particular, it is hoped that organizers will develop *campaigns*, when and where possible.

The movement frequently is divided over how much to get involved with the establishment. This manual does not seek to take sides in that dispute, but simply offers suggestions on how to use establishment channels. And that is the purpose of the final section "Working With the Establishment."

Recognizing that if we are to make fundamental changes in this country we need more local organizers and more effective organizing, the War Resisters League offers this book as a contribution to that end.

Ed Hedemann
June 1981

This revised edition differs from the first edition primarily by corrections of typographical errors; updating of resources and references; substantial revisions of the "Notes on Public Speaking," "War Tax Resistance," "Theater for Use," and "Feminism" chapters; and minor revisions of some other chapters.

E.H.
March 1986

Politics

NONVIOLENCE

By Ed Hedemann

There are four standard responses to a conflict situation*: ignore it and not become involved; give in and beg for mercy; get the hell out of there; and fight back violently. There is a fifth response, often ignored and little understood: nonviolence. Nonviolence excludes neutrality, excludes capitulation, excludes flight, and excludes fighting violently.

Because nonviolence has the power to make fundamental changes without personal threat or sacrificing militance, because nonviolence contrasts dramatically with the methods of the powers-that-be, and because nonviolence is so often misunderstood, this organizer's manual would be incomplete if the nuts and bolts of organizing contained herein were not put in the context of a broader vision of social change.

Standard Perceptions of Nonviolence

Most people understand "nonviolence" to be passive or that which is not violent. At the same time some of these people will often perceive a nonviolent action as being violent. A 1969 survey revealed that 58% of American males viewed draft card burnings as violent, while 57% felt that police shooting looters was not violent.†

Most movement people are able to see beyond these misunderstandings of violence and nonviolence. But they often identify nonviolence with a number of other myths, which frequently prevents adequate experimentation and exploration of effective ways to achieve fundamental social change.

Myths About Nonviolence

Passive

Passivity—a form of violence—is the opposite of nonviolence. The use of nonviolence does not mean avoidance of conflict, but a different approach to conflict, through militant nonviolent struggle if necessary.

Reformist

Many feel nonviolence is simply prayerful action and petitioning to what is assumed to be responsive and benevolent authorities, thereby reinforcing and strengthening the oppressors.

Nonviolence at its most creative seeks to make radical changes in society—altering even the methods of overcoming oppression and achieving justice.

A Way To Avoid Harm

Though likely to result in fewer casualties, nonviolence does not guarantee no one will be hurt. Those primarily interested in personal safety should stay home. As Barbara Deming said, "Nonviolent battle is still battle...people do get hurt."*

Suicidal

A common view of nonviolent struggle is that it is suicidal: "relying on nonviolence means being defenseless—sheep being led to slaughter."

Adopting a nonviolent discipline will generally result in fewer casualties, in the long run, since opponents cannot as easily justify the use of violence against people who are not physically threatening them.

"A nonviolent revolution is not a program of seizure of power. It is a program of transformation of relationships, ending in a peaceful transfer of power."

M.K. Gandhi

---

*Lanza del Vasto, "Definitions of Nonviolence"
†*Science News,* July 3, 1971, pp. 14-15

Revolution and Equilibrium, 1968.

"Nonviolence to be a potent force must begin with the mind. Nonviolence of the mere body without cooperation of the mind is nonviolence of the weak or cowardly and therefore has no potency. If we bear malice and hatred in our bosoms and pretend not to retaliate, it must recoil upon us and lead to our destruction."

—M.K. Gandhi

Just a Tactic

On a purely mechanical or tactical level, nonviolence can be of considerable value. However, its greatest effectiveness comes when it is persistently clung to, even in the face of violent repression. It is not a method of the weak or cowardly. Nonviolence is also not a substitute method to punish, harass, or seek vengeance over an opponent. It is a way to achieve justice through seeking to change, rather than conquer, the antagonist.

If it is seen as only a tactic, then it may well be discarded when the going gets rough, rather than carried to a logical conclusion.

History of Mass Nonviolent Action

The use of nonviolence is as old as, or older than, recorded history—and so is violence. There have been numerous instances of people who have courageously and nonviolently refused to cooperate with injustice.

However, what is relatively new in the history of nonviolent action is the fusion of nonviolence with mass struggle. Organized warfare is 30 centuries old, but organized mass nonviolent action as we know it is less than one century old. The synthesis of mass struggle with nonviolence was developed largely by Mohandas Gandhi beginning with the onset of the South African campaign for Indian rights in 1906.

Gandhi continued to experiment and develop mass nonviolence in the 28-year struggle for Indian independence from the most powerful nation on the face of the earth, Great Britain. From the beginning of the first nationwide civil disobedience campaign in 1919 to independence in 1947, India was transformed from a splintered, downtrodden mass of people to a unified, self-respecting society largely through nonviolent action. This was not without incredible suffering at the hands of the British imperialists: 300,000 jailed (100,000 alone in the year-long Salt campaign); hundreds killed; many more beaten, injured, and abused; and property confiscated.

Since 1906, mass nonviolent struggle was used successfully in many different social and political situations. The militant campaign for women's suffrage in Britain included a variety of nonviolent tactics such as boycotts, noncooperation, limited property destruction, civil disobedience, mass marches and demonstrations, filling the jails, hunger strikes, and disruption of public ceremonies.

The United States labor movement has used nonviolent action with great effectiveness in a number of instances, such as the Industrial Workers of the World (IWW) free speech confrontations in Spokane, San Diego, Fresno, etc.; the Congress of Industrial Organizations (CIO) sit-down strikes from 1935 through 1937 in automobile plants; the UFW grape and lettuce boycotts; and, of course, the strike.

Using mass nonviolent action, the civil rights movement changed the face of the South. The Congress of Racial Equality (CORE), initiated nonviolent action for civil rights with sit-ins and an interracial, interstate "freedom ride" in the 1940's. The successful 1956 Montgomery bus boycott electrified the nation. Then, the early 1960's movement exploded with nonviolent action: sit-ins at lunch counters and other facilities, organized by the Student Nonviolent Coordinating Committee (SNCC); Freedom Rides through the South organized by CORE; the nonviolent battle against segregation in Birmingham, Alabama, by the Southern Christian Leadership Conference (SCLC); the 1963 March on Washington, which drew 250,000 participants; and the voting rights drives in the early sixties.

Opponents of the Vietnam War employed the use of draft card burnings, draft file destruction, mass demonstrations (such as the 500,000 who turned out in 1969 to protest the Vietnam War in Washington, D.C.), sit-ins, blocking induction centers, draft and tax resistance, and the historic 1971 May Day traffic blocking in Washington, D.C., in which 13,000 people were arrested.

Nonviolent action has also led to the overthrow of authoritarian regimes in Germany (1920), Guatemala (1944), and Iran (1979); and the creation of instability for such regimes in Saigon (1963), Russia (1917), and Norway (1942), among other countries.

Methods

The variety of nonviolent methods and tactics is about as limited as the imagination. Gene Sharp has isolated 198 distinct methods* which have been used in the past. What follows is Sharp's categorization of the types of nonviolent action:

---

*The Politics of Nonviolent Action, volume 2: Methods; 1973.

PROTEST AND PERSUASION
leafleting, picketing, marches, teach-ins

NONCOOPERATION

Social
student strike, social boycott

Economic
tax resistance, consumer boycotts,
labor strikes

Political
draft resistance, civil disobedience of
"illegitimate" laws

INTERVENTION
civil disobedience of "neutral" laws,
nonviolent blockage, sit-in,
nonviolent obstruction.

The Politics and Dynamics of Nonviolence

In order to use nonviolence effectively, an understanding of the basic concepts and operating dynamics is essential. What is described below represents one brief formulation of the fundamental elements of nonviolence and how it works. This formulation is derived from an analysis of power, an understanding of human nature, a study of history and politics, a theory of nonviolence, and experimentation through practice.

Ends and Means. If we wish to achieve a society without wars, violence, and injustice, then it is counterproductive to use wars, violence, and injustice. What we do and how we do it determines what we get. Nonviolence is rooted in the understanding that ends and means are fundamentally linked, and are simply different forms of the same thing; means are ends in the making.

Separation of the Role from the Person. Nonviolence recognizes that the system or the injustice is the problem which needs to be overcome, not the individual. An individual committing an injustice needs to be confronted and changed, not killed. Simply changing the personnel in an oppressive system, without changing the existing power relationships or structure of the system, will not end the injustice.

Nonviolence seeks a victory over injustice, not vengeance or punishment. Opponents are more likely to change if offered a way out, rather than backed up against a wall under personal attack, so that they continue to fight violently well beyond the point of reason.

Nature of Power. * The theory of nonviolence is based on the understanding that all power depends completely on the obedience, consent, and/or cooperation of the governed. The power of governments is often so fragile that if a small but significant number of the governed were to disobey or noncooperate, the government would have to change, or collapse.

Conflict and Struggle. Recognizing that those who oppress have seldom willingly stopped their oppression, we must be willing to engage in a struggle to overcome injustice whatever its manifestation (whether that be war, sexism, racism, classism or any other form of violence and domination). Nonviolence seeks to resolve conflicts, not avoid them. Passivity in the face of injustice is complicity with it. To quote Barbara Deming again, "The challenge to those who believe in nonviolent struggle is to learn to be aggressive enough."

Nonviolence Is More Than a Tactic. To use nonviolence solely on a tactical basis is like saying "I'll use nonviolence at the moment, but I'll have a knife behind my back, just in case." The assumption is that violence is not nice, but more effective; and there exists a willingness to abandon nonviolence should the opportunity present itself. In order for nonviolence to be truly effective, the user must have enough confidence in it to persist in its use—especially at the point where the challenge is the toughest and the stress is the highest.

More Control. † The more the real issues are dramatized and the struggle separated from the personal, the more control those in nonviolent rebellion gain over their adversary. In a violent struggle, the adversary is put on the defensive, reacting out of resentment and desperation. The violence often escalates with both sides becoming more entrapped in a scenario which neither chose.

A greater pressure of defiance can be placed on opponents; if we simultaneously show a respect for their lives they are less likely to react out of fear and more likely to listen to us. Thus one major barrier in the path of change is removed.

Undercut Support of Opponent. Even if nonviolence cannot persuade an oppressor, its use will begin to erode support

"Without a direct action expression of it, nonviolence, to my mind, is meaningless."

—**M.K. Gandhi**

---

*Gene Sharp, *The Politics of Nonviolent Action,* volume 1: Power and Struggle, 1973.

†Extracted largely from Barbara Deming, "On Revolution and Equilibrium," 1968.

from the oppressor. An antagonist will find it harder to justify the use of violence. Nonviolence can move into action on our behalf those who are not naturally inclined to act for us. The more support our opponents lose, the less likely they will be able to sustain their oppression, and the more they will be forced to change. A desirable outcome of a conflict depends not only on the unity and morale of one side, but also on the morale—or lack of it—on the other side.

Liberation Struggles

Some pacifists feel that all violence should be equally condemned no matter the ends or the circumstances which lead to the violence. Violence of the oppressed is just as reprehensible as violence of the oppressor.

However, the War Resisters League believes it is impossible to be morally neutral. Our unwavering commitment to nonviolence does not mean that we are hostile to revolutionary movements. Clearly we have to distinguish between the violence of the current regime in South Africa—which is criminal—and that of those struggling against it—which, by contrast, is tragic.

Those who remain neutral are to a degree complicit with the status quo which perpetuates violence. While we do not support the violent means used by some movements, we do support their objective in seeking liberation from oppression.

The greatest single contribution we can make to liberation movements is not by becoming entangled in the debate over whether or not such movements should use violence, but by actively working to bring an end to colonialism, imperialism, racism, and sexism. This can be accomplished by attacking the factors and social conditions which drive people towards the tragedy of violence, often seeming to exclude options they might otherwise have of nonviolent social revolution.

"We salute those people who are using nonviolent action in their struggle despite the current trends and pressures towards violence. We also salute our brothers and sisters in the various liberation movements. We will work with them when it is possible—but without yielding up our belief that the foundation of the future must be laid in the present, that a society without violence must begin with revolutionists who will

not use violence."*

Nonviolence Controversies

The nonviolence movement, as any other movement, contains a variety of differences and controversies. Listed below are some of the most prominent ones.

Persuasion vs. Coercion

Some nonviolence advocates (particularly religious pacifists) feel that change should be attempted only through conversion of, love for, and persuasion of an opponent. Love prevents the development of fear and anger. Coercion is violent and is less likely to bring about permanent change.

Such arguments do not recognize that nonviolent action, while more aggressive, is no more violent than persuasion. Coercion is often essential in campaigns to end oppression, which may have long been entrenched through vested interests. Persuasion may not be sufficient to get the attention of opponents, let alone change them. The use of nonviolent force in a creative manner may provide a way to break through barriers often thrown up by adversaries.

Secrecy

Some actions—particularly ones which are small in number rely heavily on surprise for their success. In totalitarian societies, it is difficult to accomplish anything with openness. Getting Jews out of Nazi Germany would have been impossible without secrecy.

On the other hand, secrecy breeds mistrust among friends, and encourages fear and government spying, sometimes leading to violence. Effective nonviolent activity can be carried out even in totalitarian countries without secrecy. Secrecy generally runs counter to our intention of building an open and honest society (means and ends).

Property Destruction

Property destruction or sabotage is likely to escalate the struggle to a level where we may lose control. In a property-conscious society, such an act may be extremely provocative. It is usually not necessary to achieve our goals (e.g., we can climb a fence, rather than cut it, to

*From a working document of War Resisters' International Council, Vienna, 1968.

"At this point in our history, nonviolent action had better be taken boldly or one need hardly bother to take it at all, for one will be taking it alone."

—Barbara Deming, 1968

gain access to a site).

On the other hand, some property has no right to exist (e.g., nuclear weapons, napalm, electric chairs). Other property, such as fences around nuclear power plants or military bases, while "neutral," serve only to protect facilities which are harming all of us. The concern is not their destruction, but how they are destroyed. No one has suggested blowing them up or indiscriminate property destruction, but a calm deliberate cutting of a fence with a minimum of hardware can gain entry into a site otherwise not accessible.

Anger*

Anger and hatred are often the bases of violence, putting opponents on the defensive, inhibiting dialogue, and placing additional barriers in the way of constructive change. Hatred clouds thinking and does not separate the person from his or her role. It weakens the distinction between ego-tripping and social change.

On the other hand, anger and hatred can be separated. Anger can serve a good purpose if it is channeled into constructive action, and aids in motivating the desire for change.

Suffering

If there is no other choice, we must be prepared to undergo suffering (e.g., fasting, being beaten) rather than inflict it on others. Suffering for a good cause can build discipline, and may also rouse considerable sympathy of friends and even opponents. All of us endure some measure of suffering—whether that of a soldier undergoing the rigors of boot camp or battle, or the discomforts many of us impose on ourselves through various disciplines or exercise to improve ourselves. This ability to accept suffering can be put to good use when an injustice is being resisted, though its main purpose should be to *prevent* suffering of others, rather than to draw attention to our own suffering.

Suffering to gain sympathy can easily be seen as masochistic, if it is sought for itself rather than accepted in the course of a positive action. Deliberate self-mutilation or self-destruction is generally an act of desperation and a type of aggression turned inward, which is perceived (often rightly) as hostile and coercive, therefore having a negative effect. In extreme situations, however—such as those of the Buddhist monks in Vietnam—self-destruction may appear to be the only course of action, especially if it is in the context of a cultural tradition. In general one must weigh the particular situation in trying to determine to what extent one's acceptance of suffering is necessary and effective (though the latter is not always calculable), or to what extent it may be self-serving and masochistically out of proportion to the principle for which one is demonstrating.

Further Reading

This chapter has been far too brief to give anyone unfamiliar with nonviolence an adequate understanding of its history and politics. The reader is encouraged to explore the following books and articles.

Revolution and Equilibrium, Barbara Deming, 1968. This is one of the best essays on the dynamics of nonviolence. Essential reading. Part of A.J. Muste Memorial Institute Series.

On Wars of Liberation, A.J. Muste Memorial Institute Series. Three essays on pacifist response to armed freedom struggles.

The Handbook of Nonviolence, Robert Seeley, 1986. Includes Aldous Huxley's classic 104-page "An Encyclopedia of Pacifism."

The Politics of Nonviolent Action, Gene Sharp, 1973. A lengthy (900 pages), but thorough, analysis of the nature of power, the dynamics of nonviolence, and variety of nonviolent methods.

Conquest of Violence: The Gandhian Philosophy of Conflict, Joan Bondurant, 1965. One of the best political analyses of Gandhian nonviolence.

The Power of Nonviolence, Richard Gregg, 1966. A classic study and explanation of the psychology of nonviolence.

The Power of the People, edited by Robert Cooney and Helen Michalowski, 1977. The most readable and graphic account of history of nonviolent action in the United States.

Nonviolent Resistance, M.K. Gandhi, 1951. A collection of essays giving a basic understanding of Gandhi.

"Nonviolent action is a means of combat, as is war. It involves the matching of forces and the waging of 'battle,' requires wise strategy and tactics, and demands of its 'soldiers' courage, discipline, and sacrifice.

"This view of nonviolent action as a technique of active combat is diametrically opposed to the popular assumption that, at its strongest, nonviolent action relies on rational persuasion of the opponent, and more commonly it consists simply of passive submission.

"Nonviolent action is just what it says: action which is nonviolent, not inaction. This technique consists, not simply of words, but of active protest, noncooperation, and intervention.

"Overwhelmingly it is group or mass action."

—Gene Sharp

---

*See "On Anger," *Liberation,* Barbara Deming, 1971.

SOCIALISM

By David McReynolds

I begin with the reasonable assumption that you may know very little about socialism and quite possibly the little you know is wrong. You should begin with the reasonable assumption that something really important usually cannot be explained in a few pages. It requires not only more study, but also practice. Because one thing socialism is not—it is not an academic subject. It shares with pacifism the characteristic of *being involved with changing the way things are.* Marx said it: "Before us, philosophers sought to explain the world; we seek to change it." Lenin said it—and Gandhi and Mao said it in somewhat different ways—that unless one tests theory against practice, the theory has no value.

You may think socialism means that the State will own your collection of records, strangers will walk onto your family farm and walk off with your cows, police will arrest you for wrong thought, your children will be taken by the State, all private business will be outlawed, and churches will be closed. None of these things represent socialism. (Some of these things did happen in the Soviet Union—and China—in a special category, and I'll take them up in a moment.)

One of the books you may want to read is *To the Finland Station* by Edmund Wilson, which gives a long sweep of history from the earliest beginnings of socialist thought to the thunderous moment of the Russian Revolution. You may also want to get hold of the WRL *Reading List* which lists several exceptionally good books on the socialist experience and the events in Russia and China, some not in print but available at good libraries. This article can only introduce you to the topic. It can coax you toward the door—but to open that door and enter into the theory and action of socialism, and to join in shaping history, is something only you can do.

What Is Socialism?

It is the social ownership and democratic control of the means of production. It is easier to state this than define it. Socialists do not agree on whether workers should directly own the factories they work in, whether the community as a whole should own the factories in that community, or whether the government should own the means of production.

The answers are harder to find now than in the beginning of the socialist movement. In the middle of the last century there were farmers, there were the small number of men who actually owned the property, and there were workers—men, women and children who worked in mines, in steel mills, in shipyards, in great clanging noisy factories. There were very few "service" workers—school teachers, bank clerks, social workers, barbers, publicity agents, etc. The number of people who engage in "productive" labor—who actually at the end of the day have changed a log into slabs of wood, or taken ore and made it into steel—has dropped. It is harder to imagine workers today taking over the factories—because most workers don't work in factories. They work in offices, shops, etc. Our society today is a great deal more complex than it was when Marx made his critique of capitalism.

It is difficult to imagine—today—workers rushing into the factories, hoisting the red flag, and "taking control." I think the experience in the Soviet Union should make us equally skeptical about letting the State take over things and run them "for us." It was all very well for Lenin to talk about "seizing State pow-

---

"Before us, philosophers sought to explain the world; we seek to change it."
—Karl Marx

Socialism is the social ownership and democratic control of the means of production.

Our society today is a great deal more complex than it was when Marx made his critique of capitalism.

er"—but it turned out the "State" is not a piece of machinery which our side can use as easily as "their side." The problem with prisons, for example, is not that "the wrong people are in them," but that prisons are the wrong solution for the problem. There just isn't any right way, or clever way, to use prisons. I think we will have some use for governments for quite a long time to come—socialists are not anarchists. We will need to use governments to collect garbage, educate our children, provide farmers with weather information, and a great many other things. But if the government is given the job of owning the means of production then the real power goes to the government—it is a Marxist axiom that where economic power is, there will you find political power. (Pacifists have learned this in our work in fighting the military—their economic power to give out military contracts translates into political power to intimidate members of Congress by threatening to withdraw military contracts from their districts.) The problem with the state socialism of the Soviet Union is that political power ends up in the hands of the one party that is allowed to operate, because that party—the Soviet Communist Party—controls the State and the State owns the factories. *All* political power in the Soviet Union is concentrated in the hands of the Party. Workers do not run their own factories—they work for the State, which is not a great deal different from any other boss. (Bad as the situation in the Soviet Union is, there are at least two things which have been taken care of. There is no permanent ruling class which can pass on power through inherited wealth. There is an upper class, and it takes special advantages of its position, it tries to get its children into the best schools, etc., but compared to the enormous power of the DuPonts, the Mellons, and the Rockefellers, the Soviet ruling class has very limited ability *to transmit its power.* Lenin did not leave behind a private fortune, nor did Stalin. The other thing the Soviet Union has done very effectively is end the pattern of "boom or bust." There is essentially full employment, full medical coverage, and enough to eat—though a great lack of variety.)

The Irrationality of Capitalism

Socialism should have two objectives. One is to "rationalize" the economy—though in some ways I think we really mean to make the economy respond to moral values. It is irrational when our society generates a need for a product solely in order to make a profit. It is particularly irrational when that product kills people. The best case in point would be cigarettes. In 1920 very few women smoked—smoking was a male habit. Cigarette firms saw a mass market waiting to be tapped, they sold women on the idea of reaching for a cigarette instead of a candy, of using cigarettes to be fashionable. It worked. Profits went up—and so has the rate of lung cancer and heart disease among women.

An equally disturbing example of the irrationality of capitalism is that it produces for profit, not need. At first glance it seems reasonable enough no one will produce if they can't get a fair price for their product. But far too often we have seen capitalism produce champagne when it wasn't producing enough milk for babies—because the babies (and their parents) were too poor to pay for the milk, but those with great wealth could afford the champagne. This is an example of an "irrational" economy, which has its priorities mixed up. Any economy which delivers champagne and cadillacs to the wealthy and cannot get medical care and housing to the poor is irrational and immoral. It is working for the minority and against the majority.

Socialists would, therefore, "rationalize" the production and distribution of goods and services to make sure that production was for social need rather than private profit.

This is not so easy to do. In capitalism the "market" allocates goods and services and socialists probably would need to use an economy which permits *some* play to market forces. But a socialist society would not be a society geared to *creating* new products which people did not need. In a fundamental sense a socialist society would be *less materialistic* than a capitalist society. The quality of education, of medical care, of the arts would have greater value in economic planning than the sheer production of tangible *goods*, such as cars or televisions with annual changes in the model, and every model offered in five colors.

I think most socialists would agree that for a long period of time to come—certainly for our life times—we will have enough trouble taking over ownership of the top 500 corporations, and simply do not have time *now* to debate whether a business that hires 100 workers should be socialized. That simply isn't an urgent question. So socialism does *not* mean that every single business from the corner barber shop to General Motors

Socialism does not mean that every single business from the corner barber shop to General Motors will get "taken over by the workers."

If David Rockefeller asks if I would seize his toothbrush the answer is no, but if he asks if I would take his bank, the answer is yes.

We want workers to run and own the factories not only because that is more "rational," but because we seek to end the alienation of workers from the means of production.

will get "taken over by the workers." (In any case the "workers" already own that barber shop on the corner.) Socialism is a question of how *we* take control of the *basic parts* of our economy: the steel plants, coal mines, autos, chemicals, oil.

Socialists and Private Property

Right away you can see that socialists do *not* want to seize your aunt Milly's candy store with her two helpers or your uncle Walter's machine tool shop with its ten workers. (Ironically aunt Milly and uncle Walter are safer with socialism than capitalism—because capitalism tends to drive small business to the wall, while socialists prefer to see the variety of a society which is economically pluralistic. MacDonalds hamburger stands have driven the small coffee shop bankrupt.)

Socialists have no interest in your *private* property. I don't want your toothbrush and I don't think you want mine. You can keep your collection of Bing Crosby and Elvis Presley and I'll keep my Pink Floyd and Beethoven. But if you just happen to own General Motors, then it is true socialists would take it away from you. If David Rockefeller asks if I would seize his toothbrush the answer is no, but if he asks if I would take his bank, the answer is yes. A socialist society would take his bank away

from him. Because he never *earned* that bank, it was created by the sweat of the working class, and the wealth and power of Chase Manhattan bank must be placed under the control and ownership of the working class.

Note how often I refer to working people or the working class. The socialist movement is based on the working class. We want workers to run and own the factories not only because that is more "rational" but because our second objective is to end the alienation of workers from the means of production. Before capitalism, workers did own the means of production. The potter owned the kiln, the potters wheel, and skill. He or she put these together and made pots and sold them and took satisfaction in seeing a pot through from the casting to the firing to the sale. There was a sense of pride, *of wholeness*, to what the worker did. Then capitalism introduced the factory system in which the man who had large amounts of capital bought the means of production. (Today one must have a vast fortune to own the means of production—a potter needed only the wheel and a kiln, but to open a steel mill requires an investment of hundreds of millions of dollars!) The early capitalist bought the machines and hired men and women and children to work in the factories at machines which they did not own. They did not have control over production from beginning to end—some workers would make one part of the product, other workers another part.

When the assembly line was invented the worker was completely alienated, standing all day in one spot doing, again, and again, and again, a single simple action. Capitalism first reduced the worker to one factor of the productive process—"labor"—and the worker, having lost control of the means of production, had to sell his or her labor or starve. Next, the assembly line broke down the tasks into small and simple things which even workers who were not clever could do. The worker—a human being—had become a cog in the machine of production. Machines were not built to human scale—people were used in ways that were most effective for machines. (Charlie Chaplin made his laugh and cry when he did a movie about this—"Modern Times.")

Involved in this is a sense both of alienation that workers experienced, and of raw anger and rage that the Marxist movement has expressed against capitalism for the human freedom it took from the worker. Once the worker could offer a finished product to the market for sale, saying "this pot was shaped by me, designed by me, and I am proud of it." Now the worker can only say "I didn't even know what it would look like when it was done—I just tightened one screw as it went past."

In such a society it is hard to have values. Who is to blame? Who is responsible? The rise of someone such as Hitler becomes easy, and the terrible excuse "I only followed orders" becomes understandable. Capitalism trains men and women to follow orders. (Capitalism is only *part* of the problem—technology itself can be dehumanizing in socialist as well as capitalist societies.)

Let me sum up where we have gone thus far. Socialism means that the basic means of production will be owned in some way by society. I would hope in a decentralized way, with ownership located in the community. Second, socialism means that the workers will have the *primary* role in running the factories. Third, socialism is not concerned with your toothbrush—but with factories, with oil wells, steel mills, *means of production*, with *social wealth*, not private goods. Kenneth Patchen, the poet, said it perfectly when he said "no man can own what belongs to all." Factories, by their nature, belong to the community.

Socialism and Freedom

Fourth, socialism believes in political freedom, in religious freedom (and *also* in the freedom not to be religious), in free speech, in democracy. How else can we run a society if we cannot openly and vigorously debate the issues? And who wants to live in a society which is not free? Socialists have traditionally stood for greater political freedom. It has been capitalists who sought laws to repress dissent, and socialists which have sought to have more debate and discussion.

I have said socialists would plan the economy with greater stress on human need than on private profit. Let me carry that a step further. I personally love gadgets and new things—"toys for grown men." But socialism would not lay stress on creating needs that did not exist. I can make a powerful case that the human spirit cries out for beauty, theatre, art, poems, music, dancing. The business of a radical movement is to affirm that people need bread—*and roses*. And the right to choose the color of the roses for themselves, or to choose carnations instead of roses. A society will be judged primarily on how well it meets those needs. All of history tells me that human beings grope toward this light. But I will tell you that history gives me no evidence at all that people hunger for a low-tar filter cigarette. I think a socialist society would be bad at producing such trivia. Please don't misunderstand me—producing such trivia wouldn't be illegal, it just wouldn't have a priority.

Socialism would not solve our problems. People would still be lonely, would drink too much, would be . . . people. But socialism would make sure everyone had a job, had medical care, had housing, and in a sense we would find out what people were really made of when the material needs were met. The paradox is that we materialists—and I am a Marxist and a materialist—are vastly *less* materialistic than the capitalists. I believe people are motivated by *more* than the profit motive. I believe people care about more than simply the material side of things. We may be wrong. But let us liberate the human race from the primary concern with making sure they get enough to eat and see if they care, as I believe they do, for a little music.

Up to this moment all history has been a struggle over who controlled the means of production. Socialism sets the stage for the next step in history. And no one knows what kind of history will be created. Socialism won't solve our problems—but it is a precondition for creating a *human* society which has an orientation other than entirely material concern.

Capitalism trains men and women to follow orders.

Socialism believes in political freedom, in religious freedom, in free speech, in democracy.

Socialism would not lay stress on creating needs that did not exist.

Though socialism would not solve all our problems, it would make sure everyone had a job, medical care, housing, and other material needs.

Russia and China

Now let's turn to Russia and China, to Marxism, Marxist-Leninism, and then wrap it up and go to bed. (Or I'm going to bed, you can jolly well do what you want.) There isn't any question that Russia has done us a lot of harm, those of us who are socialists. Folks say "oh you mean that nonsense over there, where workers get shot if they strike and writers get jailed if they dissent?" I do not know anyone in the world who wants to repeat the Russian experience. But let's not be quite so self-righteous. From the *white male* point of view our own Revolution looked pretty good—but you need to remember we carried into our Revolution a lot of trash from the pre-revolutionary society. Slavery. Voting permitted only by men. (And only for men with property!) The Russians carried a lot of Russian habits into their revolution. None of that takes away from the drama that in October of 1917 the workers of Russia actually set up the first workers' state. Whatever its faults, and problems—and later the crimes—it was a moment of supreme drama. But Russia failed to produce a democratic socialist society for a lot of reasons, two of which stand out clearly. There was absolutely no tradition of democracy in Russia or in the revolutionary party led by Lenin. The revolution was led by men and women who hoped *later* to introduce democracy. But they did not practice it themselves and Russia simply had no experience of it.

Second, Russia had a very small working class. It was largely a peasent economy, and Marx had written of socialism as something which came first to the most industrialized nations—to Germany, France, England, or America. Not to Russia. Lenin himself never expected the Revolution to last unless it could spread to Germany. He looked on the Soviet Revolution as a kind of holding action, and for months and months he waited—in vain—for the working class of Western Europe to take power. Lenin knew that "socialism in one country" would be impossible—and he was correct.

Isolated, cut off by a trade blockade imposed by the West, barely surviving the Western military intervention that tried to topple it, Lenin's revolutionary regime turned inward. Whatever democratic tendencies it had were destroyed by a combination of outside pressure seeking to destroy the first workers' state, and the internal problems of Lenin's own anti-democratic tendencies. Some of the problems with Lenin's theories were outlined in Issac Deutcher's study of Trotsky, an exciting three volume work. And of course Rosa Luxemburg, the great Polish Marxist revolutionary leader, pointed clearly to the dangers in Lenin's approach to revolution. That danger rested in Lenin's theory that his party was the "vanguard," that it had a scientific answer to social problems, and that because it was a vanguard party made up of professional, trained revolutionists, it was logical that instead of the working class selecting its own leadership, the Bolshevik Party should appoint itself to the leadership and rule in the name of the working class—ultimately to *rule over the working class.* Most socialists—whether Marxists or non-Marxists—felt that the working class should argue things out, and stumble toward the best possible solution after debate, that the mass—"the uninstructed and non-professional mass"—would make many, many mistakes, but as Rosa Luxemburg argued, the mistakes made by the working class were vastly more valuable than the most correct position handed down by a Central Committee. To those of us who are not Leninists, the ideas come from the community, the leadership is selected by working people. Change will occur slowly, with many mistakes. But without political prisoners, without summary executions, without the silencing of the poets.

Non-Leninist Marxism

I suspect many of you, when you hear the word "Marxist" assume it means "Marxist-Leninist"—as I've tried to suggest there is another tradition which, while respecting Lenin, broke with him on the role of the Party, how it should be organized, and how much democracy would be allowed within the Party and within a socialist society. This other side of socialism is seen in Scandanavia, in the British Labour Party, in the Canadian New Democratic Party, in Japan, in parts of Latin America. None of those parties is perfect—some of these parties are pretty bad. (The German Socialist Party backs nuclear power and if I had time and space I could list a good many sins of these parties.) What I have never understood is why some on the Left dismiss the Swedish Socialist Party because there hasn't been a "proper Revolution." Most Russians would prefer to live in Sweden, if they could, or at least to have

The Russians carried a lot of Russian habits into their revolution.

Russia failed to produce a democratic socialist society because, among other reasons, it had no tradition of democracy in Russia.

One of the dangers in Lenin's approach to revolution was that his party was the "vanguard," which should rule in the name of—later, in place of—the working class.

the problems of Swedish socialism. Sweden has had no violent upheaval, no executions, it doesn't lock up right wing opponents. Our party there even loses elections sometimes! (One must admit at once that it has been a great deal easier for the Swedish socialists to provide a good and decent life—they did not suffer from World War II. However, the Swedish example, compared to American society, shows how much better things could be here if we had a socialist government.)

Again to summarize, there are Marxists, such as myself, who strongly believe in democracy. There are socialists who do not feel fully in agreement with Marx's philosophy—and who also share a deep belief in democracy. (One advantage in Wilson's *To the Finland Station*, mentioned earlier, is that it lifts up Marx's concern for the liberation of humanity, and restores for us Marx as he appeared at the time—not the Marx we are offered too often by too many "Marxists" or by the media—dogmatic, anti-democratic, and violent.) Those who take the general position of Lenin, the Marxist-Leninists, are simply not as committed to democracy and human rights—or mean something different than I do when they use those terms. The governments of Vietnam, of Cuba, of China, etc., share with the Soviet Union a belief in a one-Party system, and are willing to use the prisons to silence dissent.

Nothing is ever as simple as it appears. For the issue of Leninism is certainly being re-examined, and it is just not possible to dismiss any and all Marxist-Leninists as anti-democratic. We have the Italian Communist Party, which has been clear that it does want a "plural" society. We have the Japanese and Australian Communist Parties, which broke with Moscow's political line and are searching for the contemporary meaning of Marxism. There is some indication that the splits in the world of socialism and communism are being re-examined.

There is also the more recent development of the break of China and the Soviet Union—which, for loyal Communists, is a little confusing—as if you were a Catholic and woke up to find you had to choose between two Popes and two Romes. Where is the "real" truth—Peking or Moscow? The answer, of course, is to be discovered in our own lives and our own societies and through our own experience and discussion—it simply cannot be imported from Peking or Moscow.

In Summary

There are three summary statements to make to this chapter. First I must admit that it is a hopeless task to try here to outline *all* the groups on the Left. But the main ones would include the *Socialist Party USA*, which is the old party of Eugene Debs and Norman Thomas, and, small as it is today, I am biased toward it because I belong to it. It puts out a good list of suggested reading free of charge—write the Socialist Party, 7109 N. Glenwood Avenue, Chicago, IL 60626. There is the *Communist Party*, which is a "Moscow-oriented" party. The *Socialist Workers Party* is the largest of the Trotskyist groups. There are other significant groups—the *Democratic Socialists of America* is a group of moderate socialists primarily working as a caucus in the Democratic Party.

There is a fair amount of cooperation at the local level between the Socialist Party and the DSA—often the same people will belong to both groups, as I do myself. There is *no* dual membership, however, between the Socialist and Communist Parties, or the Communist Party and the Socialist Workers Party. There is cooperation at the local or even national level in coalitions, but the political differences are too great for dual membership. It is impossible at this time to list the groups that take the Chinese position because they are small and shift a good deal.

Second, as a socialist *and a pacifist* I want to urge pacifists to cure themselves of a bad habit of trying to find the middle ground between good and evil. Socialism is an ideology of conflict—no question about it. We do believe in struggle, and in the final victory of working people over and against the institutions of capitalism. Many pacifists, uneasy about that struggle, keep looking for some movement that will give us a new society without really having to be socialist or being political. I have a lot of repect for anarchists who reject the whole concept of centralized socialism, but I have very little patience for people who say "well, capitalism is pretty bad and we need to find a third way between socialism and capitalism." This always seems to me to reflect extremely shallow thinking—as if one is looking for a comfortable third way between peace and war, or slavery and freedom. There *is* conflict in society, and the job of pacifists is to find *nonviolent resolutions to conflict*, not to devise ways of avoiding the conflict. Politics is not for everyone, but

The "real" socialism is to be discovered in our own lives and our own societies and through our own experience and discussion—it simply cannot be imported from Peking or Moscow.

Socialism is an ideology of conflict. We believe in struggle, and in the final victory of working people over and against the institutions of capitalism.

The job of pacifists is to find non-violent resolutions to conflict, not to devise ways of avoiding the conflict.

Socialists look far ahead to some vision of what might be and seek to give it form in the present.

I really think pacifists have a tremendous contribution to make to the socialist movement in keeping it compassionate and in helping give it values.

Third, the thing we all have to live with is that no answer really works completely. India was liberated with non-violence and things are still a mess there. China was liberated with violence and the Chinese leadership itself is telling us how bad things were under Mao. (Incidentally, I would recommend Edgar Snow's *Red Star Over China* as an exciting look at the early days of Mao's movement, before it had taken power—and some sense of just how bloody a violent revolution can be, in terms of how many of the young Communists were killed by Chiang Kai-Shek.) Martin Luther King, Jr., freed the South of Jim Crow—but America is still racist and blacks can't truly be part of America if they have no jobs.

Pacifists know that no answer is perfect or complete. (Or we *should* know this.) Yet the efforts to take short cuts—through killing, through war, through a revolution that is violent—almost always seem to be the long way after all. Few things are harder than trying to bring moral values to bear in the political world. There are times when I feel that trying to make morality political, or politics moral is like trying to mix fire and water. Yet this is what must be done. There is no "third way," there is no alternative to this impossible but necessary effort to be as politically realistic as we can while never losing sight of the transcendent set of values that brought us into the radical movement. In this sense, and I will close with this, while as a Marxist I absolutely reject the utopian approach to social change, the Utopian vision is essential, it is the yardstick which permits us to judge and measure our actions in the here and now. Other movements looked back to a golden age and sought to recreate it in the present. Socialists look far ahead to some vision of what might be and seek to give it form in the present. Radicals and revolutionists seek to take the dreams that animate us and give them substance. Thus the most practical among us is drawn toward the future by the impractical and impossible dream of what human beings *might* be like. And—paradox!—we help to make that future possible as we carry it into our own lives here and now. In this sense—if a Marxist can be forgiven borrowing from scripture—Jesus caught his listeners off guard when they prodded him on the Kingdom of Heaven, where it was, and when it would come, and he replied that it was here, now, within us. It was an answer at once mystical, and also political.

Resources

The Socialist. Monthly publication of the Socialist Party, USA. Sample copy free on request from The Socialist, 422 So. Western Avenue, Los Angeles, CA 90020.

Democratic Left. Monthly publication of Democratic Socialists of America. Sample copy free on request from DSA, 853 Broadway, Suite 617, New York, NY 10003.

THE NATURE OF ANARCHISM

By Carol Ehrlich and Howard J. Ehrlich

Anarchism is a theory of society, a political philosophy, an ethical guide for behavior, and a strategy for social change. Like all theories, parts of it have been tested, parts have never been tested; and parts must be taken on faith. Anarchists accept as a matter of faith, for example, the belief that people are capable of governing themselves.

Politics and Philosophy

The underlying philosophical basis of anarchism consists of a positive and a negative principle. Anarchists are *against* all forms of institutionalized authority (symbolized by ''government'' or ''the State''), and are *for* the freedom of the individual to control her or his life.

On one end of the spectrum, anarcho-capitalists and right-wing Libertarians believe that getting government out of our lives should be sufficient to remove the restraints on our liberties. On the other end, anarcho-communists, sometimes called ''libertarian socialists'' or ''left anarchists,'' believe that freedom cannot exist without equality. Equality requires the cooperation of individuals; and it is this left, or *social* anarchism, that we are concerned with.

Social anarchism is a theory of social organization based on voluntary association, mutual aid, decision-making by consensus, full participation by everyone, and an end to all power relationships (relationships of domination and subordination). Because it stresses the communal control of the workplace, because it stresses cooperation and not in-dividual acts, it is a form of socialism. But it is socialism without Marx or Lenin, without centralism (''democratic'' or otherwise), without a Party or Party cadre, without a government. Its organizational units are the working/living collective, the neighborhood, the affinity group, the community. These units form, when necessary, into networks across wider geographical areas in order to coordinate responses to issues and necessities such as transportation, defense, environmental issues, economic production and distribution, communications, and so on.

Social anarchism is a political philosophy for activists more than for theorists. Essentially, it is an ethical and practical guide to one's everyday behavior. This gives anarchists a perspective on revolutionary change as a process: a changed society is to be built out of a succession of present actions. One must act today, and not wait until some future revolutionary event. The revolution *is* the organized actions of people. And those actions themselves become the basis of our freedom. Though we can't entirely predict the outcome of our organizing, we can decide what our goals are, and can control the means we employ to try to reach those goals. The principle of the consistency of means and ends is central to anarchist thought and action.

In day-to-day terms, social anarchists employ direct action tactics, are non-violent, and treat everyone (including oneself) with respect. It means that they reject being placed in positions where they can dominate others, and equally that they refuse to assume positions of obedience to others. And it means that they build the sorts of organizational

Anarchists are against all forms of in institutionalized authority, and are for the freedom of the individual to control her or his life.

Because social anarchism stresses communal control of the workplace, because it stresses cooperation and not individual acts, it is a form of socialism.

Social anarchism is socialism without centralism, without a party, and without a government.

Social anarchism is a political philosophy for activists more than for theorists.

The principle of the consistency of means and ends is central to anarchist thought and action.

Anarchism is not chaos, or destruction, or disorganization or inaction.

forms that are consistent with anarchist principles.

In short, anarchists believe there are *both* structural and ideological—social and psychological—bases for the existing inequalities (class, race, sex, and so on). Neither one can be reduced to the other. It is essential to work on both forms of social pathology, simultaneously. Do anarchists always succeed in living by this political philosophy? Since no one (not even anarchists) is perfect, of course not. But they do try—and, we hope, learn from both failures and successes—and then try again.

Myths of Anarchy

There are loads of them. A group of terrorists plants a bomb in a railroad station and the media label them as "anarchists." Recession and inflation worsen and some expert declares the economy to be in a "state of anarchy." The proposed solutions for these social ills, of course, are inevitably some form of increased central control.

The myths aside, anarchism is not chaos, or destruction, or disorganization or inaction. On the contrary—it requires a high degree of internal organization, continued action towards commonly-agreed upon goals, and a great deal of social responsibility.

Another commonly-heard myth is that in an anarchist community no one would work, and the whole thing would fall apart. There would be the big rock candy mountain, or the pie in the sky (choose your favorite food metaphor), and everyone would fall greedily to it, neglecting the chores.

More likely, in a genuinely anarchist organization, most people would work more willingly than they do now, because they would be working for *themselves*. The *nature* of much of the work in society would change. For example, there wouldn't need to be jobs that exploit others, or terrorize them, or make a killing off them, or tell everyone else what to do. There is a high degree of motivation in knowing that you're doing good work. There's even more satisfaction when you know that you and your comrades will benefit, not the state or some anonymous investor.

People also hear that all anarchists want to reject city life and technology, and go back to the simple life in the country—no electric toothbrushes, no frozen foods, no jet planes. Some people do feel this way—and some of them are anarchists. But other anarchists like living in cities, and want to use and improve technology to help create an anarchist society.

Finally—and the most serious misconception of all—there's the myth that there has never been a successful anarchist group. That's not so. Many groups, and even some societies, have been organized without centralized government, hierarchy, formal authority, or special privilege. That's anarchism, although it is seldom labeled as such. Feminist small groups, learning networks, working and living collectives, anti-nuke groups, food co-ops—many of these are anarchist in structure, whether or not their members consciously are aware of that, and whether or not they stay that way over time. So are the sorts of spontaneous groupings that form in response to disasters, strikes, revolutionary situations, and emergencies. We read about these quite often, though they are never called "anarchist." If people in fact *knew* that's what they had built, they might well try hard to maintain it as such—and even fleeting anarchist formations would last longer than most have. (This points to the need for us to "politicize" those settings—that is, to help people understand the political meaning of what they are doing.)

History

The history of any group can basically be handled two ways: by writing about "notable" figures and important events, or by presenting the everyday lives and work of ordinary people. This is as true for anarchism as for any other movement. We could tell you about important early figures such as Godwin, Proudhon, Bakunin, Ferrer, Kropotkin, Goldman, Berkman (and more). But we won't. You should read about them: they were important figures who had much to do with shaping the political developments of their time. But to focus on individuals, particularly in such a small space as this one, creates a kind of "elite" (even if unintentionally) and is thus very anti-anarchist.

Literally, the history of anarchism begins with the first person who opposed the idea that any social group had the right to structure itself so that some of its members dominated other members. According to some writers, the word "anarchist" was first applied to those English and French revolutionaries of the 18th and 19th centuries as an insult. The term was used to suggest that these people wanted chaos and disorder. That stereotype has continued to plague anarchists to this day.

With the continued growth of nation-states in the 19th century, anarchism developed as a self-conscious political philosophy based on the opposition to all forms of government. In the 19th century, anarchism and Marxism both opposed the state (recall Engels' famous phrase about the need for the state to "wither away"), and also opposed each other. As early as the 1840s, Marxists and anarchists were in bitter disagreement as to how the dissolution of the state would come about. The disagreement on the best means to the revolutionary end was and is crucial. The issues include disagreement on the need for a "dictatorship of the proletariat"; on the revolutionary nature of the working class; on the necessity of historical stages; on class as the "motor" of revolution; on the need for a leadership elite, on centralism and mass society, among other things. Anarchists do not place faith in any of these. Instead, anarchists believe that the impulse to create societies based on freedom and equality can come from all sectors of society; that the conflicts between authority and freedom transcend "stages." Power is the root cause of all forms of inequality; and centralism, as an organizational form, leads to differences in power.

These beliefs have made anarchists "enemies of the state," and the state has responded by systematically harassing and murdering many anarchists. For example, in the U.S. alone, there was the frame-up and execution of anarchists in the Haymarket case of 1886 in Chicago; the mass jailings and deportations after World War I when J. Edgar Hoover, founding director of the FBI, began to build his career; and the Sacco and Vanzetti murders in the late 1920s.

What of anarchism in recent years? Although Marxism has received major praise (or blame) for sparking contemporary revolutionary activity, anarchism's contributions have gone relatively unnoticed. Like the person who discovered that s/he had been speaking prose all their life, many people have begun to discover that they have been practicing anarchism without knowing it. Much of the New Left of the 1960s and early 70s, the counterculture, the women's liberation movement, the free school and anti-draft and anti-nuke movements, even "libertarian Marxism" and socialist-feminism, is at its core, anarchist. And just as ethnic historians, feminist historians, and gay historians have spoken of the need to recover their history so that they can know who they are now, so anarchists have to recover their history. The project of the anarchist historian is to help us understand the present and to help us build upon the undercurrents of our anarchist past.

Controversies

There are many ongoing controversies

In a genuinely anarchist organization, most people would work more willingly than they do now, because they would be working for themselves.

Originally both anarchists and Marxists opposed the state.

Motivation in work comes from the benefit it gives to all.

within the left, or social anarchist movement. Some are issues of organizing within the larger society; others reflect problems of living our lives, of carrying out anarchist ideals. We are all, to some extent, products of the stratified society. The "political" and the "personal" blend into each other. Each contains components of the other.

Styles of Living. Should anarchists live collectively, that is, in groups of three or more? Some think so, and argue that single or couple living is wrong because it fosters isolation and exclusivity. Those who disagree—either in principle or because they believe people should live in ways that are emotionally most rewarding for them now—argue that anarchists should not tell other anarchists how they should want to live.

Mutual Aid. How strictly should anarchists share income, property, and other resources now—particularly if the work load is not shared more or less equitably? Is it un-anarchist for someone to have more than someone else? If so, how much more is too much more?

Principles of Group Structure. How do we organize among ourselves to achieve maximum empowerment and cooperation? Some anarchists think that strict rotation of work is essential so that everyone learn skills and no one hoard them. Others argue that those with particular talents and interests should be allowed to pursue them, so long as no rewards of power or status result.

Anarchists try to operate by consensus, but this creates some hard questions for which there are no facile answers. Where is the line between holding fast to one's ideas and blocking consensus? Where is the line between group solidarity and being suppressed by an informal power elite? The arguments aren't so much over the principle of consensus as over the means of implementing it. But the means aren't always clear.

How Do We Organize, and Whom Do We Organize? Some anarchists think it most important to organize ourselves (i.e., groups of already committed anarchists who will then organize others indirectly through education and example). Others emphasize outreach to non-anarchists, on the grounds that if we can't convert others, we aren't doing our job of changing society. It's a little like the old "mass vs. cadre" organizing debate in marxist circles, but without the built-in hierarchies.

What About Coalitions? Do we ever enter into coalitions with other (non-anarchist) groups? When, and with whom? Related to this question: do we ever support reforms (which by definition are tied into the system) such as rent control, moratoriums on nuclear plant building, affirmative action, ERA, legislation against sterilization abuse, etc? If so, aren't we strengthening the system we oppose? If not, aren't we impossibly purist?

What Is Our Relation To the State? Could an anarchist accept a job from a state agency? Or does it matter since so many employers (and benefits) are state-subsidized? What about grant funds? If we accept such money are we contradicting anarchism's denial of the state? If not, are we passing up a chance to put what the State has expropriated (i.e., our and others' tax money) to good use? And what about taxes? Should they be resisted totally or selectively, privately or publicly?

The Question of Violence. Most social anarchists do not advocate violence. Some believe that it is an inescapable dimension of revolutionary change. The problem for them is how to minimize violence in the process of building a good (and nonviolent) society. Some anarchists believe that we cannot build a good society through violent means. For them, revolutionary nonviolence is the principled way to go. For them, however, the question remains: What is violence? Is it killing people? Yes, of course. But is it blowing up a building with no one in it? Some say yes—since you can't ever be sure it is vacant.

Is bombing a military building the same as burning draft board files? What about cutting down a fence in front of a nuclear plant site? Is that a violent act? Does it become defined as such if you know that act will provoke the police into violence? And what about self-defense? Resisting a rapist? Among anarchists committed to nonviolence, these questions are all matters of some controversy.

The issues and controversies of the anarchist movement are, of course, not unique. They are the issues central to all persons and movements working for social change. Fundamentally, however, anarchists reject the beliefs that basic change can come about through electoral reform, or that change requires the seizure of state power, or that change requires first the destruction of all existing institutional forms. If social anarchists were to carry a banner, it would doubtless read "We are building the new society in the vacant lots of the old."

Resources

Probably the best place to start is with the catalogs of the major anarchist book distributors. These are Circle A Books, Bound Together Bookstore, 1369 Haight Street, San Francisco, CA 94117; Soil of Liberty Books, Box 7056, Powderhorn Station, Minneapolis, MN 55407; Fifth Estate Bookservice, Box 02548, Detroit, MI 48202; and Wooden Shoe Books, 112 S. 20th Street, Philadelphia, PA 19103. When requesting their catalogs, you should send a donation of a dollar to help them cover their costs.

There are three national periodicals of general anarchist concern. These are *Social Anarchism,* 2743 Maryland Avenue, Baltimore, MD 21218; *Black Rose,* Box 1075, Boston, MA 02103; and *Fifth Estate,* Box 02548, Detroit, MI 48202.

Two regional periodicals of high quality are *Circle A* in Atlanta, Box 57114, Atlanta, GA 30343 and *Anarchy: A Journal of Desire Armed,* Box 380, Columbia, MO 65205.

From Canada comes *Our Generation,* 3981 Boulevard St. Laurent, Montreal, Quebec H2W 1Y5 and *Kick It Over,* Box 5811, Station A, Toronto, Ontario M5W 1P2.

Among the nonprint media, the Great Atlantic Radio Conspiracy has an extensive catalog of audiotapes. Ask for their anarchist catalog at 2603 Talbot Road, Baltimore, MD 21216.

FEMINISM

By Donna Warnock

> "Patriarchy is the power of the fathers: a familial-social ideological, political system in which men—by force, direct pressure, or through ritual, tradition, law and language, customs, etiquette, education, and the division of labor, determine what part women shall or shall not play, and in which the female is everywhere subsumed under the male. It does not necessarily imply that no woman has power or that all women in a given culture may not have certain powers. . . .
>
> "The power of the fathers has been difficult to grasp because it permeates everything, even the language in which we try to describe it. It is diffuse and concrete; symbolic and literal; universal, and expressed with local variations which obscure its universality."
>
> —Adrienne Rich
> Of Woman Born

Every three minutes a woman is beaten by her male partner—a man who often claims to love her. Every five minutes a woman is raped, and they call that "making love" too. And every ten minutes a little girl is molested, sometimes by a relative, perhaps her own father. The violence mounts. "Every few seconds in America a woman is slapped, slugged, punched, chopped, slashed, choked, kicked, raped, sodomized, mutilated, or murdered. She loses an eye, a kidney, a baby, a life. "That's a fact," writes Ann Jones in *Take Back the Night*.[1] "And if the statistics are anywhere near right, at least one of every four women reading this paragraph will feel that fact through firsthand experience."

That these tragedies are so overlooked and unappreciated as the horrible acts of war they are is testimony to how much damage has already been done in the hearts and minds of the people. Andrea Dworkin writes in "Remembering the Witches," "(T)hey think of us today what the Inquisitors thought of us yesterday." She goes on to quote the witchhunters, "Carnal lust...is in women insatiable."[2] We "asked for it." We "wanted it." We "*loved* it." They try to drum it into our brains: *The victim is to blame.* Nowhere are we safe. "(T)he world, even a girl's neighborhood, becomes a mined field," writes the poet Susan Griffin.[3] The fear of rape keeps us prisoners in our own homes. Still there is no security: Over half of all rapes involve break-ins.

Numerous studies confirm that rapists are, for the most part, "normal" men. And more and more normal men are becoming rapists. Rape is the most frequently committed and fastest growing violent crime in America. Increasingly it incorporates other acts of violence against women, as virility and violence become more closely linked in the pornographic masculine model.

"Pornography," writes Adrienne Rich, "is relentless in its message, which is the message of the master to the slave: *This is what you are; this is what I can do to you.*"[4] Violence aganist women[5] has proliferated in pornography. Magazines as common as *Playboy, Penthouse, Oui* and *Hustler* feature pain-filled scenes; women handcuffed, gagged, shipped, beaten, hanging from chains, sucking guns, having their fingernails pierced. Porn shops sell the really hard core and specialty publications like *Bondage*, in which women have torches or knives held to their breasts or vaginas, and worse. Theatres across the country attract eager crowds with the film *Snuff*, which purportedly shows the *actual murder and butchering* of one of its actresses. In the final scene, the Director reaches into the victim's abdomen and waves her insides high above his head in orgastic delight. "*Snuff* forced us to stop turning the other way each time we passed an X-rated movie house," wrote Beverly LaBelle who saw the film and reported on it in *Take Back the Night*.

Military Virility

While films like *Snuff* "entertain" male viewers, the military has offered hands-on experience. Veteran Richard Hale reports that on the way to Vietnam troops were told, "There's a lot of loose ass over there men, and they just love GI dick. And best of all, they are only Gooks, so if you get tired of them, you can cram a grenade up their cunt and 'waste' them."[6] Many soldiers seized the opportunity; stories of wartime atrocities abound. "This is my rifle," the troops chant, "this is my gun," they slap their crotches; "One is for killing, the other's for fun." Four-hundred thousand Bengali women were systematically raped by Pakistani soldiers; how many women have our boys raped? After all, women have been bounty in every war.

Misogyny[7] and homophobia[8] are basic components in military indoctrination. "When you want to create a solidary [sic] group of male killers," goes the Marine philosophy, "you kill 'the woman' in them."

In a society where each man is trained to equate violence with virility, it follows that public policy, dominated as it is by males, will also adopt such a posture. In 1977, for example, Henry Kissinger told Congress that the U.S. would be "emasculating itself" by not providing military funds for Angola.

"War is simply an extension of the colonial policy of the subjugation of the female culture and 'weaker' male cultures, i.e., 'weaker' national cultures," Barbara Burris and others pointed out in "The Fourth World Manifesto."[9] Men have been conditioned to respond with patriotic bellicosity at the suggestion that a foreign military target is somehow effeminate. And so "Fuck Iran!" became a slogan of the times during the Iranian hostage episode. This kind of merger of violence and lewdity permeates military thinking even in the highest echelons of government. After President Johnson ordered North Vietnam PT boat bases and oil depots bombed, he bragged to a reporter, "I didn't just screw Ho Chi Minh. I cut his pecker off."

The logical extension of this lascivious violence is articulated on a plaque which hangs on the wall of the Syracuse Research Corporation, a private "think tank" with large military contracts. Illustrated with a missile in flight, the inscription reads:

I LOVE YOU BECAUSE
—Your sensors glow in the dark
—Your sidelobes swing in the breeze
—Your hair looks like clutter
—Your multipath quivers
—Your reaction time is superb
—Your missile has thrust; it accurately hones in on its target
—The fuse ignites, the warhead goes;
     SWEET OBLIVION!

If a missile launching can be sexually fantasized by leading militarists as "sweet oblivion," it follows that total annihilation would be the ultimate orgasm. And they'd claim they did it for our welfare. Patriarchy has turned our worst nightmare into a frightening possibility.

Because the socialized violence of "masculinity" has been widely accepted as normal, indeed cultivated, the illness it has produced has been treated with increased dosages. The nuclear arms race itself is an example of violent, spiraling male chauvinism: Though the United States can destroy the USSR fifty times over, and that country can only destroy us twenty times over, and, in any case, no country can be destroyed more than once, the U.S. continues competition for competition's sake. It is preoccupied with size and power. We need to be more potent in order to feel more secure, the argument goes. We want to stay on top, don't we? But the ultimate effect of chauvinist behavior is increased vulnerability, and so the vicious cycle is perpetuated. Such is life under Patriarchy.[10]

It's a Man's World

Patriarchy is a society which worships the masculine identity, granting power and privilege to those who reflect and respect the socially-determined masculine sex role. The cliche, "It's a man's world" provides an apt description. In fact, the word "Patriarchy" is derived from the Latin "pater," which means "to own." That's it in a nutshell: Under Patriarchy men are entitled to everything. It follows that Patriarchy is inherently violent because it thrives on captured prey.

The underpinning of Patriarchal philosophy and science is the absolute separation of mind and matter (or spirit and body). The former is identified as "male," and deemed superior while the latter is called "female" and deemed inferior.[11] On one side is posited rationality, objectivity, aggression, order, dominance; on the other is intuition ("irrationality"), emotionalism, passivity, chaos, submission. This artificial male/female polarity exists throughout man's[12] value system and sets a pattern for domination in Patriarchal society.

Thus man has come to deify "rational" thought, also known as mechanistic thinking, in which each component of a problem to be solved is analyzed in-

Whereas some feminists would reform marriage, radicals want it abolished.

Under Patriarchy every woman's identity is linked to that of a man through monogamy, marriage, and heterosexuality.

The underpinning of man's philosophy and science has been the absolute separation of mind and matter.

Estimates are that somewhere between 1 and 9 million women were burned as witches during the Inquisition.

Witchburning has a contemporary parallel in the sterilization of Native American women in this country.

The Women's Pentagon Action, November 1980.   *Photo by Dorothy Marder.*

"The servant role of women is critical for the expansion of consumption in the modern economy."

—John Kenneth Galbraith

The objectification of women has become the main theme of popular culture.

dependently, mechanistically, isolated from its environment. Ecological and human consequences are overlooked. Emotion is absent. Feminists Nina Swaim and Susan Koen explain in their *Handbook for Women on the Nuclear Mentality:*

When the intellect and the dominating, controlling, aggressive tendencies within each individual are defined as the most valuable parts of their being, and those same attributes are emphasized in the political and economic arena, the result is a society characterized by violence, exploitation, a reverence for the scientific as absolute, and a systematic 'rape' of nature for man's enjoyment. This result is patriarchy.

When the patriarchal paradigm becomes operational on the economic and political level, and the exploitation of nature for the sake of technological advancement and profit becomes the modus operandi *of society, we find ourselves in the interlocking horror story of the nuclear mentality. This mentality is a belief system, an ideology, that would foster the use of destructive technology in order to sustain the expansion and domination which characterizes capitalist patriarchy.*[13]

Mechanistic thinking was originally a way for men to conquer the mysteries of nature. But to conquer nature, they had to conquer women. Pre-Patriarchal cultures believed that, because women alone brought forth life, women therefore held the secrets of nature and the keys to wisdom. To counter such no-

tions, the Catholic Church imposed the Divine Doctrine that the male had domination over creation. There was tremendous opposition to this idea; it was seen as unnatural. This blasphemous opposition outraged the Church leaders and, more importantly, threatened their power. Consequently, between the fourteenth and seventeenth centuries, they attacked women with brute force: *Somewhere between one and nine million women were burned as witches during the Inquisition.* Two villages were left with only one woman in each.

Times have changed. Women are no longer burned at the stake. We have been allowed to enter the public sphere previously denied us. While the high incidence of rape and wife beating should be sufficient to raise serious questions about the current state of women's liberation, we feminists are nonetheless repeatedly asked to exclude these so-called "exceptional" acts of violence and instead be grateful for the improvements in the day-to-day lives of "average" women in this "advanced" country. "You've come a long way, *baby*," we're told.

Let's get rid of this notion that the only women whose status counts are the so-called "average" ones, that is, those from the white middle class. Indeed, if we look at the women whose ancestors were on this land before colonization, we find that witchburning has a contemporary parallel in the sterilization of Native American women in the United States. The National

Center for Health Statistics estimates that *25 percent of all Native American women have been sterilized—many of them involuntarily*. There is one tribe in Oklahoma in which *all* of the full-blooded women have been sterilized. The implications of sterilizing Native American women should be seen in full. It is anti-woman. It is racism and genocide. It represents an attempt, like the witchhunts, to kill a culture which challenges the anti-nature bias of Christian theology.

And, that's not the only remnant of feudalism women face today.

A Man's Home Is His Castle

The saying that every man, regardless of social position, can be king in his own home does far more than hark back to a romanticized notion of the days of old. It reveals that truth about the social structure we have adopted. It is significant that the word "family" is derived from "famel," meaning "slave," and that the United Nations has declared marriage a "slavery-like practice."

Wives are viewed under U.S. law as their husbands' property in marriage, with few rights of their own. Sex is among the legal requirements, but love and affection are *not*. And marital rape is legal in all but a few states. Courts have further held that husbands are entitled to free domestic services. Freedom of domicile is denied married women in most places in the United States; that is, a woman must live with her husband where he chooses or be guilty of abandonment under the law, which could result in the loss of child custody, possessions and other financial entitlements such as alimony. This holds true even if it is actually the husband who relocates. If a husband wants his wife to live with him she must, or risk forfeiting her marital privileges.

Until recently, a woman's title indicated her marital status. If unwed, a woman is ridiculed as an "old maid," "spinster," or worst of all, "lesbian." And pity the poor widow! Again language is our teacher: The word "widow" is from the Sanskrit; it means "empty."[14] Similarly, if a woman bears no children, she is considered "barren." Families are what give meaning to a woman's life according to Patriarchal dictate.

Under Patriarchy, every woman's identity is linked to that of a man through the institutions of monogamy, marriage, motherhood and enforced heterosexuality. These institutions are maintained through rigorous promotion, reinforced by legal sanctions and social pressures which punish their transgressors. These are important interrelated components of the Patriarchal structure, for together they maintain patrilineage, the primary power base of the fathers.

Whereas agrarian cultures benefitted from large extended families where women had relatively more support and dignity, the nuclear family has been promoted by today's capitalist leaders because it benefits them politically and financially. When nuclear families form the base of a social structure they divide the society into small, easily-controlled and relatively powerless units which provide a ready vehicle for the perpetuation of hierarchy and domination and the expansion of consumption.

The Good Life

Values based on the idealized middle class life are promoted not because they're idyllic, but because there's power and profit in them for the men who run this country. Women are exploited as consumers, with 75% of corporate advertising aimed at us. These ads are designed to destroy our self-images, to deceive us into thinking that "The Good Life" is a product of American industry. They rob us of our individuality, defining us instead by our possessions and social status. They script us as sex objects and housewives. The media standards set for women are especially damaging to those of us who come from the lower income brackets. We are made to feel like failures when our economic status prohibits achievement of the middle class ideal. The damage has taken its toll in high rates of alcoholism, drug addiction, mental problems and suicide among women.[16] So much for the myth about pedestals.

The truth is that "The servant role of women is critical for the expansion of consumption in the modern economy," as economist John Kenneth Galbraith points out. The housewife market, with its endless array of energy-intensive appliances and ecologically disastrous cleaning agents, has become Big Business. But despite and, ironically, because of these so-called "labor-saving" devices, the woman at home with one

"Pornography is the theory; rape is the practice."

—Robin Morgan

The fear of rape keeps us prisoners in our own homes.

Mysogyny and homophobia are basic components in military indoctrination.

The feminist movement has become the most potent force for nonviolent revolution in practice.

The principles of feminism and nonviolence turn out to be remarkably similar.

Both contest the notion that the end justifies the means.

Feminism and nonviolence both agree that everything is connected.

child spends, on the average, more than eighty hours a week on household chores, according to the U.S. Women's Bureau.

Women with jobs outside the home work a double shift. Which brings us to yet another middle class myth; namely, that we only work for "pin money." We work because we have to. Yet women are considered the "surplus labor force," the expendable ones. And if conservative political leaders have their way in eliminating workplace affirmative action programs, things will get much worse. Right now fully-employed women make only sixty percent as much as our male counterparts. Women of color make only fifty percent as much as white men. The fifteen million women who head families do it with less than half the income of male heads of households. It is no wonder, then, that women comprise two-thirds of the 25 million people living below poverty. Households headed by women increased fifty percent in the 1970s, and almost one-third of them are below the poverty level (compared to 12% of the population as a whole).

Grace Paley at the Pentagon, 1980.
Photo by Dorothy Marder.

Fifty-one percent of the Black female-headed households are below the poverty level. Mothers' economic problems are compounded by lack of childcare facilities, fathers who refuse their childcare responsibilities and welfare regulations which encourage paternal abandonment.

Sexual Politics and Peace

The battlefield in the war against women is in the workplace, on the streets, in our homes, in our most intimate relationships. It is physical and psychological, visited upon us by others and internalized within ourselves. It is manifested in atomic power development and ecological destruction. The mentality that builds nuclear weapons is the same one that rapes women and destroys the natural environment. No political philosophy or strategy for peace can be complete without addressing sexual politics.

If the peace movement is to be successful in putting an end to war, it must work to eliminate the sex-role system which is killing us all by rewarding dominating aggressive behavior in men.

If the peace movement is to be consistent in its opposition to violence, it must address violence against women.

If the peace movement is truly committed to social justice, it must join the movement for women's liberation.

If the peace movement is to make nonviolent revolution, it must commit itself to overthrowing Patriarchy.

Feminism and Nonviolence

The power of Patriarchy is such that to see through it requires a special kind of vision, a consciousness of the most "ordinary" experience. To understand it requires "thinking across boundaries," as Mary Daly says. To overcome it demands the reinvention of revolution. This consciousness, this vision, this experience, this understanding, this revolutionary politic is feminism.

While the feminist movement has not overtly defined itself as nonviolent, by opposing oppressive institutions of domination, by employing nonviolent tactics, by pioneering in non-hierarchical structures, by formulating principles and identifying visions of harmony and liberation, it has become, I believe, the

WRL "Feminism & Militarism" Conference, April 12, 1981, Dingman's Ferry, PA. Photo by Kate Donnelly.

most powerful force for nonviolent revolution in practice.

The principles of feminism and nonviolence are remarkably similar. Both uphold the rights of all individuals in society to dignity, justice and freedom. Both understand that the revolution is not a before and after affair in which one group of men exchanges weapons and privileges with another, but instead measure revolutionary progress in terms of collective consciousness practiced in present tense. This consciousness challenges the polarized belief system which defines aggression as good and submission as bad, which fosters dominance and stifles nurturance, which glorifies mechanism and suppresses sensitivity. Feminism and nonviolence place ecological laws in social perspective: both understand that social strength depends on social diversity. Both agree that everything is connected, every act has repercussions. The political-economic apparatus, the social structure, the eco-system, the production system, the military-industrial complex, the moral and psychological health of a people are all part of a continuum. Exploitation at any point along the way affects it all. Both feminism and nonviolence see that power, in its healthy form, comes from the strength and sensitivity of this wholistic understanding and leads naturally to the cooperative and nurturing behavior necessary for harmonious existence. Both feminism and nonviolence oppose power which is exploitive or manipulative. Competition and dehumanizing objectification of individuals are seen as forms of domination and aggression

and precursors or components of physical violence.

Despite major theoretical commonalities, feminists are not necessarily nonviolent, and nonviolent activists are not necessarily feminist. This merger is our challenge. We are saying that feminism is crucial to pacifism, for we must dismantle the mental weaponry as well as the military. For us, nonviolence is a logical extension of feminism. To call ourselves feminist pacifists is to use neither as an adjective, but to integrate both. We are talking about a philosophy of its own. We are experiencing a leap in consciousness, and we are recoginzing that it is revolutionary.

[1] **Take Back the Night: Women on Pornography,** edited by Laura Lederer, 1980.

[2] *Remembering the Witches,* **WIN** Magazine, Andrea Dworkin, 1975.

[3] **RAPE: The Power of Consciuosness,** Susan Griffin, 1979.

[4] ibid,. **Take Back the Night,** Adrienne Rich's article.

[5] One and a half million children under sixteen are also used annually in commercial sex, including prostitution and pornography, according to the *Los Angeles Times.*

[6] Quoted in Marc Feigen Fasteau's **The Male Machine,** 1974.

[7] Hating women

[8] Fear or loathing of homosexuality

[9] "The Fourth World Manifesto," **Radical Feminism,** edited by Anne Koedt, Ellen Levine, and Anita Rapone, 1973.

[10] I capitalize "Patriarchy" here and elsewhere, not in deference, but to mock the Patriarchal tradition of self-aggrandizement.

[11] The word "man" comes from the Indo-European base "to think," and is akin to the Latin, "Mens," meaning "mind." "Woman,"

Feminism is as crucial to pacifism as is disarmament.

To call oneself a feminist/pacifist is not to use either as an adverb, but to integrate both.

If the peace movement is to make nonviolent revolution it must commit itself to overthrowing the Patriarchy.

"In each one of us the mother lives, for each one of us has been at one with the mother."

—Barbara Deming

on the other hand, means "womb of man," and "female," "the one who suckles." Make no mistake that the incorporation of the male in these words was ever meant to imply that women could have wombs, suckle *and* think. No, according to Patriarchy, intellect is the domain of men, and men alone; women are mothers, mere matter, as the Latin root "mater" indicates.

[12] I use the term "man" here in its Patriarchally-socialized, rather than biological, sense. Just as it is difficult for whites to reject all the privileges associated with race, it is difficult for men to change their behavior patterns and ways of thinking. Indeed, all too often the former is done without the latter. While there are certainly men who are to be commended for attempting to undo dominating behavior and reject male privileges, it is an infrequent enough occurence that I still use the term "male" in its socialized form. It has been my experience that men who demand that the exceptions be noted every time are, rather than showing their sensitivity, all too often using the charge as a defense mechanism to deflect substantive feminist criticism thereby actually revealing their need for further consciousness raising.

[13] **Handbook for Women on the Nuclear Mentality,** Nina Swaim and Susan Koen, 1980.

[14] In India, the rite of sutee, or *widow burning*, was openly practiced until banned in 1823. Still the practice continues disguised as "suicide." For further reading, see **Gyn/Ecology** by Mary Daly.

[15] **Women and Madness,** Phyllis Chesler.

Resources

Reweaving the Web of Life: Feminism and Nonviolence, edited by Pam McAllister, New Society Publishers, 1982.

We Are All Part of One Another: A Barbara Deming Reader, edited by Jane Meyerding, New Society Publishers, 1984.

Piecing It Together: Feminism and Nonviolence, Feminism and Nonviolence Study Group, War Resisters' International, 1983.

Ain't No Where To Run: A Handbook for Women on the Nuclear Mentality, Susan Koedt and Nina Swaim, 1980.

Three Guineas, Virginia Woolf, Harcourt, Brace, Jovanovich, 1966.

Gyn/Ecology: Metaethics of Radical Feminism, Mary Daly, Beacon, 1978.

Rape: The Power of Consciousness, Susan Griffin, Harper & Row, 1979.

Take Back the Night: Women on Pornography, edited by Laura Lederer, Morrow Press, 1980.

Radical Feminism, edited by Anne Koedt, Ellen Levine, Anita Rapone, Quadrangle, 1973.

Of Woman Born: Motherhood as Institution, Adrienne Rich, Bantam, 1976.

Basic Organizing Techniques

ORGANIZING A LOCAL GROUP

By Ed Hedemann

This chapter is not intended as a cookbook with a recipe guaranteed to result in a viable local group when all the ingredients are mixed in proper proportion. It's a discussion that we hope helps you as you begin the difficult but truly rewarding job of local organizing.

By joining or organizing a WRL local group, members can strengthen their work for the human society. They are better able to organize actions and projects consistent with their pacifist convictions. By working within a local group, WRL members can find new ways of bringing nonviolence into their lives.

The local group has some distinct advantages over an individual organizer, such as providing ideas for actions, since some of the best ideas for projects come from meetings or casual comments in discussions. In addition, a group provides a ready body of people to help organize and carry out projects. Being able to share your successes and experiences with a group of people is a tremendous boost to further involvement and action. Failures are easier to take when there are others to share the burden.

When organizing, local group members should ask themselves: "Are we reaching out to various groups in the community—minority groups, the elderly, trade unions, churches, the campus? Are we seen by other parts of the community as a resource and support group at moments of community crisis?" If our nonviolence is used to serve the community, people will learn to respect us and to hear our voice on the larger issues of disarmament and structural change in society.

Becoming an Effective Organizer

To be effective, an organizer must be psychologically prepared to meet with vocal, well-funded opposition. Preparation comes primarily in the form of information. However, information can have the effect of smothering you. An organizer must recognize that the purpose of information is to provide material for action. We can have the most devastating evidence in the world against a particular injustice, but if that information is not acted upon, it might as well be collecting dust.

An organizer must learn how to form associations and work well with others. The establishment is constantly nurturing the "do your own thing" attitude among young people. Fear—of associations, organizations, and division of labor—is another necessary precondition for the continued domination by the establishment.

Here are some guidelines to consider in preparing to work for a just and peaceful world:

- Educate yourself while keeping your mind on possible actions.
- Gather a core group incorporating as many key skills as possible.
- Take local action with a specific focus, within the context of your broader concerns. A "scattershot" approach to organizing will likely end in frustration.

To be effective, an organizer must be psychologically prepared to meet with vocal, well-funded opposition.

An organizer must recognize that the purpose of information is to provide material for action.

Continuity, persistence, and focus are prime ingredients for success.

A local group can either be formed around a broad political or social concern, or around a specific campaign, target, or injustice.

- Identify all avenues of access you might have into the political processes of your community.
- Identify and approach all possible allies.
- Target your information to the public. They are more likely to be persuaded than the establishment.
- Take yourself, your group, and your issues seriously. If you lack confidence in your cause it will soon show.
- Present viable alternatives. A forceful argument for disarmament or safe energy systems is just as powerful as a well-spoken expose of the military or atomic establishment.
- Continuity, persistence, and focus are prime ingredients for success.

How To Start A Local Group

There are a couple of strategies for forming a local group. The first is to start a group around *broad* political or social concerns (such as forming a WRL local group); and then develop specific campaigns and actions that reflect the concerns of your group.

A second strategy is to form a group around a *specific* campaign, target, or injustice (e.g., Trident campaign, grape boycott, ERA ratification); thereby attracting people who are concerned with that issue. They may not have broad political agreement with one another, but many who get involved for the first time may wish to continue working in the same vein with a broader group, such as WRL. In fact, political groups work with independent campaigns partly for recruiting purposes.

Recruitment

Obviously, the first order of business for an organizer is getting people

Atlanta WRL tax protest and petition table, April 14, 1981.

together. The most effective method to convince people to attend a meeting is one-to-one contact. If people are asked directly to come to a meeting, then they are more likely to attend than if they simply hear or read about it without being put on the spot for a commitment. The next best method is to mail a letter or postcard about a meeting, followed by a phone call reminder.

The common "mass methods" of outreach are through leafletting or setting up literature tables at speaking engagements, concerts, meetings, film showings, shopping centers, demonstrations, and so forth. Registration week on college campuses is often the best time for reaching new people. Having a petition or sign-up sheet is valuable for followup calls and mailings.

Placing an ad or announcement for a meeting in a newspaper, on the radio or community billboard, or simply postering key locations can be useful to draw people. But don't rely on these methods to act as more than a reminder. Some groups have formed as a result of being part of a caucus in a regional conference or demonstration; or an affinity group in a civil disobedience action may decide to continue as an independent local group.

The key is to be creative and continue to reach out. No group, no matter how stable at one time, will remain that way for long without continually trying to gain new members. This is especially true in communities which are in constant flux, e.g., high schools and colleges.

It is crucial that new people are made to feel welcome. When a stranger comes to a meeting, introduce her or him around and involve the person in regular meeting discussions and postmeeting activities. Also, give the new person a real task to perform, such as making posters, handing out some leaflets, reading a book for a study group, helping to organize a demonstration, or putting to use any skills s/he may have. You have to gauge what a person can take, however, so that a new person does not feel over burdened or get frightened off.

The key is to attract five to ten reliable workers, who are likely to stay past the first few meetings. This is your core group, which will be expected to know what is going on with the group at all levels.

The First Meeting

The first meeting of a group can be crucial to the initial success of that group. So plan carefully. Set a time and place before contacting people. The place should be convenient, the time should be far enough ahead so there are no conflicts and soon enough so people won't forget (that means about a week or two ahead).

Before the meeting, make an agenda—what you want to do, why you want to do it, how you'll go about it, and who will join in. Select a room a bit too small and arrive at least half an hour in advance. Try to have a beverage (e.g., coffee) and some sort of snack available. Also, display any appropriate literature you might have. Make sure someone will take notes which can be sent to all those who expressed interest but couldn't attend, as well as those who did attend.

Start the meeting with introductions to each other, giving a little more than one's name. Go over the agenda to see if there are any changes or additions, then set a reasonable time limit for the meeting to end (e.g., 2 hours) and stick to it. After there's been group acceptance of the what, why and how, get firm commitments to do something like giving money on a regular basis, giving time, attending a study group session, leafletting, vigiling, or just about anything. Without a commitment to do something, people have no reason to relate to the local group. Before the meeting breaks up be sure to set a time and place for another meeting. Ask people to bring others who are interested to the next meeting. You may want to set up task forces to meet between meetings.

Meetings are a drag only if you don't get anything done. Every time you have a meeting, decide beforehand what you want to accomplish. Here are some "accomplishment goals" for a series of initial meetings:

First Meeting. Get friends and people politically close to you. Discuss the need for a local group to act on specific issues. Work for common agreement in identifying the issues, and get commitments to work on them through the group.

Second Meeting. Get new people. Summarize previous decisions and determine how the organization will function.

Third Meeting. Plan an action (picket line, leafletting, etc.) and/or set up a study series.

Fourth Meeting. Discuss the action and plan further activities. Plan the involvment of more people.

The most effective method to convince people to attend a meeting is one-to-one contact.

Be creative and continue to reach out to gain new members.

The first meeting is *crucial* to the initial success of your group.

Without a commitment to do something, people have no reason to relate to the local group.

Though an office has a number of drawbacks, it is essential for an active, growing group.

If your meetings regularly exceed 20 to 30 people, you may want to split into two or more groups. It has been found that the ideal size group for decision making is on the order of a dozen or so.

Structure of a Local Group

Different people participate at different levels. Some people hate meetings, but love to leaflet or attend demonstrations; others have no free time, but wish to contribute money. A healthy group will encourage participation at whatever level people can offer.

A typical local group might be structured as follows:

1. **general meetings,** attended by a dozen or so of the most active people, to make business and policy decisions, weekly to monthly;

2. **the office,** staffed by 2 or 3 part time volunteers, to implement decisions of the group and provide coordination;

3. **task forces,** to carry out decisions of the group in between general meetings; may operate in place of or in addition to an office. Typical task forces might be: fundraising, outreach, coordination, newsletter, literature, public meetings, demonstrations;

4. **mailing list** of 100 to 200 people, providing a base of contributors;

5. **actions,** which may involve 25 people or so, are valuable not only for dramatizing views of the group, but as fund raising, recruiting, and building solidarity within the group.

The Office

At some point, if your group grows and is effective, you're going to need some kind of central place to store materials, have a mimeo machine or printing press, have work space, receive mail, phone calls and visitors, be able to communicate and coordinate, etc. This means an office, but an office can hinder a group as well as give it a boost.

The problems with offices are they cost money, they tend to be places where people hang around instead of working, and they tend to foster a central clique of people who are involved more or less full time. An office begun prematurely can really wreak havoc. It can turn a grow-

ing group into an organization devoted to maintaining an office.

The advantages of an office are it's a place to meet and do things. A simple thing like leafletting can be an unmanageable chore without an office. You've got to find a place to type a stencil and find a place to mimeo it. You've got to find a place to store the leaflets and a place for people to pick them up. You've got to find a phone where someone will answer when people respond to the leaflet. An office provides a solution to all these problems. And this is just dealing with leafletting. Think of the other things a group does.

Before deciding on an office, make sure your group is strong enough to sustain one. Can you get monthly pledges from the members that will cover rent, telephone, machinery and supplies? Can a schedule be set up that will keep the office staffed with volunteers? Or can you raise the money to have paid staff?

If your group decides it is ready to open on office, find an office that's cheap and near things. Some churches, the local "Y," another group, or a member's home can provide space. A storefront located near a college or high school is the best recruiting mechanism you can have. Get your office, clean up and paint it, get some furniture and literature and you're set. It's hard work to get it all done, but the process can help your group feel together.

Keeping the Local Alive

The easy part is getting started. The hard part is keeping things going. The single most important way to sustain a local group is to be active. If you don't develop regular projects and actions that people can involve themselves in, they will sense a purposelessness to the group and drop out.

There are any number of actions that can be organized on a regular basis. Leafletting the Federal Building, armed forces recruiters, or IRS once a week are examples. This ongoing program involves people in a leafletting schedule, and doing the leafletting itself. Study programs are regular activities that will involve people if you have a goal. Create study programs around issues, around politics, around prospective actions.

A newsletter that comes out regularly fills several needs. It's an ongoing activity that involves people. It disseminates information on local activities and is an outlet for political education. It serves as

The single most important way to sustain a local group is to be active.

a forum for opinion. It helps tie the membership together.

Second to having a program and doing something, what keeps a group together and helps it grow is a communitarian spirit. A sense of togetherness is really important in this alienating society. If your group is a place where people can feel wanted and part of something, they'll stay and work.

The problem is that a communitarian spirit isn't something that can be achieved in a simple step-by-step process. If you're not friendly it won't happen. Because the League is working for a better society we feel that a true community should seek to eliminate sexist, racist, or class prejudice attitudes. Given all this, there are a few things that can help foster the communitarian spirit.

Make your meetings enjoyable rather than dreary. For instance you can have them at the same time as a potluck dinner and at a regular time and place, so that going to them becomes a habit for members. Do some things that are done just for fun. Have parties and picnics or retreats. Make decisions cooperatively. That means really talk things out at your regular potluck dinner meeting. People need to feel involved, and be involved, in all the levels of the group. There's a tendency to let one person write the leaflets, one person to do the thinking, and another to do the shit work. While it's true that some people are better at a given task than others, an attempt should be made to rotate the tasks. If someone doesn't know how to operate the mimeo machine, teach him or her. If someone can't write a decent leaflet, work with the person until s/he can write a good leaflet. And everyone should help with the routine work.

Troubleshooting Common Local Group Problems

Listed below are problems local groups frequently encounter, and suggestions for overcoming them. Though we don't pretend to be able to solve these problems for *your* group, simply being aware of them is a major first step towards solving them. Also, anticipating and thus preparing for these problems can do a lot towards eliminating or minimizing their effect.

Endless Meetings with Little Action. Doing anything together, no matter how small (e.g., taking some time during a regular meeting to write a government official or setting up a leafletting event) can give an important feeling of accomplishment while beginning the ground work for a more substantial project (see "Keeping the Local Alive," above).

Failure to Attract, Integrate, and Hold New Members. Schedule one meeting to brainstorm ideas for outreach and set up a committee to implement those ideas; get firm commitments from people to do something. Make every new person feel welcome and immediately involved (see "Recruitment" and "The First Meeting" above).

Leader or Key Organizer Leaves. In many groups, problems of leadership can create jealousy, division, inefficiency, and sometimes result in the dissolution of the group. In addition, an indispensable leader can create serious problems if she or he moves away, is jailed, gets ill, is coopted by the establishment, or even goes on vacation. Though it is often more efficient (in the short run) to have the "best" person do a particular task (e.g., chair a meeting, write a leaflet, speak at a demonstration), it is much better to encourage others to take initiative, responsibility, and leadership in certain areas. (see the "Group Process" chapter).

Responsibilities Not Adequately Shared. A process of rotating responsibility or leadership can be regularized to promote a decentralization of skills, thus a strengthening of the movement. Set a time limit (e.g., every 3 months) to rotate convening and facilitating me-

A communitarian spirit is important to keep a group together and help it grow.

Make your meetings enjoyable, rather than dreary.

Encourage others to take initiatives in areas of key responsibility.

etings, or coordinating the newsletter, and so forth, depending on the job. Schedule special workshops for certain skills (e.g., writing and designing leaflets, speaking, fund raising) to develop self-confidence in those areas, and encourage new people to take on responsibility (see "Group Process" chapter).

Lack of Funding. Establish a pledge system for regular members ($1 a week or $5 a month) just to meet basic operating expenses. Plan a raffle, garage sale, film showing (see "Fund Raising" chapter). Set aside a special meeting to brainstorm ideas, get *firm* commitments, and establish a task force to implement.

Group Too Large. Meetings that get cumbersome with too many people make adequate participation difficult. You can either stay as is and after a few meetings many people will leave by attrition, or the group can split into two or more parts. The group can split by geography, interests, or meeting time (some prefer to meet on Sundays, while others prefer Monday evenings).

Division of Interests/Lack of Unity. If the group is large enough, it can undertake a number of projects. But if the in-

upon project, then followed after a given time by another project. If worse comes to worse, the group may have to split or dissolve.

Group Changes from Founding Basis. Often, as new people join a group, it begins to change from its original purpose or its politics may be altered or diluted. Sometimes this is a good process, but sometimes this happens by design (i.e., infiltration and take-over).

To avoid the latter, the group should be founded on an explicit basis. For example, a WRL group would make clear that those who join adhere to principles of nonviolence. Coalitions are more susceptible to manipulation than groups with clearly identified politics, such as WRL. Should a division occur and it is not resolved internally, then another organization could be formed as a last resort and to avoid alienating many people who wish to contribute what they can to the cause.

Government Infiltrators. The best way to deal with informers is to keep everything you do "aboveboard" and honest; that way no exposure would disrupt your activities. Often groups are disrupted more by suspicion of "who's the agent," than by what an agent could do.

For more information, the Campaign for Political Rights (201 Massachusetts Avenue, NE, Washington, DC 20002) has written an article entitled "Bugs, Taps and Infiltrators: What to Do About Political Spying."

Resources

The Organizer's Manual, O.M. Collective, 368 pp, 1971, out-of-print.

Grass Roots: An Anti-Nuke Source Book, ed. Fred Wilcox, Crossing Press, 192pp, 1980.

Resource Manual for a Living Revolution, ed. Coover, et al., New Society Publishers, 330pp, 1985.

Organizing—A Guide for Grassroots Leaders, Si Kahn, McGraw-Hill, 387pp, 1982.

terests of the members diverge too much, there may not be enough energy for any of the projects. The group needs to resolve whether individual identification with particular project ideas exceed identification with the underlying politics of the group. See if there can be agreement to do one commonly agreed

GROUP PROCESS

By Susan Pines

How we work together—the process that we use to make decisions and act together—is probably as important as *why* we are working together. Because we are working to build a society that depends on cooperation rather than competition and that recognizes the value in each of its members, the structures we set up should strive to foster these qualities.

Group Dynamics

It is necessary to understand the forces working within a group. Good internal dynamics come from an awareness by all members of how the group functions, an ability to work efficiently together and a sense of personal satisfaction and accomplishment among group members. Some general characteristics of a group are:

- Cohesiveness—the degree to which members of the group agree on basic goals and values and the degree to which group members like and support each other.

- Climate—the psychological tone of meetings and gatherings. Do participants feel comfortable to express themselves? Are goals clear? Is the room comfortable?

- Structure—interrelationship of different aspects of the group, such as the decision-making process, roles, membership, goals, style and process of communication.

- Standards—expectations regarding behavior in the group, e.g., amount of involvement, or being on time.

- Control—regulation of the group. How are new members included or excluded? How does the group insure its own continuation?

Understanding and defining your group's structure and process will keep it working efficiently.

Meetings

Meetings are probably the backbone of our groups. Most of us probably spend more time at meetings than we ever do at demonstrations (or at home, for that matter). Given that our most important strategizing and decision making is done in the context of meetings, it's important that we try to make them as exciting, challenging, involving and efficient as possible.

Set a regular meeting date and time for your group, and stick to it (e.g., the first Monday of every month at 7 pm). This will make it easier for people to remember the meeting and will make it less likely that they will schedule something else for that evening.

It's often nice to incorporate some social aspect to the meeting (people will talk whether you allow time for it or not). Start with a pot luck dinner or go out together after the meeting for pizza or beer. This gives people a chance to relax and get to know each other in a non-formal setting.

There is nothing like a long, boring meeting dominated by one or two people to discourage people from ever coming back again. There are a few key elements (often interrelated) to a successful meeting:

- involvement—a feeling of participation

- information—a feeling of having learned something

- action—the meeting was a step towards or resulted in some action, so

> Understanding and defining your group's structure and process will keep it working efficiently.

> Given that our most important strategizing and decision making is done in meetings, we should try to make them exciting, challenging, involving and efficient.

> There is nothing like a long, boring meeting dominated by one or two people to discourage people from ever coming back again.

It's good to have a proposed agenda ready before a meeting begins.

The meeting facilitator should be selected in advance in order to become familiar with the items likely to be discussed.

Follow every meeting with an evaluation.

there is a feeling of accomplishment
- socializing—this is usually incorporated in the above three but sometimes can be a separate element—something to give the sense of being part of a community.

Meeting Preparation

Your meeting will run more smoothly, and you'll accomplish more if you do a little advance work. Here are some suggestions.

Prepare an Agenda

The agenda can be changed or modified at the meeting, but it's good to have a proposed agenda ready. Arrange in advance for someone to present each item. Be prepared to give background information as to why the item is on the agenda. Estimate the time needed for each item. This will give participants an idea of the relative importance of each item and help tailor the discussion to the time available. Know what is required of each item. Is a decision necessary? Or do you just need to decide a process to deal with the item? Make tentative judgements about priorities. What could be held over to the next meeting if necessary? Try to create a balance of long and short items. If an item on the agenda is complicated or controversial consider ahead of time a process for its discussion. Try to deal with difficult items at a time on the agenda before the group is tired.

Select a Facilitator

Because the facilitator plays such an important role in the meeting its helpful if she/he is familiar with the agenda items. It is good to select the facilitator for the meeting in advance so they can work with the agenda committee.

Physical Arrangements

Prepare the room before the meeting starts. Make sure you have enough chairs, paper, marking pens, blackboard or chalk, if necessary.

Running the Meeting

Always begin with introductions. This will help all participants know each other better. Go around the room and have everyone give their names and some other information about themselves (e.g., where they live, what other groups they work with).

Review the agenda, and ask for approval, corrections and additions. Determine an ending time for the meeting.

Make sure someone is taking notes. Taking notes or minutes of a meeting helps everyone by having a written record of all discussions and decisions made by the group.

Assign someone to be timekeeper who will watch to see that discussions do not run over the time allotted to them. Running over on some items can cause other important matters to be rushed through, postponed or ignored.

Have an evaluation at the end of the meeting. Evaluations help a group learn from its mistakes and accomplishments

Small group at 1973 WRL Conference. Photo by Grace Hedemann.

and gives feedback to the people who had specific roles and tasks (e.g., facilitator, agenda committee). Evaluation often works best if there isn't a lot of discussion or comment on what people say and if people feel "safe" to say anything. The trick is not to get caught up in further discussion of the agenda items but to get concrete suggestions for improvement. Keep a list of the comments under different headings: good, problems, improvements. Time can be taken at the end of evaluation for discussion of implementation of ideas for improvement.

The Role of Facilitator

The facilitator helps to keep discussions centered on the agreed-upon topic, helps to assure that everyone who wishes to can speak and helps to keep discussions from falling into dialogues and side discussions. She/he should be sensitive to the feelings of the group and realize when some variation of process is necessary, e.g., breaking into smaller groups, going around to hear everyone's opinion, taking a break (see "Conflict Resolution" chapter for more on these techniques). The facilitator should also encourage quieter group members to participate ("I wonder if any people who haven't spoken yet have something to say?") and should be sensitive to whether people speaking are being cut off by others. A person with a strong emotional involvement in the discussion does not make a good facilitator. A facilitator who does become involved in an issue should step down and ask for someone to take over as facilitator.

Brainstorming

Brainstorming is an important tool used in meetings and group discussions to help generate as many ideas as possible on a given topic. It helps free the imagination to come up with new ideas about projects, goals, etc.

Decide on a specific question for which you wish to generate ideas, such as, "What can we do for our next fund raising event?" or "What should be the focus of our next demonstration." Set a time limit for the brainstorm.

Everyone then throws out ideas on the topic. There should be no criticism or discussion at this point. The idea is *quantity* of ideas—not quality, and to encourage creative thinking. Bizarre ideas can lead to new approaches.

Have someone record the ideas on a piece of paper on the wall. When the brainstorm is over the group should go through the list and determine which are the best ideas to work with. Or the group can divide into smaller groups, each focusing on a different project.

Decision Making

"The majority is always right...right?" NO!, in fact, the majority is often wrong. Pacifists have always been in the minority. Groups dealing in majority decision making have to be particularly sensitive to minority opinion.

Voting does have an advantage of being quicker in the short run and can be used as a "straw ballot" (non-binding) to indicate leanings or for decisions in which no one has strong feelings one way or the other. Some of the criticisms of voting, or majority rule, is that it sets up adverserial win/lose attitudes within the group and that it often leaves a disgruntled minority that feels uncomfortable with decisions and may feel alienated from the group.

Consensus

Although many WRL groups use majority vote to make decisions, many also use consensus or "sense of the meeting" decisions developed by the Quakers. The basic difference is that under consensus, the group takes no action that is not consented to by all group members. This does not mean that everyone is always in perfect agreement, but that the decision doesn't violate anyone's principles and that those who don't agree, don't disagree enough to block the group from taking an action.

Groups that use consensus feel that it has the following advantages over voting:

- It keeps people from getting into adversary attitudes where individual egos are tied to a proposal that will win or lose.

- It produces more intelligent decisions by incorporating the best thinking of everyone.

- It increases the likelihood of new and better ideas being thought up.

- Everyone has a stake in implementing a decision because all have participated in its formation. Participants have more energy for working on projects with which they are in agreement.

A basic process for reaching a decision might look something like this:

A person with a strong emotional involvement in the discussion does not make a good facilitator.

Brainstorming helps free the imagination to come up with new ideas about projects, goals, etc.

Though voting is often quicker, it frequently sets up an adversarial win/lose situation, sometimes alienating the minority.

Consensus does not mean that everyone is always in perfect agreement.

Consensus produces more intelligent decisions by incorporating the best thinking of everyone.

There are ways to object to a proposal which will allow the consensus to go forward.

First, the problem or situation needing consideration is expressed. A clear idea of what decision needs to be made is formulated. Discussion follows which can include brainstorming or breaking into small groups. After adequate discussion, people would begin to look for the "sense of the meeting." The facilitator, or anyone else, may be able to synthesize the diverse threads of the discussion into a single proposal which meets the needs of all. If there are no objections to the resulting proposal, a consensus has been reached. It is good to restate clearly what has been agreed to.

Sometimes a consensus is almost present, but there are still one or two objections. Further discussion should seek to creatively incorporate these objections into a new proposal. If the objection can be satisfied a new sense of the meeting can be seen, and the proposal has consensus. However, at times an objection is so strong that no creative alternative incorporating it can be found. There are ways to object to a proposal which allow the consensus to go forward:

1. Non-support ("I don't see the need for this but I'll go along")
2. Reservations ("I think this may be a mistake but I can live with it")
3. Standing aside ("I personally can't do this, but I won't stop others from doing it")
4. Withdrawing from the group.

New Hampshire armory after 1977 arrest of Seabrook anti-nuclear protesters. Drawing by Peg Averill.

If a new consensus cannot be reached on an issue or problem, the group can continue with the last consensual agreement reached previously, often called "falling back." Fall backs are a guarantee that we will be able to act together even when we cannot reach a new consensus (see section on fall backs in "Conflict Resolution" chapter).

Overcoming Sexism in Groups

Because sexism is an act of oppression it is important to pay special attention to it in our groups. Good group process will only come about if all members are full and equal participants. We should be aware of, and seek to change patterns of male domination. Because women traditionally fulfill nurturing functions within groups while men fill the positions of authority, we should be especially sensitive to having women take on leadership and public roles, such as facilitator or spokesperson for the group. It is important for the group to be sensitive to sexist behavior and language within the group and work together to find ways to change our behavior. A good article on this subject entitled "Overcoming Masculine Oppression in Mixed Groups," is available for $2.45 from New Society Publishers (4722 Baltimore Ave., Philadelphia, PA 19143) in a booklet entitled *Off Their Backs...And On Our Own Two Feet.*

CONFLICT RESOLUTION

By Meg Gage

What can you do when conflict develops within your group? The problem is different from conflicts arising between your group and people outside, like the police, hecklers and the uninitiated public. From these outsiders, not familiar with non-violence and nonviolent action one might anticipate a certain amount of conflict. But conflict within a group of committed nonviolent activists can be even more disconcerting because you do not expect it and may not be prepared to deal with it—surely your commitment to nonviolent social change and to nonviolence would enable you to overcome little difference of objectives, strategy, or style. So when tensions, disagreements and arguments develop between friends, we are sometimes unready to respond as creatively as we are when faced with an angry construction worker.

I have identified six guidelines which can help in dealing with this kind of conflict:

1. Learn to differentiate between conflict your group can live with and conflict it cannot live with.
2. Try to identify exactly *what* the problem is and *whose* problem it is.
3. Avoid blaming one person or faction for the conflict.
4. Assume good will on the part of those involved.
5. Always try to improve communication.
6. Learn to see conflict among friends as an opportunity for better understanding of each other.

A short essay like this can provide only the barest outline of these techniques and guidelines. They must be discussed, worked on, and developed to meet your group's needs. They sound easy and obvious, but at the moment of conflict, all of us have trouble remembering them.

1. Learn to differentiate between conflict your group can live with and conflict it cannot live with.

There is a misconception around that any group operating under consensus is continually in the process of finding things that everyone in the group can agree on. Consensus process means that everyone, every single person, has opinions which are important and should be heard. Consensus does not require agreement at all unless there is some action which needs to be taken; when action is required and there is no agreement, there are procedures for acting. Consensus is a process in which there should be conflict and differences of opinion. If a large dynamic group never had conflict, one might wonder whether people were really expressing themselves.

Often a conflict will arise for which there is no need to find a resolution. For example, in the disarmament group I work with we have some permanent conflict about how to relate disarmament work to other social justice issues. Some of us feel that while issues are inherently related, in order to get anything done and to be taken seriously by the community, it is necessary to focus only on disarmament, and to count on other groups to work on other issues. Others of us feel that our work is invalid if we do not reach out to those oppressed by racism,

> When tensions develop among friends, we are sometimes unready to respond as creatively as when we are faced with an angry construction worker.

> Consensus is a process in which there should be conflict and differences of opinion.

> If a large dynamic group never had conflict, one might wonder whether people were really expressing themselves.

Often a conflict will arise for which there is no need to find a resolution.

Sometimes a conflict will arise within a group, but its origins may relate to an incident outside the group.

One approach to conflict resolution is "owning" the problem—taking responsbility for our own problems.

One technique to help identify a problem is active listening.

poverty, sexism, corporate capitalism and the polluted environment. This is a conflict we do not have to resolve. In fact it is a conflict which helps keep us honest. We *do* have to deal with it when we plan specific actions or projects. Then through consensus and hard work we come up with plans which are probably more sound because of the different, sometimes conflicting, points of view from which they spring.

Another example comes from the Manchester Armory where over 600 of the Seabrook 1415 were incarcerated for two weeks. There was a tremendous amount of conflict about whether or not we should cooperate with the guards. Some, citing Gandhi's recommendation to be model prisoners, helped with cleaning and with administration, providing lists of names, passing on communications from the prison officials, and distributing toiletry items and food—generally helping things to run smoothly. Others felt that we should not cooperate with or in any way help the prison system to imprison us. This group felt that, not only were our actions at Seabrook legal, but that jails are a part of the same oppressive system which built the nuke we were trying to stop. The non-cooperators ranged from simply not helping the guards to a total refusal to eat or drink water.

This conflict was not so much between two opposing sides as a wide spectrum of people pretty much spread along the way. It was not necessary or appropriate for the group as a whole to have taken a position and to have "decided" what we were going to do. The question of how to deal with jail is profoundly personal and complex. No one should be pressured into fasting. And obviously it would be a gross violation of individual integrity to suggest that someone who felt the need to fast should not.

The conflict over this issue was very intense, but because conflict occurred and because the group did not try to push through a group position (although some were trying to do just that), many of us in small groups and talking one-to-one, watching each other's cooperation or lack of cooperation, thought about the question of non-cooperation with the prison system more deeply than ever before.

Sometimes conflict will arise which your group cannot live with. Then you have to try to find some sort of resolution. For example if you are planning an action in which all of the people in your group will participate, all of the people must feel satisfied with the decision.

2. Try to identify exactly what the problem is and whose problem it is.

Sometimes a conflict can arise because of someone's personal agenda of needs and wants. The person may not even be aware of that hidden agenda him/herself but may inflict the problem on the group in a distorted way. Sometimes a bad mood or a disruptive experience at home may become displaced conflict in a group hours or days later. Or a conflict between two people in one situation will carry over into another situation. Most of us have had the experience of becoming angry at someone close to us because of something upsetting that happened earlier that day. And everyone knows what lack of sleep can do to our ability to resolve conflict.

Sometimes a person's particular life situation will give them a different perspective which can come out as conflict. A friend of mine told me of becoming angry at hearing some of his friends reminisce about childhood memories of staying overnight at friends' houses. He had been so poor as a child that he was not able to have anyone overnight; hearing middle class people talk about their experience as if it were universal, made him angry. That anger could have come out as a putdown of his friends. Fortunately he understood his anger and he confronted them unaccusingly with their classism.

This approach to conflict resolution, analysing what the problem is, whose problem it is, and "owning" ones problems, has become very popular over the last fifteen years or so. Techniques have been developed which we see in transactional analysis, the "effectiveness training" movement, and re-evaluation co-counseling. This variously applied approach has some extremely helpful tools for nonviolent conflict resolution.

Any time a person feels distress or conflict, that person has a problem. It is that person's problem. Each of us is responsible for trying to resolve our own problems. We may need help in resolving them, but we are the primary person responsible for them. It is up to us to recognize our problems and to ask for the help we need. If I am feeling angry with someone, that is my problem and it is my responsibilty to do something about it. My friend was angry at his friends' discussion about staying overnight as children. The anger was *his* problem, not theirs. He dealt with it by *owning* his anger, understanding where it came from, and discharging it appropriately so that his friends became more aware of their class attitudes without resenting him.

In a conflict within a group, the problem belongs to those who feel distress or pain. It is not necessarily the problem of the whole group. If one person in a group is upset about a decision, the group can help the person define the problem and perhaps deal with it, but it is not necessarily something the whole group should take on. It may be that it is the behavior of the group which is bothering the person. It is the responsibility of that person to tell the group, and then the group can decide how to deal with it.

One technique which can help someone identify her/his problem is popularly known as creative or active listening. Listening is a communication skill few of us have learned very well, and so it is sometimes necessary to *practice* listening. There are now workshops and courses offered in listening skills which can be helpful. In active listening the listener tries to help the speaker hear what she is saying and feeling, by saying back to the speaker what he, the listener, has heard. The speaker can then clarify or further explain what she meant. The listener must not give advice, judge, or in any way comment on what he has heard so that the speaker reflects only on what she has said. If the speaker is trying to identify a problem or clarify a feeling, it is important that the listener not interfere with personal observations and opinions.

This is a technique which much be practiced to be learned. It is a basic counseling tool which is most effective in a one-to-one situation. It can be used in a group as long as the speaker is not ganged-up on by the group. The purpose of the technique of active listening is to help people clarify and understand their feelings and problems. If the speaker is intimidated, it will backfire. For a more complete description of this technique you can read any of the many books on transactional analysis, re-evaluation co-counseling or effectiveness training.

Once you have identified exactly what the problem is and whose problem it is, your group will have a much easier time resolving the conflict. If you are trying to decide whether to be dragged or to walk to the courtroom, and it turns out two or three people don't want to be dragged because they are afraid, then the group can help them face their fear, rather than debating for hours the ideological pros and cons of being dragged. It is not a problem for the whole group, but for those three people, unless the group decides that everyone should do the same thing— then it becomes a problem for the whole group. Perhaps those three people should walk and the rest can be dragged. Many conflicts which may seem irresolvable have easier solutions once the real problem is identified, and those people whose problem it is take responsibility for solving it.

3. Avoid blaming one person or faction for the conflict.

While the problem may "belong" to one person or group of people, it can be very counterproductive to blame someone for a conflict. There is a big difference between saying "This problem is yours," and "This problem is your *fault*." Guilt makes people feel defensive and outside of the group, and sometimes the group loses its ability to help someone solve a problem by making them feel guilty and therefore alienated. Our society has somehow afflicted many of us with a deep sense of guilt. We must constantly struggle in our work together to minimize that feeling because guilt and blame are inherently violent. They take away our dignity and reduce us to becoming less effective members of the group. The hidden message in saying "You are guilty" is "I am not guilty." If we can blame someone else then surely we are not guilty ourselves. By saying "You are guilty" we are also relieving ourselves of any responsibility for helping solve the problem. While it may not be our problem, we, as members of a group of nonviolent activists, have responsibility to help our friends with their problems, if they want that help.

Sometimes someone will do something which is unhelpful or even destructive to the functioning of the group. It is important to distinguish between the action which was harmful and the person

IT'S BEEN ONE OF THOSE ALL STRUGGLE, NO UNITY DAYS.

Once your have identified exactly what the problem is and whose problem it is, your groups will have a much easier time resolving the conflict.

There is a big difference between saying "This problem is yours," and "This problem is your *fault*."

We should criticize the act but not the person.

who did the action, between the deed and the doer. We should criticize the act but not the person.

Sometimes there can be a member of a group who is constantly disruptive or negative. A group may be infiltrated by a provocateur, or there may be someone who is emotionally unwell. In these cases it is especially appropriate to criticize the actions of the person rather than to blame the person her/himself. If you suspect someone of being an infiltrator, it is much more effective to confront them with their suspicious actions rather than accuse them of being an agent. In the first place you may be wrong; if an innocent person acts suspiciously, it would be helpful for them to know it. If you really do have an infiltrator in your group, it is important for them to see that nonviolence is not just a tactic, but is a way with which you relate to all people. For the nonviolent revolution to come about and be successful, we need to learn to use nonviolent responses in all situations.

In learning not to blame people for inadequate behavior, it is good to start with ourselves. Self-blaming can be the unrecognized source of conflict among people in groups.

4. Assume good will on the part of those in conflict.

Not only should we not blame each other for things that go wrong, we should also try to assume that people's intentions are good. Often we pick up cues of how others feel about us and we start to feel that way about ourselves. Children especially are very quick to see themselves the way others see them. Sometimes parents' expectations that one child is clumsy or stupid get lived out by the child who takes on the projected characteristics. Children who are treated as if they are bright and pleasant seem to become bright and pleasant. And in groups of adults, individuals can take on a role in the group because of the way the group treats them. It we treat our friends as if they are just trying to pick a fight or to be difficult, they will often fulfill our expectations. A resolution to conflict is more likely if we act as if there will be one and not as if someone is trying to cause trouble.

Furthermore, we complicate the conflict if we do not assume good will. We have the original conflict and then on top of that we heap negative feelings about those involved in the conflict. Where there are layers of conflict like

this, and the original problem is buried deep beneath many hidden attitudes and feelings, it is almost impossible to extricate the original problem and solve it.

5. Always try to improve communication.

When people are angry or upset and feelings are hurt, the cheerful suggestion: "Let's try to communicate better!" can cause more anger and resentment than a cooling of tempers. Sometimes it is helpful to rely on a technique or procedure which you have ready for conflict situations. There are several tools which your group can practice to help resolve conflict nonviolently by improving communication.

Breaking down into smaller groups. You can break down into special interest groups, or special concern groups. For example if some people have conflict because they represent a special concern, it can be helpful for them to get together and more clearly articulate their concern. Or the conflict may involve only a few people in the group, with most people neutral. Those people in conflict can often communicate better if they go off into another room, perhaps with one or two neutral facilitators, and discuss the conflict in a less public situation. Or you can break down into small groups to talk about the conflict. This way everyone gets to say more and to have more chance for dialogue, especially if there are only 2 or 3 in each group. Sometimes conflict can be resolved just by giving people a chance to talk about it more.

Straw vote. Sometimes the conflict is not as great as you may think. By taking a straw vote you can find out how many people actually feel a certain way. Sometimes one or two very vocal or concerned people can create the impression that the whole group is in conflict, which may not in fact be the case.

Go around the room. Another way of gauging the depth of the conflict is to go around the group, giving everyone an equal chance to say what they think about the issue. You can set a time limit to be sure that each contribution is equal and to prevent those who have the greatest conflict from dominating the group.

Silence. A short period of silence for reflection and cooling off can have a magical effect on communication.

List objections and amend proposal. If the conflict is about a specific proposal it can be helpful to have those who do not support the proposal list their specific objections. Then the group may be able to amend the proposal so that it reflects everyone's concerns. Listing specific objections can help clarify which part of the conflict is substantive and which is emotional.

Confrontation. Sometimes one or two people can be causing conflict. If the group has made every effort to resolve the conflict and that person or people seem to be resisting a resolution and holding up the group, it is sometimes helpful to confront them with the group's frustrations and feeling of antagonism. This can be done in a positive way, if it is free of anger and in a calm tone of voice, perhaps by someone who has not been part of the debate. A lot has been written and said about confrontation. While it is a strong and effective way to improve communication with someone who may not be aware of his/her role in a group, it can be misused and further exacerbate a conflict.

Fall-backs. If it is necessary to make a decision and the conflict is so deep that no decision is possible, you can fall-back to a previous decision. For example, imagine your group is doing civil disobedience by sitting-in at a spot picked after weeks of planning. While you are sitting at the pre-arranged spot, someone in the group suggests moving to another place where she thinks you will get more media coverage. After a lengthy and heated discussion no consensus is reached. So everyone agrees to fall-back to the original plan and stay where you are. This technique is very helpful when conflict has caused your group to feel that they can't agree on anything, but a decision has to be made. Falling-back to a previous decision helps create security and improves communication.

6. Learn to see conflict among friends as an opportunity for better understanding.

In the midst of a heated argument it is very difficult to see conflict as an opportunity for anything. But in situations of conflict we can be pushed to think more carefully about our attitudes, assumptions, and plans. Without conflict one is less likely to think about and evaluate one's views and prejudices. If we can learn to approach conflict nonviolently and openly, without defensiveness and guilt, then conflict can create an occasion for growth and understanding. If we are listening to each other, caring about each other, and trying to take from each person's point of view the best we each have to offer, then conflict can be seen as an especially intense form of interaction where we are highly attuned to each other's different needs and we can benefit from each other's contributions. This is hard to do, but worth the struggle, it seems to me. We have all been in situations where there was a consensus and then someone brought up one contradictory point, and then over the course of the ensuing discussion, everyone slowly moved over to the other point of view. By accepting each individual and the conflict which that acceptance guarantees, we have an opportunity for growth.

Conflict is an opportunity in another way: it gives us a chance to practice our conflict resolution skills. Our society has not prepared us very well for nonviolent conflict resolution and we need all the practice we can get. We must practice and then discuss and evaluate how we are doing, constantly improving our response to conflict, so that individual needs are met and our groups can function more and more effectively.

Falling-back to a previous decision helps create security and improves communication.

Without conflict one is less likely to be pushed to really think about and evaluate one's views and prejudices.

FUNDRAISING

By Dorie Wilsnack

It is not helpful to support your work through a scatter-shot method selling a few buttons and praying silently for donations.

Money is an essential tool to organizing, much as people's time is essential to organizing.

Fundraising is actually just another form of education.

Scene I. *You make all the proper arrangements—setting up an appointment with a potential donor, sending your literature packet, bringing one of your advisors with you. The conversation flows easily as you discuss the latest political crisis and the need to organize your local community around the issues. Your potential contributor is enthusiastic about your efforts. The time flies. You finally take your leave, having had a most enjoyable morning. Halfway out the door, the gnawing truth hits you—you never asked for a donation!*

Even though that was what you came for, it never felt like the "right moment" to bring the subject up. The words got stuck in your throat because you kept envisioning a rejection and an air of polite coolness falling on the room. Now you are in trouble because you needed that contribution. All the organizing ideas you had just been discussing will never be a reality if you have no money to send out the mailings and stage the rallies.

Scene II. *Your disarmament program is going strong, attracting new participants, and developing good organizing strategies. You begin planning a major action for the spring but you are stymied about how you are going to pay for it. Someone on your mailing list agrees to temporarily loan you the money. Great! Your mind rests; you can delay your financial worries until the event is over.*

These two scenes are dangerous ruts in which organizers commonly find themselves. It is not helpful to support your work through a scatter-shot method of selling a few buttons and praying silently for donations. The following comments and ideas are offered to help set you on a better path. They cover basic attitudes and plans you

will need, and some specifics about fundraising activities.

Attitudes

We have a terrible ambivalence about money. We see it at the roots of the violent system we are trying to change, yet we are personally dependent on money and our organizations don't operate well without it. We carry with us childhood histories where we had too much or too little, and where money was often intertwined with love and attention. We need to be aware of and have opportunities to talk about this complicated mixture of emotions if we are to develop new attitudes about fundraising.

We need to build our projects around a simpler notion—money is an essential tool to organizing, much as people's time is essential to organizing. No matter how important the money is, it is always a tool and a tactic, not a goal. It is a challenge to our nonviolent politics to use money in ways that build on our value system. How can we use funds to encourage more sharing, collective structures? How can we put money to use in more creative ways? If we see ourselves actively making our finances work in a nonviolent manner, we will probably feel a whole lot easier about asking for funds.

Fundraising often gets postponed because a group's political work of educating the public is more compelling and more fun. There are some myths operating in this assumption. Fundraising is actually just another form of education. You are educating people about your financial needs as well as the issues, and you are educating a constituency with financial resources as well as your other supporters. Working with this definition, and using your imagination, fundraising can be as much a source of enthusiasm among your members as all your other activities. Bake sales can double as information tables and attract even more people. Organizing a benefit houseparty is quite similar to presenting a small seminar with a keynote speaker. Working with a foundation staff will require the same kinds of approaches that you use with the press. They have a lot of clout, but they need a lot of political re-education.

Fundraising will bring you into close proximity with other groups much like yours. Your initial thought may be simply "we need to get there first." But is this consistent with the nonviolent, non-competitive society you want to build? How can you share information and coordinate fund raising calendars with other groups? What kinds of joint fundraising can you do that would not be feasible alone? When a competitive situation arises that can't be avoided, is your project willing to step back or compromise?

Your major source of funds is probably going to be individual contributors. This is where our mixed emotions are most apparent. We tend to assign donors a lot of power and then resent that power. None of this is healthy or quite accurate. Keep the thought that people who contribute to your work do so because *you* are doing them a favor, not vice versa. You are out there holding the rallies and press conferences and distributing the literature for something that they deeply believe in but don't have the time or inclination to work on actively. What they can do comfortably is make a financial gift. Respect them for that, and recognize that the work you are doing merits the money.

When we ask someone for funds and they say "no," we can't help but take it personally. We read lots into their response, e.g., that they don't like us or they don't like our project. In truth, there are many other possible reasons, such as cash-flow problems and political indecision, to name just two. Look at this from another perspective...when we ask someone for a few hours volunteer time and they say "no," we calmly take their response as reasonable and move on. We make a mental note to ask them again in a few weeks. We don't take their rejection personally. The trick is to see financial gifts in the same light. We need to include our donors as members of our community and think of them as important human beings, not pocketbooks or numbers. This principle is central to a nonviolent organization and it also produces more financial secu-

rity in the long run.

There are ways to analyze attitudes about money, donors, and fundraising in your organization's development. Have discussions on the agenda of the full group. Use role playing as a way to define emotions and to understand the perspective of the donor. Analyze and review fundraising activities from an emotional/political perspective as well as by financial returns. Take notes on these evaluations for the people who come after you.

There is a tendency to leave all fundraising considerations to one or two stalwarts. However, this not only encourages the myth that fundraising should be separate from "real program" work, but it will burn out the lonely individual who shoulders the responsibility. A good structure is to have a fundraising committee of 4 or 5 active members, and to include fundraising and finances on the whole group agenda regularly. If you have a fundraising coordinator, make sure the emphasis in on the *coordination* and not on being the sole fundraiser.

Planning

One result of our emotional ambivalence about fundraising is our refusal to look too far into the future. (This probably reflects some political insecurities, too.) We resist developing one or two-year financial plans because we are afraid we'll never bring in the money we will need. Why make a plan that we're convinced will end in failure? Why not just wing it, one step at a time?

This is where you need to grit your teeth and think logically. Operating as you go is actually more emotionally wearing and draining on your project; it gives your donors a shaky image. Funding will come easier, believe it or not, if you plan ahead.

1. Set your program for the year ahead down in writing. Second-guess and project where you have to, but write a full year's program.

2. Develop an expense budget for the year. Talk with other organizations to glean estimates for your printing, mailing, telephone expenses, etc. You now have a goal for your fundraising.

3. List all your possible sources of funds by category (mail fund appeals, benefits, newsletter subscriptions, etc.).

4. Make realistic estimates of how much income you can raise in each area. Your aim is to come up with a fund-

Your major source of funds is probably going to be individual contributors.

Set up a fundraising committee, and discuss fundraising regularly at your general meetings.

We resist developing one- or two-year financial plans because we are afraid we'll never bring in the money we need.

raising plan that can bring in a little more money than you anticipate needing. For example, this may require cutting back on your expense budget in one area and pushing for higher results at one of your houseparties.

5. Lay out your fundraising activities on a calendar, making sure they are spread realistically throughout the year. If you can set your expense plans down on a similar calendar grid, you can foresee cash-flow problems ahead of time, and alter your plans to avoid them.

At this planning stage, it would be invaluable to create a "model proposal"— a two- or three-page description of your project; including purpose, program, and projected budget. Such a summary can serve to help your whole project in clarifying definitions, program goals, and strategies. It will also provide you with the basic first draft for foundation proposals, letters to individual donors, fund-appeals, and magazine articles your project may write.

A resource piece like this will provide consistency and give newer members a starting point.

Consider long range program projections. What do you see your project doing over the next five years? Where do you want your finances to come from? Your first year is the time to set up fundraising patterns that will ultimately provide you with self-sufficiency.

Political activists worry about the compromises and strings attached to the money they raise, especially from foundation grants and large donors. Some discomfort along these lines may have to be tolerated at first, but in making your long range funding plans, you can insure yourselves against such constraints. You just need to work toward an ever growing financial base of small and medium sized donations. Count on them for a third of your money at first, and aim to increase in small steps over the five-year period. This will mean a constant search for new supporters, and expanding op-

portunities to which people can contribute (e.g., newsletter subscriptions, a yearly raffle, an annual dinner or poetry reading).

A variety of activities like the examples above serves another important function. If one of your fundraising events fails, you have a dozen other activities to fall back on. Your whole financial security was not resting on that one item. Remember that you don't need to plan a whole set of fundraising efforts above and beyond your group's political activities. Every film showing and public speaker, every pamphlet and button can serve as a fundraising opportunity as well.

Mail Fund Appeals

- Develop your house mailing list. Send information materials as well as fund appeals out regularly (3 to 6 times a year is common). People will count on receiving them at the same time each year, and will plan their contribution schedule around that.

- Decide how many mail appeals to send, spreading them over the year. Time them to coincide with certain events (e.g., tax day, Hiroshima day, your project's anniversary). Fund appeals have been found to be the most effective in the early fall, the December holidays, and the spring.

- Personalize your mailing as much as you can. If you have the time, hand address the envelopes and personally sign each letter. If you have the money, send them first class.

- Include a return envelope with your mailing, postage paid if possible. Also enclose a return card where contributors can fill in their name and address and check a box identifying their contribution size. Filling out such a card has the effect of encouraging donors, and labeling the boxes with $10 to $500 encourages them to give a larger amount.

- You can also leave space on the return card for the suggested names of other people who would be interested in your project. Encourage your donors to recommend their friends.

- To add new names to your contributors list, you may want to do a mass fund appeal once each year. This is a very basic introduction to your project sent to "new" lists, such as subscribers to a publication, church rosters, and organization mailing lists. Include a nicely designed brochure with your letter. The goal of a mass mailing is more to acquire names than to make a lot of money; if you can break even on the mailing costs, you have been successful.

- Though your letter will have the most integrity if signed by one of your group's members, you occasionally may have the opportunity to send an appeal signed by a well-known public figure. Or you can combine the two by having someone famous write a supportive "P.S." at the bottom of the page.

- A *successful* mailing to your own list will bring in a 7% or better return. A *successful* mass mailing to another list will bring in a 1% return.

- If bulk rate mailings are used have a postage meter imprint on the envelope, rather than an imprint put on by the printer. It looks more like postage at first glance, thus more important and more likely to be opened.

- Large donors should be given an annual budget. It indicates you're serious about planning and have a good grasp on financial matters.

Assorted Notes on Fundraising Possibilities

- Encourage people to become pledgers. That will assure you of some consistent income.

- Donors identified as capable of giving more can be phoned. If you are unsure of yourself, phoning allows you to have a list of reminders in front of you, and it is less threatening than getting all dressed up and ringing a doorbell.

- Every project should have a built in fundraising aspect. Literature can always have at least a soft sell and events can always have a verbal pitch as part of the program.

- *Pass the hat* at all meetings, marches, and rallies generally advertised to the public. Make an announcement and appeal sometime during the meeting, then pass around buckets appropriately labeled. Make sure you have enough 1-quart buckets, about one per 50 people is sufficient.

- *Literature* does not usually bring in a great deal of money but can be a fairly reliable and steady source of income if handled carefully (see "Literature Program" chapter).

- If you think you can attract large donations or foundation grants, you should investigate the possibility of acquiring tax-exempt status. This can be done through applying to the IRS, or finding a "fiscal sponsor" who will act as your fiscal umbrella. Tax-exempt monies cannot be used for political lobbying or illegal activities, but they can be used for "educational" purposes. They require clear financial record-keeping.

- *Foundation grants* are for puddle-jumping. They can help a project get off the ground, or they can help an ongoing organization start a new program. They are one-time gifts, rarely more. The require lengthy preparation time, but they are large enough to be worth it usually. They involve researching the most appropriate foundations to approach, writing a proposal and letters of inquiry, following-up with personal visits to foundation staff.

- Sale of *unusual items* such as posters, T-shirts with silk screened slogans and graphics, balloons, prints, buttons, plants, stamp albums, etc., can bring in more money than usual items, such as books.

- *Bake sales* are another fairly reliable, but financially small, way to bring in money. The idea is simple enough: several people volunteer to bake cookies, cakes, pies, candy, and other goods that have sufficient eye-appeal to sell. The food is set up in a busy area and at a time when the flow of hungry traffic is greatest, around lunch time. Prices can be set at about double the cost of the ingredients. Work this out in advance and set up index cards with prices and names of the items being sold. A neatly painted sign is helpful to draw attention. Always have literature next to the food. If done carefully, $50-100 can be raised each day.

  Selling the goods can be fun if you are careful not to put the burden of the baking or selling on one or a small number of people. Share recipes and

Every project should have a built in fundraising aspect.

Foundation grants are for puddle-jumping—they can help a project get off the ground, or they can help an ongoing organization start a new program.

kitchens to encourage those who are shy about their cooking. To avoid a situation where women do most of the cooking, try alternating days where women cook one day and the men the next.

Variations on bake sales might be to sell coffee and breakfast rolls in mornings, some sort of cool drink and sandwiches in the afternoon.

- *Film showings* are potentially excellent ways to raise money but, because of the overhead, can be financial flops if not done properly (see "Film Program" chapter).

- *Benefits* for your group by bands, theater groups, singers, poets, and other sympathetic performers can be potentially good money raisers (see the "Organizing a Benefit Concert" chapter).

- *Peace fairs* set up in a central location can bring in hundreds of dollars, if planned and executed carefully. Have one area where a central platform can be set up for the entertainment. Literature tables, concession stands, booths of hand-made articles to be sold, potted plants, and so forth should be set up.

Other sympathetic community groups should be invited to put up their booths of literature, etc. This is particularly important as an additional attraction to potential fairgoers but also allows these other groups to spread the word of your fair around the community. Well-planned publicity (posters, leaflets, press releases, balloons) is essential.

- *Garage sales* (or yard-, lawn-, attic-sales) can bring in hundreds of dollars, especially if everyone in your group donates unwanted furniture, appliances, National Geographics, etc. Advertise in the classified section of the paper, put a sign in front of your house, post signs on telephone poles around the neighborhood. You must really slash prices or people won't come and things won't move. There must be real bargains. Always have literature on hand. Rummage sales or street fairs are other possibilities (see chapter on "Street Fairs").

- *"Peace work day"* can be a day that everyone in the group is committed to doing odd-jobs (together if possible) around the community. Mow lawns, wash cars, paint houses, sell flowers on street corners, etc. This sort of thing can be beneficial for group solidarity as well as bringing in money.

- *Giving up* smoking, drinking, movies, food, etc., for a particular period of time and then donating the money saved to the group can bring in considerable sums with some groups.

Follow Up

Many people have gone before you in the anxious search for funds. You can benefit from their experience, particularly from other social change activists. Some of their advice is available in writing:

Search for Security, 1985, available from the Forum Institute, 1225 15th St. NW, Washington, DC 20005. Features profiles of foundations which make grants to organizations working on international security and prevention of nuclear war issues.

Grant Seekers Guide, ed., Jill R. Shellow, 1985, available from National Network of Grantmakers, 2000 P Street NW, Suite 410, Washington, DC 20036. Provides information on grantmakers and their programs; geared towards community-based, social and economic justice projects.

The Grassroots Fundraising Book, Joan Flanagan, 1977, available from the Youth Project, 1000 Wisconsin, NW, Washington, DC 20007. An outline of steps for every fundraising activity you might be considering.

The Bread Game, ed. Herb Allen, 1975, available from Glide Publications, 330 Ellis Street, San Francisco, CA 94102. A how-to-do-it manual for those seeking funding from foundations.

The Grantsmanship News, 1031 South Grand Avenue, Los Angeles, CA 90015. A bi-monthly magazine full of articles that de-mystify the moneyed world, and articles on important organizational advice. It uses wonderful graphics, and there is a strong sense of humor running throughout (very important!).

The rest of your advice will come from talking, and being observant. Read and learn from the fund appeals that arrive in your mailbox. Pay close attention at the benefits you attend. Ask other activist fundraisers questions. Set up appointments with them. Corner them at parties. They won't give you the names of their donors, but they will give you ideas.

LOCAL LITERATURE PROGRAM

By Jerry Coffin

The production and distribution of relevant printed materials—literature—is an important activity of any organization. The National WRL literature program consists of a regularly updated list of about 200 items: books, pamphlets, etc. Last year we sold about $20,000 worth of literature, apart from 13,000 Peace Calendars. We distributed about 120,000 copies of *The Nonviolent Activist*, sold hundreds of maps, posters, buttons, organizing packets, and T-shirts.

Literature in all its forms is an important way of spreading ideas and educating people on issues, programs and politics. A well-organized literature program can also be a major source of funds for local, regional and national groups. For instance, the National WRL raises a significant part of its annual budget by selling the annual Peace Calendar. In addition, the literature program is a regular source of operating money.

This chapter deals with whys and hows of organizing and maintaining a local literature program. Remember, this is only a sample of what can be done to create a literature program.

Why Have a Local Literature Program?

The most important reason for developing a strong local literature program is education. In most areas of the country, books, periodicals, and pamphlets related to radical and pacifist subjects are not readily available. If they are available at all, it's only after a long search for a particular title. In order for radical and pacifist literature to be widely read and accepted, people must have access to the literature.

By creating an active literature program you can win converts and raise consciousness. By bringing literature to the people, you're opening them up to new ideas and concepts, and providing them with the opportunity to learn about, understand, and eventually participate in the movement for social change.

Beyond its educative and outreach function, a literature program can be a significant source of funds for your local organization. A literature program is one of the few ways of raising money while you're engaged in the education and outreach work you'd normally be doing.

Setting Up a Local Literature Program

First, and most important, is finding one person in your organization who will make the literature program her/his primary responsibility. To be successful, the program must be persistent. One-shot attempts at a program will not work. The person who volunteers to handle the literature should be prepared to keep good records, develop a regular system

A well-organized literature program can also be a major source of funds.

Find one person in your group who will make the literature program their primary responsibility.

of ordering literature for resale, and organize a regular system for selling the literature.

Ordering Literature

For local WRL's, almost any item on the WRL literature list may be ordered at a 30% discount. The WRL will advance a certain number of books on consignment to locals. For other groups, you need to deal directly with publishers. This entails: 1) developing a list of books you wish to handle; 2) writing to the publishers and requesting their bookstore catalog; 3) ordering from the publisher (usually you have to order in lots of from 10 to 40 copies of each title). The drawbacks are that you need to pay in advance for the books and order a large number of copies of each title. The usual publishers discount to retailers is 40%. The reason WRL gives only a 30% discount to locals is because we need to cover postage and handling costs, and sometimes we get less than a 40% discount.

Selling the Literature

Once you've selected and ordered the items you wish to sell from the WRL list and other sources, you should develop your selling plan. Simply putting the literature in your office and waiting for people to come buy the stuff is not enough. You must go to the people. This means taking your literature to places where sympathetic people gather and setting up a literature table. It also means

going to places like your campus library or dining hall at a regular time each week (say, every Tuesday and Thursday from 6 pm to 10 pm in front of the library and/or every Monday, Wednesday and Friday at lunch time in front of the dining hall and/or one evening a week at a dormitory) and selling the literature on a regular basis. The key here is regularity.

If the word gets around that you're in front of the library every week at a certain time, you'll develop a regular clientele and word will spread that you're there. In addition, if you have regular hours and places for your table, you can put out advertising leaflets telling people where they can buy radical literature. You can feature a certain title each week and offer a discount on that title.

Whenever there's a demonstration or large gathering of almost any character (conference, concert, basketball game, etc.) you should set up your literature display and sell. Stand by your table and call attention to what you're offering for sale. If you can get into this type of selling, you'll be surprised how many items you can sell. After a while you'll know which large gatherings are best for selling literature and you can concentrate on them.

Mechanics of Selling

While you have to be persistent in selling literature, you can make it simple. Get an old trunk, or construct a literature display case (see drawing) and keep all your books and pamphlets in the trunk

Literature table at 50th Anniversary conference of WRL in 1973, Asliomar, California. Photo by Grace Hedemann.

Literature Case

Make the case out of ½ " plywood with 2" x 2" frame. Glue and screw all joints. To maintain structural integrity (i.e., so it won't fall apart), the lid and front must be secured to each other and the sides when the case is closed. Hasps seem to work best for holding lid and front to each other and the sides. A hasp is what you use to lock something with a padlock. The best hinges to use are piano hinges. A piano hinge is one long hinge that you cut to size. It runs the length of the hinged joint.

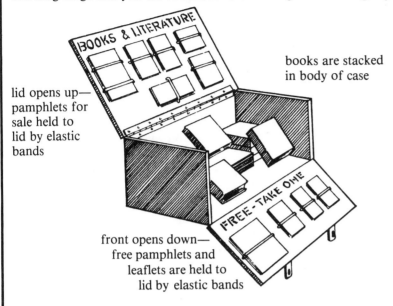

books are stacked in body of case

lid opens up—pamphlets for sale held to lid by elastic bands

front opens down—free pamphlets and leaflets are held to lid by elastic bands

dimensions should be determined by number of books and pamphlets you wish to sell

or case. Also keep a money can with change stored inside the trunk or case. Get a folding table and folding chair and make a sign that gives the name of your group and has "books and pamphlets" written on it. The sign needs to be on cloth so it can be folded up and put in the trunk/case or on cardboard small enough to fit inside the trunk/case. Using this method you have a self-contained literature-selling outfit. When you go out to sell literature, throw the trunk/case, table and chair in the trunk of a car, go to your location and in minutes you're set up and selling. If you use the trunk you'll have to spread the books on the table, but that doesn't take much time.

Record Keeping

Your program will be more successful

Your program wil be more successful if you keep accurate records.

Sample Inventory List

On this form you have a record of each title and a cumulative inventory list. You can tell how many books you've sold by subtracting current number of books on hand for a given title from the previous week's inventory. A quick glance at this form will tell you which titles are your best sellers. You need only xerox a few such forms.

Title & Inventory No.	1/28 copies on hand	2/4 copies on hand	2/11 copies on hand	2/18 copies on hand	2/25 copies on hand
Power of People #1	2	2	1	5	4
Gandhi #2	4	3	1	5	3
Living My Life #3	2	1	0	4	3

Don't get caught with a static literature list, or you lose your regular buyers.

if you keep accurate records. This means some method of knowing how many of a given title you sell in a week, and always having enough of the title on hand to cover sales. If you don't keep records and inventory of your literature every week, you'll discover that you only order a book when you're out of it. This results in poor sales, since you'll always be out of a number of your better sellers. Illustrated is a sample (and simple) form designed to keep track of a single book. The best system seems to be to have one sheet that has a running record of sales for each book. This way you know when you're running low on a book so you can reorder before you run out and you also can see which books sell the best. Some of the best books politically are poor sellers, so you have to develop a poor-seller-to-good ratio that makes sense, such as one "good politics poor seller" to every three "good politics good seller."

Finally, don't get caught with a static literature list. Either update the list every couple of months or constantly add and drop titles. Whichever system you use, be sure that list doesn't become static or you lose your regular buyers.

Conclusion

The program outlined in this chapter has worked well in many areas of the country. It has been a proven method of outreach and gained new workers for local groups. It has been a proven method of fundraising, in some cases paying all the operating costs of a local group. Again, the key points in making it work are:

- have one responsible, committed person make literature her/his primary job
- keep records and keep up your inventory
- always go to large gatherings of sympathetic people and develop places where you sell literature at a regular time each week.

Sample Inventory Card

This card can be used as a way of keeping track of each book or pamphlet in your inventory. Mimeograph or xerox a blank copy of the form for each item. Inventory should be noted each week or so on a regular schedule. Orders should be placed far enough in advance to guarantee you won't run out of a title. The reason you note when you order and when you receive an order is so you know how long it takes to get delivery. Also, this form will tell you if you owe money or if you've already paid a bill you're getting hounded about. The form will tell you when you've ordered books so you can follow up on the wholesaler if delivery is delayed.

Inventory No. _____1_____

Title ___Power of the People___

Author ___Edited by R. Cooney + H. Michalowski___

Publisher ___Peace Press___

Retail Price ___$9.95___

Order from ___WRL, 339 Lafayette St., NYC 10012___

Minimum Order ___2___

Date	Inventory	Ordered	Received	Paid for Order
1/28/81	2 copies	4 copies	—	ck. #201
2/16/81	1 copy	—	4 copies	—
2/25/81	4 copies	—	—	—
3/12/81	2 copies	—	—	—

A LOCAL FILM PROGRAM

By Lynne Shatzkin Coffin

Local groups have two basic problems. The first is outreach—spreading your message in the community. The second is finances—making enough money to sustain yourselves while you organize part or full time. A film program can be helpful in solving both of these problems. By the films you select, you can spread your message in a medium that may be more palatable to folks in your community than methods such as leafletting or literature campaigns. Also, if you plan and organize your film program with care, you can provide your group with a regular income.

How to Select Your Films

The first problem after deciding to initiate a film program will be to decide what films to show. You will need to reserve your films at least one month to perhaps as much as six months in advance. So planning is important. Sit down with your group and some film catalogues, and map out a strategy. This should take into consideration the following elements:

1. **Make-up of the Community You Are Trying To Reach**

   Are you primarily involved with organizing students? Is your group mixed between students and community people? Films for student audiences may not be appropriate for the general community. If your group is mixed, your problem may be more difficult. Trying to find a common denominator is not always easy. The important thing is "Who am I going to attract?" and "Who do I want to reach?"

2. **What Other Events Are Taking Place?**

   In mapping out your strategy of what films to show it is very important to take into consideration several factors which may be beyond your control, such as

   Other Film Programs. In most communities, especially around universities, there will probably be another film program already in existence. Find out as much information as possible about films they have planned, when, where, how much they charge, etc. It is usually not a good idea to have two films on the same topic showing at the same time, even in the same week. Most people don't go to movies more than once a week; and if they do, they want variety in what they see. An exception to this might be a film festival or program with a particular theme.

   Political and Cultural Events. Take advantage of being able to build an audience by showing a film that is relevant to a specific issue or program important to your community. This is not always easy to predict in advance, but when you have prior knowledge, use it. For example, if you or other groups are engaging in a campaign for welfare reform, use the interest in that campaign to stimulate interest in your film. Of course, this also works in reverse, because your film can build interest in the campaign you are already engaging in.

   Also, if the local State College is having a week-long symposium on

A film program can be helpful in solving problems in outreach and finances.

Reserve your films at least a month to six months in advance.

Take care your films are not scheduled in competition with a major event.

law, you might want to schedule a film on repression and the law. The advantages are two-fold. You get free publicity for your film and are able to present a political side to a discussion which might not have been included.

3. The Message You Want To Get Across

Uppermost in your mind when you select your film should be your own political position. Don't choose films with which you have fundamental disagreements simply because you think they might attract large audiences and raise money. Remember, your group is sponsoring the film and people will connect what the film has to say with you.

> **Uppermost in your mind when you select your film should be your own political position.**

Ordering Films

There are several groups from whom movement-oriented films can be ordered. Media Network (see end of chapter) produces several film guides on various social issues. Also see the 1987 WRL Calendar "Films for Peace & Justice." Major film distributors (e.g., Audio Brandon) will send you a catalog of films they carry.

Photo by Karl Bissinger.

Costs of films vary widely, but commercial distributors usually charge 50% of the gross take or a minimum fee (from $40 to $200 or more), whichever is greater. Movement groups and non-commercial distributors (universities and public libraries) usually charge a flat rate, such as $5 to $15, and sometimes offer free films. Many non-commercial distrubutors stipulate that there be no admission charge. When ordering films, make sure there is enough lead time in order to receive the film before the showing. The U.S. Postal Service, UPS,

> **The key expenses to minimize are the film rental, room, projector, and advertising.**

and Greyhound have all been known to deliver late. Nothing can be more devastating than to have a sellout crowd for a showing with no film. Also, do not order a cinemascope film unless you have a cinemascope projector.

Setting Up the Showing

The Room. If you are near a college campus and have contacts there, you should be able to arrange an auditorium through the school. Make sure that you fill out all the necessary forms and go through all the "channels" so that you end up with written confirmation of the auditorium with a date and time specified. At most colleges there is a person who is specifically assigned the task of reserving and scheduling rooms. It will help you in the long run to be as friendly to this person as possible. She/he wields a tremendous amount of power and has a lot of leeway in decision making. A good personal contact in this office can make the difference in a good turnout for your film by giving you a good location.

Because competition is stiff, some universities hold lotteries for auditoriums and dates for the whole school year among those campus groups who wish to show films. Since Friday and Saturday night competition is so keen, you might consider showing films on other nights.

If there is no space available to you on a campus, you can arrange to show your films in a church or other community meeting place. If all these options fail, try to find a person with a large living room or recreation room who is willing to let you use it for your film showing.

The Projector. You will need a 16mm sound projector. In fact, some groups use two projectors so that there will not be a break in the film if there is more than one reel. Projectors can sometimes be obtained free from a college or library or church or possibly a community group like the YWCA, if you have contacts there. If not, you will have to rent one. Remember, it is important to have a firm commitment on the loan of the projector.

You will also need a qualified person to run the projector. If there is no one in your group who is qualified, make sure you train at least one person and preferably two in the use of the machine. Be sure that these people are able not only to turn the machine on and off, but understand how it works so that they will be able to repair it if something goes wrong. They should also know how to repair the film in case it breaks or is damaged.

Projection Suggestions. If you do not have a projection room, you'll want to make sure your projector is not a noisy one (e.g., with a lot of chatter), which can be a major distraction during the showing. Make sure you have a take-up reel, an extra projection lamp, an extra exciter lamp (for the sound), an extension cord (if necessary), equipment to make a proper splice (tape may damage the film). Check out the film well enough in advance to make sure it is rewound. Can the room be darkened properly? If the projector is not in good shape, it may "chew-up" the film. Use a soft brush, air bulb, or Q-tip to clean away dust in the film "gate," before the showing.

Tickets and the Collection of Money

It is important to have tickets ready at the showing. These can be purchased on rolls at an inexpensive price or you can make your own. The reason for this is to enable you to keep order with a large number of people, to keep count of the number of people attending, and sell in advance if so desired.

You will need a box of some kind to keep your money in. Security of the box is essential; so one person should be responsible for it at all times. Be sure to have some change for the first people to arrive. It is possible to lose sales simply because people don't have anything smaller than a ten dollar bill.

For proper staffing of the event you will want 5 to 10 people: 2 to sell tickets, 1 or 2 to take tickets, 1 or 2 projectionists, 1 or 2 on the literature table, and perhaps one person on security.

Security and Fire Regulations

On most college campuses, as well as in public buildings of all types, there are rules about public meetings. These rules will also apply to your movie if they take place in a college auditorium or public place. Find out what they are in advance so that you do not run the risk of having your movie closed in the middle of a showing. You may be required in some places to hire a security guard for a fee. Again, know these things in advance. Try to get around the rule by providing your own "security," pay the fee if you can afford it (and want to), or decide to hold your showing in another place. If you want to challenge the rulings, remember that you may end up having your movie disrupted. Whatever the circumstances, the most important thing is to find out all the facts in advance.

The other problem which you will face in terms of regulations is fire laws. Find out the rules which apply to your building and the size of the crowd which you think you will have. Usually the rules involve "No Smoking." This rule can be enforced by one of the two people who have responsibility for the film showing. Before the film starts, remind people of this regulation and explain that their cigarette money is helping the military, as well as creating discomfort for non-smokers.

Records

Keep a record of the amount you gross each month and your profit. Include the name and category of the film and where it was shown. This will help you to determine after a few months what kinds of films are attracting large audiences and help you in the selection of new films. You may also decide on the basis of this information that you are attracting large enough crowds that you may want to do more showings of your films.

Literature Table

One of the major reasons for having a regular film program is to publicize the work and politics of your group. One effective way to take advantage of the group which has assembled to see your film is to have a literature table set up outside of the room. Make sure that you have someone who will be responsible for setting up the table and being there to answer any questions. Have a sheet of paper which people can sign to join your mailing list and a box for contributions. (See the chapter on "Local Literature Program.")

Publicity

One of the most important aspects of a film program is the amount and quality of the publicity that you produce. You can have a fantastic program but if

Be sure to have a well-qualified projectionist who not only can run a projecter but who can make repairs.

One of the most important aspects of a film program is the amount and quality of the publicity that you produce.

the publicity is sloppy, late, or simply not done, then your program has little chance of being successful. Designate someone from your group whose sole responsiblity is coordinating the publicity for your films. This can be an enormous task if you take your film program seriously—and you should—if you are serious about building your group and spreading your philosophy.

Posters. You can produce a large number of mimeographed posters (8½ " × 11") for little money. They can be distributed as leaflets, and posted all around. The key here, as in any leaflet, is the design. Make sure that they are clear as to time and place. Get an artist to design your leaflet/poster around the theme of your movie. But remember to be careful that the design does not detract from or obscure the time and place. Make sure the name, address, phone number of your organization are listed.

You can attract people to your group by leaflets. People can get a sense of participation this way. On college campuses, organize by dormitories. Be sure that your announcements are posted in every elevator and on every floor, as well as on the doors leading in and out of the dorm. Get them up early and then, a few days before the film showing, go around again and make sure that they are still up and if they aren't, post them again. Post your announcements in store windows and in places where people you think would be interested gather.

If you have a regularly functioning film program, it will pay for you to design and produce a larger poster on heavy stock. This can be used throughout your program by simply leaving a blank space for the title, time and place of your movie. In this way people will become aware of your program as well as individual movies and you will attract a regular crowd by your reputation. Be careful in selecting the spots for these posters. Choose places where they will get maximum attention and have minimum chance of being immediately ripped down. If possible, try to obtain access to the glass cases that are used to post announcements in universities and churches.

Radio. Have your movie announced on the local radio "community bulletin board" on your campus or in the community. Again be sure that the time, place, and price or requested contribution are included as well as your organization's name and phone number.

Newspapers. At some point you may want to spend the money to place an ad in the school paper or local alternative or community paper. Be sure that they are well designed to receive maximum attention. If you don't want to or can't spend the money, get your event placed in the announcement or calendar section of the paper. Check the deadlines and get your copy submitted in plenty of time.

You may also be able to obtain a free display ad by convincing the editor of the paper of the importance and worth of your organization. Another way to gain free newspaper publicity is to have someone interview you on the start of your "new project." For instance, a college newspaper may be interested in writing an article on "WRL Southwest's New Film Program" which would discuss the political as well as social aspects of your program.

Other Publicity. There are several additional ways to publicize your film program. One way is to have all the teachers in area high schools and colleges whose subjects even vaguely relate to your movie announce it in their classes. Of course, it is even better if they recommend that their class attend.

Another method in initial scheduling of the movies is to have them relate to other programs such as speakers, symposiums, community events, etc.

Making Your Program Profitable

All the previously discussed techniques or approaches to publicity, scheduling, etc., will help to make your film program successful in terms of monetary profit as well as community work. The final step in this is to set your prices so that they will be in line with the community you are trying to reach as well as the other movie projects that are already going in your community. You could charge a dollar or two. In some situations it may be reasonable to request more. Remember to calculate how many people your auditorium or room can seat, how many people to expect, and total what your expenses will be.

For example, you can rent "Fail Safe" from Audio Brandon for 50% of the gross or $35, whichever is higher. Projector rental costs $35, posters and leaflets are $25, classified ads are $35, and miscellaneous expenses (e.g., tickets) are $5; making a total of $100.

If you have a regularly functioning film program, it will pay to design and produce a larger poster with blanks for the title, time and place of showing.

You are showing it at 7:30 and 9:30 on a Friday in an auditorium which seats 200. Considering the competition, you expect to draw 150 per showing. If you ask $1, the fee to Audio Brandon is $150, making your total expenses $250, resulting in $50 proceeds. Or looking at it in another way, you must have 100 per showing to break even.

If you wish to determine the value of your various forms of advertising, just before you turn out the lights before each showing ask for a quick show of hands for "How many heard about this showing from the poster?", etc.

Community Organizing

One of the most important aspects of your film program is how you use it in terms of your ongoing work. As stated previously, a film program can be of tremendous help in carrying your message to other folks. Make sure that you select films that will interest and challenge the folks you are trying to reach, and most important, that reflect your feelings and politics. Be comfortable with your films and use them to the fullest advantage. It will require work to get the program going, but the benefits from a creative, effective program will be well worth the effort.

recommended sources to help you develop a film program.

Films for Peace & Justice, 1987 WRL Calendar, available for $6.75 in the Fall of 1986 from WRL.

Reel Change—A Guide to Social Issue Films, 140 pp., The Film Fund, 1979. This book has 500 titles. A new edition jointly produced by The Film Fund and Media Network will be available in late 1986. The current edition can be obtained from Media Network, 121 Fulton Street, Fifth Floor, New York, NY 10038, for $7.45.

In Focus: A Guide To Using Films, Blackaby, Georgakas, Margolis, Cine Information, Inc., 1980, available from Media Network for $10.45. This is the best resource for organizers who want to set up a film program. It tells you how to use a projector, how to find a place for a showing, figuring a budget, conducting a discussion afterwards, and where to write for catalogs.

And finally, the Media Network has a series of specific guides to films on the following issues: disarmament, Central America, South Africa and apartheid, reproductive rights, the Third World, community organizing issues, labor, and the environment. Each guide is available for $2.50.

It will require work to get a film program going, but the benefits from a creative, effective program will be well worth the effort.

Check List

The following is a check list to refer to when you think that you are ready to show your film.

☐ Has the film been confirmed with the distributor as to title and date?

☐ Is there a confirmed room to show the film?

☐ Is the room dark enough? Does it have proper wall plugs? A screen?

☐ Have I checked with security and fire officials?

☐ Are tickets ready?

☐ Who are the two people responsible for the showing?

☐ Is there a box to keep money in?

☐ Are there enough volunteers to sell tickets, take tickets, be on the literature table, run the projector, clean up, etc.?

☐ Have I done as much publicity as I can?

☐ Is there a record of the expenses?

☐ Has there been an arrangement to set up a literature table?

☐ Am I prepared for film or projector breakdowns?

☐ Is the film wound properly?

☐ Will volunteers be at the auditorium an hour in advance (or more) to put up signs advertising the show, etc.?

Resources

Listed below are several highly

ORGANIZING A BENEFIT CONCERT

By David Catanzarite

Benefits educate, as well as raise money.

There are aspects of every social issue that cannot be articulated in words, but can be communicated through art.

Determine how political the event is to be.

Concerts, dances, and poetry readings are a good way to raise funds, if you know what you're doing. Far too many benefits raise very little money or even lose money; more often than not, this kind of bust could have been avoided with a little thoughtful planning.

To view benefits *only* as a way to raise money overlooks a great deal of their potential. They are also an important organizing tool. Many people who will pass up leaflets, newsletters, and speeches will learn and get inspired to act from the words and feelings presented in political song or theater; often people who avoid rallies will listen attentively to a political rap during the break between bands. There are aspects of every social issue that cannot be articulated in words, but can be communicated through art. Moreover, the group feeling of a good cultural event can help build a sense of community among diverse people.

The following outline explains primarily how to promote a small or medium sized event (200-1000 people). Most of the information will, however, apply to shows on a larger scale with some modifications.

Choosing an Event

The first questions to ask when organizing an event are, "What kind of a show do we want?" and "Who are we trying to reach?" What kind of tone will the event establish? Celebration? Mourning? Urging people to act? You wouldn't want a good-time dance band for a Hiroshima Day commemoration. What kind of audience do you want to attract? Draft age teenagers? Black? Latino? White? Women? Lesbians and gay men? This may seem an obvious question but I have seen more than one occasion where, for instance, a group doing anti-racist work books a rock band popular with white audiences, into a hall usually attended by the white community, and then is surprised when lots of whites and very few non-whites turn up for the show.

In a political fundraiser, there are four major factors that determine what kind of audience you draw, roughly in this order of importance: 1) who the performers are, and what other shows are in town that night; 2) the kind of publicity you use; 3) the political issue(s) being addressed and the "name recognition" of your organization; 4) where the event is held. Price of admission can vary; a general rule is to set the price at roughly the same amount as a comparable non-political show.

Another question to ask is, "How overtly political will the event be?" There are a number of performing artists who devote their lives to political cultural work. Often their performance alone is a thoroughly political event. But there are many other musicians and performing artists who will contribute their talents to a cause, although their work is not overtly political.

When working with such performers, a promoter must decide how many political speeches and announcements (if any) should be given time in the program. Bear in mind that people usually pay to attend a benefit primarily to be entertained, and not to be talked to. One compromise is to find a funny M.C. who can talk politics. In some shows the only political information you may want to present is a prominently displayed literature table staffed by a member of your organization.

Production

Sometimes there are one or two nightclubs or coffeehouses in town that are willing to sponsor benefits for political causes. Such places are worth approaching, but remember that donating a night's worth of business, especially on a weekend, isn't easy to afford. Unless you have booked a ''star'' who can bring the club good publicity, the manager may ask for a part of the door sales or bar. It is worth weighing the advantages of making more money but doing a lot more work yourself.

Occasionally an independent producer, or perhaps a student-run production group at a large university, will be interested in co-producing a show with you. You may be asked to provide part of the front money and volunteer workers. Especially for very large concerts, this may be the best way to go; most big-name performers are reluctant to work with amateur promoters. Again, the more work the professional promoters do, the more of your proceeds you may be asked to split.

Budget

Before you start booking halls and performers, give some thought to at least a rough budget. *This is the best guarantee against losing money on a show.* Attention should be paid to the following items:

1. Front money. The larger the show, the more you will need to pay for items in advance. Sometimes you can get short-term loans from people who are well off.

2. Publicity costs.

3. Sound, lights, security. Shop around, prices for sound systems vary a lot.

4. Hall rental, insurance, cleaning deposit

5. Investment in concessions (food, beer, cups, etc.).

6. ''Miscellaneous.'' Don't let incidentals such as postage, long distance phone calls, gas, etc., slip by unaccounted for. They can add up to hundreds of bucks, and then take you by surprise after the show, when you thought you'd paid everything off.

7. Expenses or fees to performers. Big stars may be willing and able to perform for travel expenses only. But the majority of poets and musicians have a hard time just getting by, especially if their work is politically oriented. It is not unreasonable of them to ask for a set fee or a profit-sharing arrangement (the latter is usually preferable for you.) Naturally, your organization shouldn't be expected to pay as well as a commercial promoter, since the show *is* a benefit. At the very least you should try to cover travel.

8. Signing for the deaf. Especially in the case of a poetry reading, you might consider providing a sign language interpreter. Good signers are cultural workers, and should be booked and paid like any performing artist. It's also helpful to provide the signer ahead of time with lyrics or poems that will be performed, so that s/he can practice interpreting the material.

9. Break-even. Estimate total expenses and income from ticket sales. It is wise *not* to depend on income from concessions when estimating income, especially for smaller shows. Estimate how many tickets you can *reasonably expect to sell* (not simply sell-out for the hall). Make your break-even figure *half* the expected attendance. If expenses exceed the break-even figure (times your ticket price), you're taking too many chances. Raise the ticket price, cut back on expenses, or find another show to do. *Note:* Plan on selling tickets or taking a specified donation at the door. Don't count on passing the hat once people are inside.

Booking

1. *Lead time.* Give yourself as much lead time as possible; even the smallest show needs about six weeks. Finding your talent and a date they can perform, and then finding a hall that is open on that date (or vice-versa) are half the job of promoting.

2. *Booking the hall.* There are probably a number of halls around worth looking into, depending on the size and type of crowd you expect. It is preferable to pack a small hall and turn people away at the door, than to

Estimate a budget before starting work on a benefit.

Keep expenses to a minimum or it won't be a benefit.

Give yourself as much lead time as possible.

half-fill a large hall. Check out churches, schools, nightclubs, community centers, and concert halls.

Ask about available dates; rental fees; insurance; sound and lights available; wheelchair access; security and cleanup deposits and arrangements; childcare facilities. Providing your own security and cleanup can often get you a substantial price break. Check out sound/amplifying systems (and air conditioning in summer).

3. *Finding and booking the acts.* Be assertive and be persistent. Personal contact is best, but approaching a performer backstage before s/he goes on will probably get you nowhere. Nobody likes to be bothered while they're working and full of adrenaline. Contact performers or their manager by phone, or by mail as a last resort. Always follow up an initial contact within a week or so. Performers who just start out or come to town for the first time are usually very open to doing benefits for the sake of publicity. This is where keeping track of the local cultural scene pays off. Be wary of booking an act that has already played in town recently. It can only draw audiences so many nights in a row. Since you're not paying the performers much, they won't be as worried about drawing as they are for their commercial appearances.

Ask the performers about their needs for the event—what kind of sound system; do they want sound checks prior to the show; transportation; etc. If the performer is a celebrity, ask if s/he's willing to do media interviews in the week or so prior to the show.

Be sure performers are informed about when they appear in the program—in some cases, s/he will not want to open the show, or follow certain other acts. Your best-known performer should appear at the end or near to the end of the program.

A week or more in advance, send each performer a letter describing final details of the performance, including a schedule and directions to the hall. If possible, give a phone call during the week to remind the performers one last time and answer last-minute questions. Consider sending thank-you notes to performers after the benefit.

Many people will base their decision about whether to attend your benefit upon the artistic quality of posters and ads.

Selling tickets in advance can help promote the show.

Publicity

Issue news releases and set up interviews with the local media, especially if the performer is famous. Send public service announcements to the local media (see the "Media" chapter). Many people will base their decision about whether to attend your benefit upon the artistic quality of posters and ads, particularly if they're not familiar with the performers or your group. Take the time to make your posters as "professional" as possible. The first posters should go

Designed by Peg Averill.

up 10 days in advance. Make sure dependable people are doing the postering and take care in coordinating their distribution. Newspaper ads should start about a week in advance.

Selling tickets in advance can help promote the show. Cheaper advance tickets encourages people to commit themselves before the last minute. Bookstores or bars may be willing to carry your tickets for you. Check to see that your publicity mentions where tickets can be purchased in advance, whether you have a deaf signer, wheelchair access, or childcare.

Production Volunteers

Depending on the event, you will probably need people for some or all of the following jobs on the night of the show. Treat volunteer workers as well as performers, and both will be willing to work with you again. Developing a pool of experienced volunteers makes each show you do a little easier and more professional. Explain jobs to them *before* the day of the event. It's best if they can work in shifts, so that they can relax and enjoy at least part of the show. They should get in for free, but ask them to pay for food and drinks at the bar or your profits may get "eaten up."

- One or two managers
- "Accountant" to keep track of money (don't carry large sums of money around, lock it in an inconspicuous room or a car, since benefits are a good target for thieves)
- Stage manager and stage crew
- Backstage manager (attends to the performers backstage—consider buying the performers flowers; provide munchies, drinks and plenty of water)
- Ticket takers (in teams of two) at the door
- Volunteer coordinator
- Bar/concessions manager and crew; preferably people who don't drink, and are willing to rush a lot
- Childcare
- Security coordinator and security people (give them basic nonviolence training if possible)
- Literature table
- Back-up people (extra volunteers to fill in for absentees)
- Set-up (usually two hours before show) and cleanup (two hours after the show).

After each show, it can be very useful to have a feedback session with performers and/or volunteers and crew. Make notes; a thorough evaluation can teach you a lot for the next time around.

Conclusion

This outline includes suggestions based on a few people's experience. You will inevitably learn more than this outline can tell you each time you do a show. Try everything you can for the first few events. After that, make adjustments according to what works best in your situation and location.

Promoting can be exciting and even "glamorous" at times. But it is also a se-rious part of social change. In our society, art is treated as a luxury commodity to be bought and sold; sometimes this attitude shows up in the movement too. Creating culture and community for social change is frequently viewed as a lower priority than disseminating facts and analysis. I personally feel that one of these tasks cannot go forward without the other. Organizing a political cultural event is a very important and powerful act of resistance!

Audience at Women on Wheels concert in Santa Barbara, with Margie Adam, Meg Christian, Holly Near, and Chris Williamson. Photo by Adrienne Adam.

Follow Up

Besides going to benefits, observing how they are produced, and talking to those who have organized successful ones, the following book is a valuable resource:

Making a Show of It—A Guide to Concert Production, Genny Berson, available from Redwood Records, (P.O. Box 996, Ukiah, CA 95482, 101 pp., 1980.

Good volunteers are the key to a well-run show and successful benefit.

Creating culture is essential to building a better world.

STREET FAIRS

By Ed Hedemann

As with most other fundraising efforts, street fairs are also usually designed to educate and recruit. The key elements to producing a successful street fair consist of

- a committee and competent, hard-working coordinator
- sufficient lead time for preparation (e.g., 2 to 3 months)
- detailed and realistic planning
- adequate publicity and a good location
- a lot of donated items
- plenty of volunteers.

Planning

Determining the location and time are the first steps to organizing your street fair. Obviously you want a high trafficked area for the location. Don't secure such a large area that spreads you so thin that few are aware something is going on. WRL has found May and September to be good months for street fairs in New York City. We've found the first weekend after Labor Day particularly good. Students have just returned for school and the weather is still warm, but not too hot.

Form a planning committee and select one or two people as coordinators, who can be easily reached by phone. This committee should take on responsibilities for certain tasks: permits, vendors, advertising, volunteer coordination, food, literature, rummage pick up, booths (such as the flea market), and other logistical elements.

Get your street, beer, sound, health, and other necessary permits as far ahead as possible. Make sure you have a rain date. You also need to decide whether you will have amplified music. It may be good to attract a crowd, but it could alienate those who live or work in the area.

For the annual WRL street fair, money is made primarily through donated rummage, selling space to vendors, food, and literature. Other street fairs bring in a lot of money through raffling off a prize (preferably, donated), auctions, games and rides, arts and crafts, among countless other possibilities. But keep in mind that you need to maximize the number of donated items in order to raise the most money.

After determining how many spaces you have available for booths (e.g., 10 feet per booth lining both sides of a street), figure out how many you wish to make available and at what cost to other groups or vendors outside your organization. Then advertise the fair to those who might be interested in buying space. In 1981, WRL charged $80 per day or $125* for the weekend to outside vendors. Some fairs charge a percentage of the vendor's take (e.g., 10%). You may wish to charge a lower price (or donate space) to friendly political groups selling their literature.

Very early in the planning, advertise to your own constituency and friends for donated items: clothing, appliances, books, records, plants, crafts, anything which works and is likely to sell. Ask them "If you moved tomorrow, what would you leave behind or give away?" If they cannot deliver these items to you or an appropriate storage location, be prepared to make pick ups. Try consolidating pick ups to the final week before the fair.

Begin to line up volunteers a month or so before the fair. Make a chart of categories and fill in names and phones of

Allow plenty of lead time in planning and preparing for your fair.

A successful fair depends on getting a lot of donated items to sell.

*These figures are for New York City, therefore likely to be much lower elsewhere.

Charlie King at WRL Street Fair, New York City, 1976. Photo by Ed Hedemann.

volunteers for set up, clean up, staffing your booths (food, rummage, literature, etc.), baking food, picking up rummage, and making crafts. Volunteers can also be solicited to lend their talents in creating a festive atmosphere (e.g., clowns, mime, theater, music), valuable to drawing a good crowd. Events such as a fiddling contest or "battle of the rock bands" also work. Get volunteers to convince local merchants to donate items to the fair.

The sort of literature-type items which we have found to sell well are buttons, stickers, posters, T-shirts, fliers or brochures, inexpensive or used books. As a rule, books don't sell. Display is the key to selling literature. Be sure to have something to hold down literature in any breeze (e.g., string is preferable to weights). Clearly label all prices.

If you have the fair in a good location, there is no need to advertise it to the general public. In fact, such advertising in New York City tends to attract pickpockets. But the day of the fair, or possibly a few days before, you may wish to string a banner across the street announcing your event.

Other items to consider in advance: rest rooms, ice, barbeque pits, a sound system, change for your booths, pricing rummage and books, rental of tables and chairs, lost and found area, a way to deal with cars that remain on the street, brooms and garbage bags for clean up, trash cans, plastic to cover table in case of rain, first aid, heating and refrigeration facilities, electrical outlets, items for food sale (forks, serving spoons, plates, cups, napkins, etc.), and make up a chart of which booths go where.

The sort of food items which generally sell well are drinks (beer, soda, cider, coffee), hamburgers and hot dogs, baked goods (cakes, cookies, brownies, quiche, bread). Pick up the food as close to the event itself to minimize spoilage and storage problems. Put notices on the street and cars the day before, asking them to move before the fair begins.

The Event

Start setting up several hours before the announced beginning of the fair, especially if you have to build a stage. Block vehicular traffic with sawhorses. Get up any decorations needed. Make sure spaces for booths are clearly marked, that someone will be in charge of telling which people set up where, and checking in groups. You should have a person to periodically make the rounds collecting money from your tables, and

If you have a fair in a good location, there is no need to advertise it to the general public.

A lot of volunteers are essential to the success of a street fair.

Be sure to include tables with your organization's literature attractively displayed.

WRL Street Fair, 1976. Photo by Ed Hedemann.

WRL Street Fair, 1976. Photo by Ed Hedemann.

keeping track of where the money came from. Take the money to a "secure" area.

As the fair nears the end and a lot of rummage remains (which you don't wish to restore or throw out), start slashing prices or offering all the rummage people can stuff into a large shopping bag (which you provide) for $2.

After the clean up, counting and depositing the money, it would be a nice gesture to write thank you notes to all who volunteered their efforts in the fair. Also, an evaluation of the event, noting which booths made how much, which lost and why, where you were short volunteers, which literature sold and which didn't, etc., is valuable for future fairs.

ORGANIZING A FESTIVAL OF NONVIOLENCE

Our expressed purposes for sponsoring a festival of nonviolence included: 1) bringing people together; 2) educating about the history, methods, styles, and traditions of nonviolence; 3) coalescing our own community by the experience of planning these events, and sharing time with the resource people we brought in; 4) offering opportunities for further involvement in nonviolent efforts; 5) "discovering" new people to involve; 6) increasing visibility for nonviolent activist efforts in this area.

Insofar as the planning group had a "message," it was made explicit to participants: we must learn from the past, realistically assess our strengths and weaknesses in the present, have an idea for what we are working, and be precise and thoughtful in our choice of strategies and actions to bring about the type of change we seek.

Overview

The planning group developed a week of activities roughly divided into four aspects:

Criticism of the Past. What were the strengths and weaknesses of past efforts at personal and social change? We had

These notes are based on a week-long series of events held in 1974 and then again in 1975 by the Thomas Merton Unity Center/WRL in Isla Vista, California. Though that group no longer exists, a number of people from that community are now part of the Resource Center for Nonviolence, P.O. Box 2324, Santa Cruz, CA 95063.

an evening panel discussing "What have we learned from the activist movements of the 1960's and 1970's?"

Analysis of the Present. What is the current status of the nonviolent activist movement? Where are its growing edges and what frustrations is it experiencing? What areas are particularly productive or instructive for work, and how do we determine where to commit our energies and efforts? We had a workshop with panelists describing the analytical perspectives of anarchism, Gandhian nonviolence, Christianity, and Marxism. Also there was a panel and daylong discussion with three well-known movement activists on "What are the prospects for change in America?" We hosted workshops on the Justice System as an institutional case study showing the things both encouraging and impeding change in the American social structure; and a workshop on the Middle East, as an international situation in which global forces came into play for and against change.

Visions of the Future. What kind of society do we want? What can we offer people of our country and the world by way of a more humane social order and more life-giving interpersonal relationships? A workshop was scheduled in which ideas were shared of how a more humane society might be structured.

Tools and Strategies. What methods does nonviolence offer for building a movement for radical personal and social change? How can we effectively create such a movement and what are the essential elements of a nonviolent

A "nonviolence festival" provides an opportunity to learn from the past while developing a strategy for change.

demonstration, campaign, or movement? Workshops were held discussing these questions as well as how to build communities of nonviolent activism and resistance.

There were at least three crucial factors in choosing to develop this model for the week. First, the content and schedule provided participants some considerations to be made when thinking of working for social change. Second, this approach showed that nonviolence offers a channel for working for societal change while demanding a simultaneous personal transformation. Third, the flow of the week (from past to present to future) had a tendency to move people in a more forward-looking way, by offering them opportunities to become personally involved. In other words, the week moved from criticism and analysis to community-building as we felt that the building of communities is essential to create a movement which will sustain prolonged political struggle and offer the support and challenge necessary for personal growth.

Additionally, each event was intended to be self-contained—of sufficient quality and interest to allow participants who chose this one event to feel thay had been challenged and had a worthwhile experience.

Format

Format ranged from large public events to smaller follow-up discussions and informal sharing. Thus, for example, an evening program on the Middle East was followed noon the next day by an informal discussion that actually succeeded in arriving at points of unity among the varied interests in attendance because it allowed for greater discussion and more time for interaction.

Events included a poetry reading, a musical performance, films, small discussions, panels, lectures, daylong workshops, etc. We consciously moved the week's events from larger to smaller and more intimate gatherings. This was done to facilitate community-building and offer people more of an opportunity to pursue interests or points which they may have wanted to raise during the earlier events. We provided periods of evaluation, both after several of the events and at the end of the week, so we could learn as much as possible from other people's experience of the activities.

Participants included a small core of people who came from a distance and who attended all or a major part of the week's events, local residents who attended all or most of the activities, local folks who attended few or just one event, and some from greater distances who came solely for the daylong workshop. The total number of participants was between 1500 to 2000.

Planning

The prime responsibility for planning was assumed by the cooperative living community, involving 8 to 10 persons. Also, we invited various persons active in other groups to join the planning committee. A person from the community was assigned responsibility to personally invite each such person. As a result we were able to involve two or three other persons in the planning. In addition, since we co-sponsored many specific workshops with other groups, one or more from our central planning group would meet regularly with such groups to coordinate individual events.

The core planning group began meeting four months ahead of the event. Initial contact with well-known resource people had been made nine months before the events themselves. At that time we simply informed them of our interest in having them visit this area, tested their interest in coming, suggested possible dates to see whether they would be free, getting an idea of how much it would cost to have them involved, etc. The final dates for the activities were chosen three to four months ahead of time.

The planning group met every other week for the first two months. For the last eight weeks we met each week for one and a half to three hours.

While hammering out the conceptual model which would govern the planning of the week, we met as a whole. The entire group chose the title, the theme, the general schematic flow of activities, who to invite, how to describe the event in publicity, and what tasks needed to be done.

As the event drew closer, specific tasks were isolated and individuals or task forces took specific responsibility (e.g., media, posters, mailings, housing, finances, logistics, literature) to pursue them at times other than during the weekly meetings.

Individual members were responsible for detailed planning and "managing" of individual events—contacting resource

The fair was structured to show that nonviolence offers a channel to work for social change while demanding a personal transformation.

Each event was self-contained to allow participants to pick and choose sessions without having to attend the whole week.

To facilitate community-building, the week's events moved from larger to smaller and more intimate gatherings.

*Continental Walk Peace Fair, Santa Cruz, California, February 7, 1976.
Photo by J.C. Stockwell/Celebrations.*

people, getting the key to a workshop room, setting up the room, introducing speakers, etc. Another person took responsibility for setting up a literature table before the event.

While individuals took responsibility for such detailed planning, any and all concerns could be brought to the weekly planning group and the entire group evaluated individual events and the week as a whole.

Other parts of the planning were: 1) a time-flow chart posted on the wall describing the tasks and when they needed to be started and completed; 2) a large chart on the wall describing various tasks needing to be done so that individuals who had time to help could ascertain which tasks needed doing, and how to do them; 3) we felt free to call on other people not part of the central planning group for specific help when necessary.

Resource Persons

A sample letter to resource people was developed by a subcommittee. Such letters were individually typed and sent to 50 potential resource people, whose names and fields of interest had been brainstormed by the entire planning group. These people were informed by the letter of who we were, what constituted the work of our center, what was the purpose of the week's events, and what specific themes we were asking them to address and in what format (e.g., speaker, panelist, workshop facilitator). We asked

each person to indicate if they were available and willing to come during the time we proposed, how many days they could be with us, if we could set up speaking dates in other nearby towns to help offset transportation costs, and how much they anticipated their expenses to be.

Nearly all persons were willing to come for travel expenses alone. When possible, we offered a modest honorarium ($20 to $300). We encouraged them to stay beyond or arrive before the event which they had been invited, and simply participate in various activities.

When resource people arrived we had for each of them a schedule of the entire week's activities, an itinerary of their time with us, who would be accompanying them to each event, maps showing where they were being housed, information on meals, and envelopes with their transportation reimbursement and honorarium, if any. This tends to make them feel more relaxed and informed about what's going on.

Fund Raising

The budget, which amounted to about $3000, included: travel and honoraria, printing, postage, rental of facilities and equipment, advertisements, etc. This was financed in three ways:

Grants. We approached local community groups for a specific part of the week or for a particular budget item. For example, we approached the Resident

The core planning group began meeting 4 months ahead.

Part of the cost for the fair was offset by the co-sponsorship of community groups.

Hall Association at the local campus to co-sponsor three of the week's major activities (including most expenses). Having access to student fees, the RHA agreed to our request and paid transportation costs for the resource people (amounting initially to nearly $1200). In return for their support: 1) they were listed as co-sponsors on all of our printed material, press releases, etc. (for many groups, such high visibility is a selling point encouraging participation); 2) residents of the dorms were given a reduced admission or free admission to events; and 3) we scheduled many of the activities on campus or in the dormitories to increase resident student participation.

We approached the lectures committee of the University student government for help with speaker's honoraria. Other groups were asked to contribute financially and in return either co-sponsored or hosted events. For example, an association of campus ministers hosted a lunchtime dialogue with Dan Berrigan for local clergy and religious studies faculty and students.

Sponsor Contributions. We sent letters asking financial support ($10 or more) of key contacts from our mailing list. Of 120 or so letters which we sent out about a third responded with contributions totalling 20% of the week's budget. This is essentially the only time of the year when we made a general appeal for contributions to our mailing list. A hundred dollars was raised through a raffle. Prizes were donated by local businesses and by national peace groups which offered books, magazine subscriptions or other items.

Receipts from Events. At some events we asked for small donations and at others we charged a registration fee ($1). A daylong workshop, co-led by two or more of our major resource people, was set up with limited registration and costing $12 to $15. We widely advertised the workshops and were able to raise enough money through registrations (30% to 40% of the budget) to carry the rest of the week.

We contacted other groups within several hundred miles of us to host various of our speakers, thereby reducing the initial cost of transportation for those coming from a distance, and nurturing contact and cooperation between us and those groups.

To help advertise the fair, we wrote reviews in local papers of recent books by resource people.

We developed a logo for all our literature to establish continuity throughout the week's activities.

Task Force Areas

Press Releases and the Media. An early notice was written and mailed a couple of months before the events to avoid calendar conflicts. This mailing was sent to our entire list and to special contacts including other nonviolent groups both regionally and nationally. A series of news releases were sent: a general release describing the entire week of events which we got published in newspapers the week prior to the first events; individual news releases for each event or series of events. Be sure to include biographies and photographs of resource people for the press releases.

We got listed in all the area's "calendar of events" each day. We wrote reviews of recent books by resource people, and either wrote or solicited others to speak personally with media people to suggest scheduling an interview. Finally, notices were published in various national movement publications.

Local radio stations were sent texts for "public service announcements" to air before events. To help promote attendance, we arranged radio and television interviews with our guests on the local university station. Also, we scheduled interviews for each noon hour, and a half hour every evening. The radio programs were hosted by members of our community who took turns at interviewing so we gained a fair amount of practice in this media.

Posters. We developed a logo to establish continuity throughout the week's activities. The same logo appeared on our letterhead, press releases, fliers and posters. One poster was developed describing the entire week, and three separate posters describing certain portions of the week and its major activities. Distribution of posters is always difficult— and we found ourselves falling short of energy when it was time to put them out.

Brochures and Mailings. We printed 10,000 brochures describing the week of activities. This brochure included a full calendar/schedule of activities, brief descriptions of events, resource people, information about registration, housing, costs, etc. This prompted our early planning and decision-making as we had the brochure ready for print weeks ahead of the events themselves.

The brochure was mailed to our mailing list, as well as those of organizations friendly with us. Such mailings vastly increased our visibility and news of the conference spread throughout southern California.

Brochures were also distributed on campus and at campus events. A reduced one-page version of the brochure was distributed as a flier in the faculty mailboxes with introductory letters indicating willingness to provide notices for their classes and encouraged their students to attend certain events. The most effective publicity was by word of mouth.

Housing. We arranged for out of town resource people to stay with members of our community. In each instance of where to place them, we considered the resource person's need for privacy and rest against exposure of people to such resources. In every case the local hosts appreciated the chance to meet and talk with the resource people in passing. Offering housing is a way that many people supported the week's activities. We also arranged for resource people to eat in the campus dining halls.

A local church provided space for out-of-town participants to roll out sleeping bags during the week.

Finances. A subcommittee of three took charge of receiving and recording all income. Specific tasks were handled by individuals, such as registration for the day-long workshop. (Keeping finances straight is a difficult task—bookkeeping is not a forte of the nonviolent movement. Still, it is important.) We made an effort to keep track of book sales (on which we paid a sales tax), donations, sponsors contributions, workshop registrations, and grants. The finance committee also took charge of writing checks. They prepared a detailed budget summary after the final events.

Logistics. It is important to anticipate as many of the transitions and special arrangements as possible to allow a more relaxed week and less surprises. We always forget small items such as having change available, not having a table for literature, forgetting blackboards, pens, etc.

We also made an effort to have a range of books available for sale during the week. We made a little money and often having books gives people something concrete to take home. We always tried to have the most recent books by the resource people we invited. Aside from various free brochures, on all our literature tables we printed a statement about our community describing who we were and how to get in touch with us.

Finally, a logistical consideration is recording (in writing and on tape) any or all of the events. We have tried to prepare transcripts of the more important parts of the week for distribution as free literature or for possible publication.

The hosts of our resource people appreciated the opportunity to meet and talk with their guests in passing.

CANVASSING

By Steve Ladd

Door-to-door canvassing can be a very effective way to reach a lot of people, or it can be a waste of time and energy. It all depends on how clear your goals are and how well organized the campaign is.

Knocking on doors is time-consuming and slow, but it can really pay off, based on the experience of many consumer, environmental, electoral, and service groups that have used this technique to solicit either support or financial contributions. Canvassing not only helps you identify and possibly activate supporters, it also provides the canvassers with experience in public speaking, among other skills.

Goals and Techniques of a Canvassing Campaign

There are two basic canvassing methods. The first is a literature drop, which is simple, quick, and non-threatening. However, personal contact is absent, and neither opinions nor money can be collected. The other method is to knock on the door in order to talk to the resident, determine their opinion, leave literature, encourage follow up from them, and possibly solicit money.

Before beginning a door-to-door campaign, your group needs to determine what it hopes to achieve. You won't get very far if you just plan to walk around knocking on doors to give your political rap. No one wants to open their doors just to be talked at. We can't realistically expect to convert people in a few minutes

Thanks to Becky Winborn and Crossing Press for permission to draw from the section on canvassing in **Grass Roots—An Anti-Nuke Source Book**. Comments by Kate Donnelly and Clay Colt were also helpful.

at the door.

The group must determine what its goals are and whether canvassing is the best way to achieve those goals, especially considering the large number of volunteers and amount of energy needed for a canvassing campaign. How much time do you have? Do you need to develop literature for the campaign? What are your costs? How much money do you have to spend on the canvassing? How will you recruit canvassers? Will there be training for the volunteers?

One of the most effective techniques is to ask people to respond to a set of questions or sign a petition. This gets them thinking and involved, and makes it less likely they will immediately disagree with you.

A questionnaire to find sympathizers or people open-minded about your issues should be carefully and simply put together. Don't ask too many questions, and those you ask should be phrased in a clear and concise manner. Yes or no questions are the easiest to answer and keep track of, but you can also use a graduated response format (agree totally, agree somewhat, somewhat disagree, totally disagree, not sure). Leave room to jot down comments people may make beyond the yes or no.

At the end of the questionnaire if they seem sympathetic, you can ask them to go to or even host a housemeeting with others in the neighborhood. Or invite them to a community forum. Be sure to leave a leaflet or other material with those who express interest.

It can also be helpful to have a more specific reason when going door-to-door such as a petition or support for a ballot referendum. Since most people feel they should know something about the issues on which they are voting, they are likely to listen.

Canvassing not only helps you identify and possibly activate supporters, it also provides experience in public speaking, among other skills.

You won't get very far if you just plan to walk around knocking on doors to give your political rap.

One of the most effective techniques is to ask people to respond to a set of questions or sign a petition.

How To Organize the Canvass

After deciding on the goals of the canvassing and the techniques to be used (e.g., questionnaire, petition, house-meeting invitation, literature), you need to figure out how to approach your community in a systematic way.

One of the easiest ways to break down a community is by voting precincts (in rural areas, by towns might be better). You can obtain a list of precincts, as well as the voters and their party registration from the local registrar of voters. You can also obtain a record of past voting trends in the community.

Unless you can cover the whole community, limit your canvassing to precincts where the canvassers live and those which have the most liberal voting records.

Canvassers can be found by asking friends and supporters, using posters, ads, mailings, or going to meetings. Ask people to give a day or several hours. Before your briefing or training session make sure you have enough maps with clearly marked routes that teams of two can reasonably be expected to cover in the time allotted. Determine how much literature each canvasser will need.

Scheduling a training session an hour before the canvassing is to begin will give people a sense of confidence and solidarity. Besides a briefing and some tips on effective canvassing, doing role plays or hassle lines (see chapter on "Nonviolence Training") are a good way to orient people. Then give out maps to the canvassers with their assigned route.

After training, canvassers should be divided into groups of 5 to 10, with each group taking a particular precinct or neighborhood. Each group should have a contact person. Canvassing should always be done in teams. Two people can do a street—one on each side—and meet at each corner before going on. The best hours to find people home are between 4 pm and 9 pm. Be sure people have clipboards for questionnaires or petitions, and an adequate supply of literature.

When knocking on a door, the canvasser should be willing to listen rather than argue. State the group you're with and why you're going door-to-door. Develop a simple, short, and friendly introductory rap. Avoid dogmatic assertions, and attempt to engage the person at the door in dialogue or some response quickly. Listen to what they have to say, and offer a response if they're willing to listen.

If it's obvious they're not interested, move on. Someone will not be converted in 5 to 10 minutes, so don't waste excessive time trying to do so. When working in your neighborhood, it might be advantageous to appear more informal and avoid the atmosphere of recruitment. Invite them to your home for an informal meeting, with refreshments available. At the gathering, go around the room and have people share their feelings on the topic, then mention your project, asking whether they'd be interested in meeting again on it.

For places where no one is at home, leave a copy of the petition/questionnaire with a cover letter and return envelope. Put it under the door or mat, since it's illegal to stick it in the mailbox. Or simply leave a leaflet or doorhanger.

After the first outing, have the canvassing crew meet to share experiences and role play some of the difficult situations to see how they could have been handled differently.

Some Helpful Hints

The Opening

- Don't talk to people indirectly— through an intercom, locked door, or their children. If they don't want to talk face-to-face, politely leave.
- Begin by identifying yourself (use your first name if you like), the name of your organization, what the organization is about, and why you have come. If you are there asking for money, say so.
- Then keep talking and move on to what it is you want to present.

General Considerations About the Rap

- Always maintain a friendly attitude and smile.
- Be brief and to the point. Choose your words carefully.
- Show enthusiasm and sincerity. If people perceive that you are convinced of what you are saying, they will be more receptive.
- Use the clipboard well. If you want them to sign something get it into their hands as soon as you can.
- Keep your rap well structured. Know what you want to say, hold the person's attention, and maintain good eye contact.
- Be sensitive to the person you are talking with. Speak in a manner which will make them feel more comfortable.

One of the easiest ways to break down a community is by voting precincts.

Schedule a training session before canvassing to give people sense of confidence and solidarity.

When knocking on a door, a canvasser should be willing to listen rather than argue.

Step out of your role as canvasser from time to time, and don't be afraid to keep the atmosphere light.

Attitude

- If you are relaxed, they will be also. Don't bury the person under an avalanche of words.

- Remember that each person is an individual, and you can never know how the person feels at the moment. Give the person the benefit of the doubt. Don't prejudge.

- Step out of your role as canvasser from time to time, and don't be afraid to keep the atmosphere light.

- When someone is rude or hostile to you, don't reply in kind; that only aggravates the situation.

- Remember: you are not there to evangelize. There is never any one person that we *must* get a positive response from. We are looking for people who agree with us, and undecided people who are willing to listen. To try to change the made-up mind of a stranger in a few minutes causes unneeded frustration.

Attention of the Person at the Door

- Dogs, telephones and screaming children present an ongoing challenge. If you see that it presents an insurmountable distraction, it means that you are probably not coming across anyway. Leave when it's clear you've lost the spotlight.

- If the person seems more interested in what is going on across the street than in talking and listening, you're not going to get anywhere. Try an attention getting fact and see if you can rescue the situation. If not, move along.

- If it appears that the person is truly busy, inquire as to whether or not you should come back later. Then do so.

The "Come Back Later" Situation

- If a person says that you should come back later (when the husband/wife/roommate/parents are home), respond that you would be happy to do so at a specific time that evening. If the individual really wants you to, they will say so. If the person says to come back next week, next month, or some vague time in the future, chances are that the person is not really interested but doesn't want to say so. Return if you wish but try to determine if it is a serious prospect.

Problems of Defensiveness and Negativity

- Don't allow yourself to be defensive or sarcastic. Stay with the issues.

Don't allow yourself to be defensive or sarcastic. Stay with the issues.

Don't get into long-winded discussions with people who obviously disagree or don't want to do anything.

- If you feel a sense of being overwhelmed by lack of response, stop and rest for a few minutes. Try to figure out what is the problem and change your rap accordingly. When in doubt, go back to the simplest approach you can use. At least you won't be wasting time talking to people if if they aren't into it.

- Determine which people are the fence-sitters. They require the most effort. Let them know how it affects them as individuals. Establish a common ground. You probably won't convince those who are automatically against you, but at least let them know that we are human and friendly, that we aren't there to cause trouble, and we certainly don't want to argue. Let them feel that we all need to work together to find common solutions to the problems confronting us.

The Discussion

- Always maintain a positive attitude. Never argue with people about the validity of their excuses. Go back to talking about the issues or what you would like out of them.

- Don't get into long-winded discussion with people who obviously disagree or don't want to do anything. Politely excuse yourself by stating, "I'm not here to change your mind," or "I'd like to talk further but I have to canvass the next three blocks before 9 pm."

Canvassing in Oklahoma on the Continental Walk, 1976. Photo by Alison Hickman Metcalf.

Asking for Money

- The legal requirements for raising money through door-to-door solicitation vary and should be checked out first with the Attorney General's office of your state. You might also consult with other citizen's organizations who canvass in your state.

- Money will only be raised from people who are sympathetic. So ask those from whom you have received a positive response.

- The more specific you are about what the money is for, the more likely that people who support your cause will give. If your cause seems vague and not well organized, they will be less likely to contribute. Be clear with people on whether the money is going to support the group, or you, or both.

- You may have to mention a number of times that one of the reasons you are canvassing is to raise money.

- Don't be apologetic about asking for money; it gives people an excuse not to give. Be confident in asking.

- Suggest an amount to people. Say, for instance, that most contributors give $5 (or whatever is reasonable). This makes it easier for people to think of a specific contribution.

- Stress that you would like a check. Experience shows that people tend to give more by check, and it's a safer way of handling money.

- Let the person sign your petition or answer the questions before they contribute. You can talk up one or two more issues while they are signing; mention your newsletter, forum, next activity, etc.

- Be sure to thank people and keep a record of who gives what. Add their names to your donors list for future mail or door-to-door solicitation.

The more specific you are about what the money is for, the more likely that people who support your cause will give.

Don't be apologetic about asking for money; it gives people an excuse not to give.

THEATER FOR USE

By Chris Brandt*

Phillip Sydney said the aim of all art is to delight and instruct.

Theater is action in public, and it seeks creative rather than destructive way to use our energies

Theater is *not* stage, costumes, actors in masquerade pretending to be someone else.

This is about using theater to serve demonstrative politics. All art—worthy of the name—exists to be used, so use it. Don't worry about the skills; they come with the doing. You already have all you need to start: talking and doing things to get a point across, and letting yourself be seen doing it, are within everyone's daily ken. Furthermore, if you have ever demonstrated, carried a placard, chanted a slogan, or participated in a die-in, sit-in, or civil disobedience, you have already used and experienced theater in the large sense. The more conscious you can be of that use, the more effective and powerful the use will be. You have something important to say. Say it with the clearest means possible. I hope this discussion of the theatrical process helps.

Theater has at least two things in common with the nonviolent movement: it is action in public, and it seeks creative rather than destructive ways to use our energies. It takes an enormous amount of energy to do theater. It's hard work, especially at the beginning, before the shape begins to show, but the more you work at it the more it energizes you. When at last you are "up there" in front of an audience, saying what you want to say and getting reactions to it, you will feel surges of excitement. An action done for others to see is charged with that excitement and therefore magnified. So the great thing is to enjoy the rapture and the power, then to try to understand and use that power for the furtherance of life. In theater and in political action we do this in public.

One other characteristic makes the-

ater a natural for political use. Theater has always found its stuff in history, myth and manners, in short, in politics. From Aristophanes' nose-thumbings to Arthur Miller's melodramas, serious theater is always concerned with the social consciousness of its time.

A political movement is a theater. We have actors and a geography. Gertrude Stein said plays are landscapes. Real landscapes. They can be internal ones or moral ones or landscapes of the heart, but always they are *real* landscapes. They have people in them and the people do things, show themselves living in the landscape and they *change* the landscape. It is very important that we change the landscape; it is why we do what we do. We would create our own lives.

How To Do It

What you have to work with is movement, colors, shapes, sound and music, and words, all delivered through the human presence of the actors.

Improvisation. Improvisation will help you feel more comfortable together as a group doing theater. And, of course, it will help you think about your statement. Some of the best theater games are in a book called *Improvisations for the Theater* by Viola Spolin. This book, available in public libraries, is valuable in both loosening up the group and suggesting structures the piece could take. Some of the games can also be easily adapted for nonviolence training role plays. So get a copy of this book and use it! What follows is a sampling of the most well known games.

---

*This chapter has been re-edited for this edition by Lisa Miller of the WRL staff. She thanks Chris for trusting her changes and hopes they don't stand out too much.

a) *Part of a Whole* (also called "machine"): One person goes on stage and becomes part of a large animate or inanimate moving object. As soon as the nature of the object becomes clear to another player, she or he joins the player on stage and becomes another part of the whole. This continues until all have participated and are working together to form the complete object. Concentrate on being part of a larger object.

b) *Involvement in Threes or More:* Group agrees on an object which cannot be used without involving all of them. They are to participate in a joint action in which all move the same thing. Concentrate on making whatever object (tugging a boat, pushing a stalled car, beating a sword into a plowshare) real.

c) *Orientation Game* (also called "world"): One person goes on stage, picks a simple activity, and begins doing it. Other players come on stage one at a time and join him or her in this activity. The group should not know ahead of time what the first person is doing. So, one person might start raking leaves, the next might get a bag to help. Then the next person might split logs, while another begins to harvest the garden. This sounds like a very tranquil world, but what if the first person seemed to be making a bomb? What would you be doing inside that world?

Music. Music will be heard. Nothing gathers people like a band, or a drum or a group song, and those who stop to listen and watch will help you make the space and the ambiance for your action. Here are some suggestions for homemade musical instruments to be used for demonstrations or street theater. The materials used are found mainly in the home or hardware store.

Pipe Bugle: Lips are pursed against end of copper tubing or aluminum electrical conduit pipe to produce bugle-like tones. Much breath required.

Shaker: Cardboard mailing tube partially filled with rice, peas, beans and sealed at ends.

Jinglestick: Bottlecaps loosely nailed on to a stick. Be sure to flatten the protruding nail against the back of the stick. This makes a nice rattle. Variations include attaching beads or buttons, anything noisy that a nail will hold to a stick.

Pot Lid Gamelan: An assortment of metal pot lids are mounted on threaded rods with nuts. The rods are inserted in drilled holes through a hollow wooden box and fastened firmly with nuts on both sides of the box. Slots are cut in the tops or sides for sound holes. The pot lids are struck with dowels or mallets to produce gong-like tones. A baby carriage, shopping cart or other wagon can be adapted to carry large instruments such as the pot lid gamelan. This carriage mounted with bicycle horns and cowbells can be played by as many as six people to great rhythmic and visual effect.

Foghorn: Purse your lips and direct a stream of air downward into the mouth of an empty bottle. With a little practice you should be able to achieve a deep foghorn tone, a mid-range tone, and an ear-piercing high note. Partial filling will change the effect.

Miscellaneous: Collect inexpensive instruments like penny whistles, kazoos, bells, toy drums, finger cymbals, maracas, castenets, tambourines. They will come in useful for actions, and your parties will be more fun, too.

Colors & Shapes. Banners or large simple symbols in strong colors catch the eye and focus the attention. Think of the Bread & Puppet's wondrous white birds. If you feel like it, try big puppets, masks, costumes, make-up, stilts, raised platforms. But remember, you don't need the fancy stuff. Try color coordination in clothes (everyone could wear some combination of three strong colors, for example).

Movement. Mass movements or

May Day specters, 1971. Photo by Diana Davies/WIN.

The most precious ability of all is the ability to make a fool of yourself.

Improvisation will help you feel more comfortable together as a group doing theater.

An action can be quite ordinary, but the purpose for which it is done transforms it into a unique gesture which lives on in the memory of the audience.

repeated individual movements magnify the action and focus it. The Vietnam Veterans Against the War storming the Capitol steps, for example, or noncooperation with arresting police, or the readings of the names of soldiers who died in Vietnam.

This all suggests a parade, and why not. Everybody loves one and it's important to remember that we are not only protesting the evils we see, not only demonstrating *against*, but exploring and creating the possibilities of life in spite of them, ultimately without them, demonstrating *for* something too.

You could also consider involving the spectators directly through some transaction. The sugar action in Freiburg, Germany, was one such action, designed to convey a specific message (see "Notes"). Another possibility, and one of my favorite stories: Chico and Harpo Marx once offered passersby in Times Square a five dollar bill for four singles. There were no takers, but a lot of people got suspicious and frightened, including the cops, who chased the two "nuts" away. In a very funny way they taught us how seriously we take money.

You could illustrate your point with a story or parable in the traditional way, using a stage and staged action, as the San Francisco Mime Troupe, the Teatro Campesino, and the Theater for the New City do, as Brecht does in his teaching pieces. Scripts are available in some collections or by writing to street theater companies (see "Resources"), usually for the cost of copying and postage. Or find research material like Senate hearings, speeches by historical figures, interviews, newspaper and magazine arti-

cles, etc., and use the "cut-and-paste" method. Or write your own script to fit the particular situation.

Rehearsals

Performers and demonstrators do an action twice. First to find out what it is, how we do it, and how we rely on each other doing it. Then to show ourselves doing it. For political activists, the first process is the planning, role-playing, nonviolence training, etc., in preparation for a demonstration. For actors, it's rehearsal and exploration. It is as brave as performance. For an exploration to be worthwhile, the territory must be unknown. And to allow ourselves to be seen acting is to share the action with others.

The basic questions have to be asked and answered before you go public. If you are sure of who you are, what you are doing, for what purpose, and that you can count on each other's support, you are free to act and react out of the present moment.

In the rehearsal process, problems of ego and personal need may arise. It's important not to deny or denigrate them, but also not to let them swamp the action. Remember the purpose, indulge your own impulses and needs, and use what serves to clarify the action. Someone who gets impatient with the process may need to play a role that way; the important question is, impatient for what. I once knew an actor who insisted on wearing her own eccentric clothes in a chorus of birds. I tried persuasion, trickery and exasperation, but without result.

Nothing gathers people like music, and those who stop to listen will help you make space for your action.

You could consider involving the spectators directly through some transaction.

You could illustrate your point with a story or parable in the traditional way using a stage, or write your own script to fit the particular situation.

The Bread & Puppet's wondrous white birds, New York City, May 27, 1978. Photo by Grace Hedemann.

Finally, at dress rehearsal, I realized what a magnificent solitary hawk she was.

You may find that some one person becomes primarily responsible for keeping track of all the pieces of the puzzle and focusing the action, and setting the order of the parts. If so, don't panic. Remember that the collective process does not exclude having an outside eye as advisor or director, and vice versa. Always, the question is, what works?

them sitting naked on toilets; or use any image that reminds you we're all humans in this boat. Finally, again in advance, imagine *in great detail* what is the worst thing that could possibly happen to you in this situation. You'll find it's not so bad after all, and the very act of sketching it out for yourself is exciting and funny (you could act this out for each other at a rehearsal) and robs it of its horror.

Getting Out There

Once the piece is ready, get a place to do it, draw a crowd, and go to it. Always remember that an audience is there by choice, to see *you*; they want you to succeed, because that's when they get the most out of it, too.

If you get "stage fright," here are five things you can do about it. First, remember that fear, shortness of breath, even depression, are excitement repressed. Second, take your time. Breathe. Smell, touch, taste, or hear something real and present. You'll find that even the smallest connection with your immediate surroundings brings you back to yourself and to what you are about. See and hear your fellow actors. They are with you. Third (and you may want to include this one in rehearsals), imagine someone near you or in the audience who *totally* approves of whatever you do. Literally. This can be someone you know, or someone fictitious, as long as you really believe in her or him. Fourth, if you feel the audience is judging you, simply imagine

Taking It To the Streets

What you are faced with in a public, outdoor situation is an audience that's not an audience. In a theater building all the people are there for the same reason; in a public place the people come and go. You can either transform them into an audience by playing on their expectations (music, drums, a charged space, heightened or compressed actions, or simply an announcement that a play is about to happen). Or you can come, act quickly and decisively, and so alter *their* landscape that they *have* to deal with your alteration. We could as well call this a nonviolent guerrilla action as guerrilla theater.

One example would be Abbie Hoffman's storm of dollar bills thrown to the floor of the New York Stock Exchange. Another is the Central America activist in the guise of a waitress who approaches some people on the street. She carries a tray. On the tray she has painted a map of Central America and glued to it a couple of toy

To allow ourselves to be seen acting is to share the action with others.

If you feel the audience is judging you, simply imagine them sitting naked on toilets.

Our theater must do three things: it must appeal to the senses, the passions, and the mind, but it must not preach.

Theater itself is not illusion, it is magic.

soldiers. She asks, "Did you order this war?" Whatever the response (usually confusion), she then says, "Well, you're paying for it." She then presents a bill for the cost of U.S. support for the dictators, puppet presidents, and Contras in Central America.

Accumulation of guerrilla actions turns out to be more than theater, for it alters the landscape of the entire culture. Part of their attractiveness lies in the fact that, unlike demonstrations and mailings and petitioning, they are *immediately* effective. If the gesture is a telling one and strikes a strong chord in the country's collective unconscious, the impact of a single action multiplies and magnifies in the social consciousness. Maybe no stockbroker or general learned anything about greed or power or role playing or the way he sees his world, but when the brokers scrambled and the generals huffed, *we* did, the *audience* did and the event became a mythic landmark in the American landscape.

Our theater must do three things and *not* do one. It must appeal for all it's worth to the senses and the passions and the mind, and it must not preach.

To appeal to the *senses*, we must desire to please and delight, for these release our energies and teach them to expand.

To appeal to the *passions*, we must desire adventure and take great risks. The greatest risk is not to know. This is often difficult for us, since we think we know what's wrong with the world, and often, how to correct it.

To appeal to the *mind*, we must desire to teach. What we teach is related to the sensible passions we arouse, to the de-

light and adventure we indulge, and thus we reveal the community of theater: actors and audience, mind and body.

We all, actors and audience, are entertaining (Latin: *inter tenere*, to hold between) each other. We hold each others' attention between "real" actions or events. Does this mean that theater is merely illusion, unreal, a waste of time better spent in consequential action?

Some trappings of theater are illusionary. Throw out the illusion. Let us see the mechanism.

Theater itself is not illusion, it is magic. Because it *is* real action in real time but without "real" consequences (nobody really dies or falls apart), it allows us to contemplate action, not in memory or imagination, but *as* we experience it. The more conscious we are of this gift, the more we can do with it.

That is why we must not preach. The preachers have turned out to be wrong and the questioners, from Socrates to Bertrand Russell have illuminated our lives. We are actors, the ones who do, and let our doing be seen. The audience will teach themselves.

NOTES

• Here is a **list of actions** which illustrates theater in the senses this article talks about: the raid on the FBI office in Media, Pennsylvania; the Plowshare actions against nuclear warheads; the die-ins, sit-ins, lie-ins, the White Train actions, blockades and attempted take-overs of nuclear plants and weapons facilities and draft registration centers. The unemployed

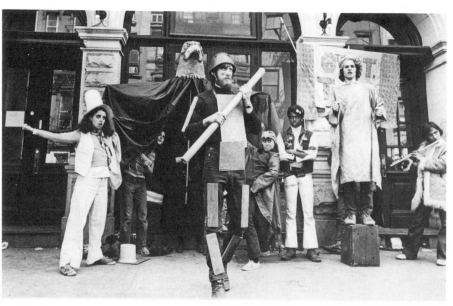

Photo by Charles Lerrigo.

marches and the Poor People's March, and their tent cities. The balloon-release actions at nuclear plants. Chicago 1968 Democratic National Convention, where many among the demonstrators and newspeople had the presence of mind to make the riot theater; the second act was the trial. People's Park in Berkeley, 1968. Sam Lovejoy's solo act on the nuclear weather tower. The Columbia University Free South Africa occupation of Hamilton Hall. The work of the Living Theater, the Teatro Campesino, the San Francisco Mime Troupe, and many other groups.

• The 1969 **Sugar Action** in Freiburg, Germany. Turbinado sugar is considered a luxury there and sold at a high price in health food shops. The Aktion Dritte Welt bought several hundred pounds from a distributor and then bagged it in half-pound quantities. It was sold at a price far below that of refined European beet sugar, but still enough to cover fair purchase, shipping and tax costs. Each bag was printed with a brief explanation of the generally high sugar prices, suggesting a parallel to other imports. With each purchase went a short stack of flyers on various aspects of Germany's neocolonial relations with Third World countries. Literature tables, petitions, a march, and street theater skits surrounded the central action. The action had a built-in guarantee of success because the political message was printed on a consumer bargain.

RESOURCES

All local groups need in order to do theater is contained within this chapter and their imaginations. However, those who wish to follow-up on the experiences of existing theater groups for practical advice could contact the following groups:

San Francisco Mime Troupe, 355 Treat Street, San Francisco, CA 94110.

Theatre for the New City, 162 Second Avenue, New York, NY 10003.

The Shared Season, St. Peter's Hall, 336 West 20th Street, New York, NY 10011. **The Modern Times Theatre, The Labor Theatre,** and the **New York Street Theatre Caravan** share space there and will gladly answer questions.

A simple, direct, practical and cheap ($1) handbook on techniques of political theater (from which many of the suggestions in this article come) is *The Art of Demonstration,* available from Cultural Correspondence, 505 West End Avenue, New York, NY 10024.

Political theater is complete theater. See Nietzsche's *Birth of Tragedy* and Norman O. Brown's *Love's Body.*

Political theater is simple theater. Read Brecht. There is a pretty good collection called *Brecht on Theatre.*

Political theater is aesthetically moral theater. Read John Berger's *Ways of Seeing* and *About Looking,* and Bertrand Russell's *Unpopular Essays.*

Political theater is dada. Read *Dadas on Art,* edited by Lucy Lippard, especially Richard Huelsenbeck's Berlin Statement.

Political theater is funny theater, silly theater, foolish theater. See lots of Marx Brothers, Chaplin, Keaton, Laurel and Hardy to get ideas. Read old vaudeville acts.

Political theater is ritual theater. Read Alan Brody's *The Mummers and Their Plays,* Hunningher's *The Origins of Theatre,* and any of the medieval ritual plays you can find.

The preachers have turned out to be wrong and the questioners have illuminated our lives.

All a local group needs in order to do theater is contained within this chapter and their imaginations.

STREET MEETING

By George Lakey and David Richards

As a quick and low-cost training and recruiting technique, the street meeting has internal value for the organization.

Street speaking stimulates the participants to do homework on the issue involved.

Street speaking is a chance for your group to sell itself to others by showing off your best style.

At street corners, factory gates, and parks many an American has found informal street meetings in progress, debating the major issues of the day. Grassroots organizations have found "soap-boxing" a useful tool. As a quick and low-cost training and recruiting technique, the street meeting has *internal value* for the organization. The *external value* of the street meeting is to serve the "movement" and the community by publicizing your viewpoint and getting other people to begin thinking. When it provides training, education of others, and is thought-provoking, a street meeting is really *direct action* on a small scale. The main features of the action are the ways in which the speaker relates to people through talk and action in unknown and hostile situations.

Internal Value

For activists who want to sharpen their skills and improve their ability to interest others in their cause, street speaking can be a valuable learning experience. By actually getting up to speak and noting the reactions of people, the speaker can learn how to communicate ideas to an unfamiliar audience. In order to interest new people in the goals of your movement, you will have to learn how first to get their interest, then present your ideas in a clear and understandable way.

This training is in turn useful for handling radio and television interviews, especially the phone-in shows on radio. Learning to respond creatively by actually doing radio work can be costly to the movement; one can alienate many people while learning not to be tongue-tied or impulsive. But the experienced street speaker will handle hostile radio and television situations well.

A further way in which it is useful is that street speaking stimulates the participants to do homework on the issues involved. They realize that they can support their case better by learning more facts, and have the motivation to learn them.

A street meeting is a low-cost tool. Usually the job can be done for under $5 including transportation. Since the sessions can be quickly arranged, the technique is always available to your group as part of training before a project or as part of a continuing program.

External Value

By using street meetings as a training tool you are not sacrificing time from the real work of the movement. The fact that you set up shop on a corner and start speaking helps to maintain the civil liberty of free speech in America. At the same time you are reaching out for potential support beyond your own members. Remember, in street speaking "the medium is the message." This is a chance for your group to sell itself to others by showing off your best style. People who see you only behind your sign on a picket line or on TV may find it hard to remember that you are human, too.

One of the problems with anti-nuclear, civil rights and anti-war efforts has been the too-often garbled accounts in the press of the goals and purposes of programs. Many ideas behind anti-nuclear actions are difficult for people to understand. Street meetings provide an inexpensive way to tell people the truth about your program. You can respond to *their* questions directly and not just hope that

Wall Street speaking by 1980 WRL Organizers' Program. Photo by Grace Hedemann.

your advertisement or press release will do the job.

One shouldn't claim too much for the street meeting as a direct action tactic. After all, it is only another type of meeting. However, in a short period of time 500-1000 pieces of your literature get handed out to a stimulated audience. The information on the leaflet interacts with the speaker. People will be encouraged to let the speaker answer any immediate questions they may have. The speaker can stimulate discussion among the people. The combination of leaflet and speaker appeals to people, sets them thinking, and opens an easy channel for their own participation.

Planning a Street Meeting

Choosing a site. When choosing a site for a street meeting, think about whom you want to speak to. The value of various types of sites vary with the kind of work the people do, the kind of neighborhood, whether the area is residential or an industrial one, the formal education level, and whether the crowd will be fairly mixed (like center city). Choose the site because of the issues involved or the characteristics of the people. For example, if you want to speak to inner city residents on the issue of getting play areas for children, you would have to go where the people normally walk and congregate at certain times of day.

The value of different sites changes according to the time of day and different days of the week. In order to be sure of having an audience, visit the proposed site during the same time of day that you will be speaking. In general, early eve-

ning is the best time for street speaking because people have more time to listen. But if you want to speak to workers, you'll probably have to catch them at lunch hour. They may be in too great a hurry to listen in the morning or evening.

In looking over a site remember the people must be able to see you, hear you, and they must have a place to stand without blocking traffic. There are a few requirements to keep in mind:

- a place for your stand
- sidewalk big enough for the crowd
- not blocking any entrances to stores or other buildings
- not too much noise from traffic or construction
- location of rest-rooms.

Equipment. The two pieces of equipment for a street speech are a sign and something to stand on. If you have resources, some literature in the form of leaflets will be helpful. The only absolute requirements for your equipment are that it is sturdy and weather proof, and that it is yours. As long as you own the equipment no one can object to what you do with it.

Something to stand on. A folding chair is often not stable enough. A convenient wall, a stairway, the back of a pickup truck, a sturdy painter's ladder, a strong straight chair, or even a box could be used.

A sign. The sign should clearly identify the group. This may be done with a slogan or a symbol with the organization's name. It is important to think in advance how the sign can be affixed to something stable. A straight chair or ladder is good for this. You can fix the sign on the top and stand on the bottom step.

When choosing a site for a street meeting, think about whom you want to speak to.

The two essential pieces of equipment for a street speech are a sign and something to stand on.

You should *not* use amplified sound since this prevents good communication between you and the listeners.

A flag. Some cities' laws require a speaker to display a flag. Some members of your group may object to this. The matter should be discussed at the briefing session for consideration of whether or not the group wants to commit civil disobedience over this issue. (The fact that the law is unconstitutional will not necessarily help your group if your failure to display a flag prevents you from speaking at all.) Look into the city regulations regarding street speakers. This can be done at the city hall or police station beforehand. A certain size and manner of display may be required. Be certain that you have a means to secure the flag. If it falls or is knocked down, violence could be touched off. (One reason that flag requirements were imposed was that authorities were convinced this would lessen chances of violent assault on the speaker.)

Literature. Leaflets and pamphlets should be kept nearby for distribution. Putting them right out in front of the crowd is risky. (They present too much temptation to steal or throw them around.) Protect the literature from rain by having a ready supply of empty plastic bags.

There is one piece of equipment you should not use in street speaking. Loudspeakers or the usual outdoor public address system prevents good communication between you and the listeners. If your meeting goes well, you will want interaction with the audience. Loud-

The best training for street speaking is simply to go and watch and get the feel of it.

speakers prevent this. Your style and personality get lost in the sound. Your audience feels a barrier between you and them. A street meeting is not a mass rally; you shouldn't need a loudspeaker to be heard. You do not want to talk to too large a crowd anyway. You want to be able to converse directly with trouble-makers. Keep it small so you will have some element of control. (See the section on crowd dynamics.)

Training. You may want to make a condition for speaking that all speakers and assistants (in some situations, team members rotate jobs as speaker and assistants) come to briefings. The best training for street speaking is simply to go and watch and get the feel of it. Role playing is useful for learning to handle hecklers.

Discipline. It is wise to agree on a plan and discipline beforehand. For example:

1. The purpose is to (a) communicate and (b) learn, and (c) express your thoughts and feelings; (c) must be in the context of (a) and (b).

2. There will be a prearranged order of speakers.

3. One person will be assigned to deal with reporters and police.

4. All team members must agree that all response to hecklers and trouble-makers will be nonviolent.

Weather. Bad weather doesn't make it impossible to hold a successful street meeting; it only makes it a little more

WRL Street Forum in Wall Street, 1941. Photo by Harry Patton/Swarthmore Peace Collection.

difficult. (In England it is done in all weather.) If you are street speaking on a regular basis, build a congregation. Don't let bad weather discourage you.

Preparing Your Literature

Most literature is not written for most people. The writer usually has a specific audience in mind. Leaflet writers should get experience as street speakers so that they will become familiar with the vocabulary and subject matter of audiences. For finding the right word to use for various groups, you might use the *Junior Thorndike Dictionary*. It tells you which vocabulary to use for groups at different levels of formal education. Use plain, concrete language in a leaflet. Use specific examples rather than large generalities. Short declarative sentences are good.

It is simply not true that people are holding their breath until you appear with the truth to lead them. You have to work for their support. Keep the readers in mind when writing a leaflet. Ask yourself the same questions you asked about the audience when choosing your meeting site.

Keep the reader in mind when designing the leaflet. The form should be attractive. The outline should be clear. A poorly designed leaflet gives readers the impression that you are incompetent and that you don't care about people.

A good leaflet gives you advantages. It provides a place for more information not mentioned by the speaker. People can use it as a reference while listening to the meeting. It continues to stimulate discussion in listener's homes after the meeting. It gives an address and telephone number where the listener can learn more. It has a tear-off coupon which can be sent in requesting more information.

Crowd Dynamics

Keep in mind from the beginning that crowds can never be totally controlled though they can often be influenced.

Three Assumptions Underlying Crowd Control

1. Crowd members are a random sample of the people who frequent the site you have chosen for your street meeting. If you have surveyed the site in advance you have a good idea of the composition of the expected crowd.

2. Tolerance of speakers of all convictions is the rule. Exceptions are obvious. George Wallace would have poor success in a street meeting in Harlem.

3. Most American crowds try to "identify" the speaker before deciding how to react. Some usual "badges" of identification are: race, clothes, length of hair, accents or dialects, and vocabulary.

Use of Assistant to Control the Crowd. One or more assistants can help the speaker control the crowd by acting as crowd members. Good assistants "join" the crowd. They assume the general characteristics of the crowd members. At the same time they divorce themselves from the content of the speech and study the group.

Training of Assistants. Speaker's assistants learn by observing all kinds of crowds. They should learn to recognize what causes crowds to react and how reaction begins and spreads. After watching small crowds, classroom, and other groups, the assistant can begin to act as a "crowd technician." By subtly "setting the pace" for the group's reactions to the speakers, the assistant will be able to move the crowd and thwart or forestall hecklers. Good assistants will place themselves at a vantage point either slightly above or at the edge of a crowd in order to observe its reactions. Their purpose is to divert interference and keep the crowd's attention fixed on the speaker.

Techniques. The assistants must remain anonymous and seem to speak for the mood of the crowd. In this way they can actually help create the mood. They may help the speaker get started and set the pace by applauding or laughing at the speaker's jokes.

When a heckler appears, the assistant should speak from the crowd and undermine the heckler's confidence to heckle. For example, someone may shout "Shut up that commie bum!" At that point the assistant could say something like, "Let her speak; this is a democracy." By appealing to the crowd's ideal of fairness, the assistant turns the crowd's sentiment against the heckler, at the same time keeping unconnected with the speaker. As long as assistants don't speak too often, they can have a good effect.

If there is only one assistant, he or she should not go over to argue with a heckler. This would draw attention away from the speaker. The assistant would also lose value as an anonymous member of the crowd. But if there is a second

Crowds can never be totally controlled though they can often be influenced.

One or more assistants can help the speaker control the crowd by acting as crowd members.

When a heckler appears, the assistant should speak from the crowd and undermine the heckler's confidence to heckle.

A meeting is easily started by appealing to everyone's natural curiosity.

Once the crowd has been collected and introduced to the subject, the team can begin distributing literature.

Experience in street speaking will teach you to present a few short points in a variety of ways.

assistant, one might talk quietly to the heckler and try to move him or her to the edge of the crowd or offer coffee while pursuing the argument. This should only be done if the heckler is very disruptive—remember, heckling can add spice to a meeting.

Timing is important for the assistant. By rebuking a disrupter early in the speech, the development of unfavorable group feelings toward the speaker is prevented. By interjecting well-timed comments, the assistant can move the crowd to action or subdue hostility.

Some points to remember:

- Try not to "stage" your statements; plan quickly and act fast.

- Speak loudly. *Shout* if you have to, but try not to sound strident or angry.

- Use short phrases. The crowd won't hear long sentences.

- Use ordinary language.

- If you have a sharp sense of humor, use it on the speaker if it will help the crowd relax. Remember, a crowd that is smiling and chuckling will not usually behave unfavorably.

- Time your statements to work with the speaker. Use his or her pauses to make your remarks. You may even interrupt sometimes; but don't steal the show. Experience will help you decide when is the right moment for a comment from the crowd.

- Don't speak too often. You will be identified as a "ringer" and your effectiveness will be lost.

Starting a Meeting

A meeting is easily started by appealing to everyone's natural curiosity. This is done by attracting attention to interesting sights or sounds. Opening with singing or musical instruments can be effective. (Don't bring expensive instruments or electric guitars.) One problem in starting with pure entertainment is that the crowd often loses interest and walks off when your speaker appears. This can be avoided by having a first speaker who can collect a crowd, then begin speaking by telling jokes or promising some impossible feat. (One speaker tells people she will make herself disappear; then the eyes really get glued on her. Since the people were first attracted by the speaker's personality, they tend to stay around when the real subject of the meeting begins.)

The first speaker should be entertaining; the initial content of the speech is not too important. Enjoy what you are doing. Your personality will set the mood; then lead the crowd into the subject and turn them over to the next speaker. The team's assistants can help the first speaker by choosing a good time to walk slowly in close and "bring the others with them." If their first move fails they can fade out and slowly move in again later.

Another job of the opening speaker is to set the size of the crowd before turning it over to the main speaker. The aim should be to get an attentive crowd. This means not more than 75 people (25-75 is a good number). With the constant turnover of the crowd your team reaches 1000 people in several hours. The value of a small crowd is that each person sees more and you can communicate individually.

Leafletting

Once the crowd has been collected and introduced to the subject, the team can begin distributing literature. Leafletters should watch the crowd and the speaker to note when the people get interested in the subject. If literature is distributed too soon, then interaction will begin before the speaker has set up a relationship with the crowd.

Leafletters can be stationed around the crowd and across the street as well. They should be pleasant and assume that people will take the literature. Don't be timid; but don't force your material on anyone. If you are too aggressive, people will react more strongly; more leaflets will be thrown down. You should pick up all discarded leaflets in the vicinity of your meeting. Be considerate of people with arms full of groceries. They won't appreciate your forcing them to take a leaflet. A good ploy is a polite "Would you read this, please?"

General Speaking

Communication of ideas to a constantly changing crowd requires a special form of speech. Your talk cannot be a logical progression of ideas that requires hearing all of the speech in order to understand it. Few people will listen more than a few minutes. Experience in street speaking will teach you to present a few short points in a variety of ways. Your speech will consist of small capsules of ideas that can be understood independently of each other. In attempting this at first you will probably have a tendency to "talk down to people." Your listeners will notice your manner immediately and will resent it. Simplifying and encapsulating your thoughts for street speech does not require talking down or a sell-out of intellect or integrity. It requires learning how to communicate.

The theme of the speech and the literature at the meeting should be directed to the type of people you are speaking to. The kind of work the people do and how much formal education they possess should always be considered. In thinking about your speech you should keep in mind this question: "In what special way can this group relate or contribute to my organization?" Your points should be directed at informing them as to how your problem or proposal affects them and how they can relate to the solution.

Humor. If you are the speaker, humor is fine when directed at yourself. As a rule, don't ridicule the government or the heckler in the crowd. In an unknown crowd that kind of humor will almost always elicit hostile response. Humor directed at yourself will get the crowd in a good mood by making them laugh. A little self-ridicule, even if facetious, will usually gain you personal sympathy from the crowd. For example, "Reagan is stupid, but not that stupid."—BAD. "My teenage daughter thinks I'm stupid, but not that stupid."—GOOD.

The speaker needs a battery of quick responses to stark questions like, "Who's this group?" "Who's paying you?" or "Who writes your speeches, Moscow?" Humor can be most helpful in answering this type of question, but a quick response is the most important. The speakers can profit by thinking about the obvious questions of this type as they prepare for the meeting. But like most street-speaking skills, proficiency will only come with practice, and experience is the best way to learn.

Your points should be directed at informing them as to how your proposal affects them and how they can relate to the solution.

If you are the speaker, humor is fine when directed at yourself.

The speaker needs a battery of quick responses to hostile questions.

NOTES ON PUBLIC SPEAKING

By Ed Hedemann

If the movement is to succeed in its efforts to change the face of the earth, we will need to produce many more public speakers.

As with many other skills, becoming a good speaker is developed through experience. So merely reading this chapter will not transform a poor speaker into a charismatic orator. However, it is hoped the suggestions which follow will give the activist some aid and confidence.

Purposes of Speaking

There are a variety of reasons and uses for public speaking. Listed below are some of the main ones.

Educate. Presenting new material, facts, or a different analysis.

Inspire. Requires a passionate speech to motivate people into action or create a sense of unity, as in a "pep rally."

Recruit and Persuade. Use the speaking engagement to gain new members in your campaign or organization, raise money, become active.

Challenge Opponents. Your speech can make clear the anger and strength of opposition.

Entertain. Ideally, this should often be part of every talk. But sometimes "to entertain" will be the main purpose.

Speaking Situations

Different speaking situations require different approaches and preparation. Some speaking formats are a combination of the following types (e.g., a radio debate).

Workshop or Class. This format is more low key than the others. Often includes dialogue with participants, is longer, and entails more detail in the subject matter. Workshops normally involve a sympathetic audience; while classes, which are often captive, may be less sympathetic; and the presentation is usually shorter.

Interview. Often very brief, with emphasis on questions rather than a presentation. Radio interviews can range from five minutes to hours, usually a half hour. Sometimes involves callers from the listening audience. Television interviews require more care on visual appearance (also, remember to look at the camera), and tend to be much briefer than radio. Press interviews may be still shorter—sometimes only a few seconds to reply to some controversial or current topic.

Speech. Remarks need to be brief (anywhere from five minutes to a half hour), and main points need to be limited. Feeling and passion are important. In a rally or teach-in, you are usually dealing with a sympathetic audience. Be aware of what other speakers have said (or will say). Try to move the audience. If you are doing street speaking the audience is generally less sympathetic, and is constantly changing and flowing. Need to keep repeating a few main points in different ways.

Grace Paley speaking to May 6, 1979, anti-nuclear rally in Washington, DC. Photo by Grace Hedemann.

Debate or Panel. Usually you have little time in preparation, but it requires a lot of preparation. Need to know your opponents and their arguments. Your points need to be clear and simple. Content will often take a back seat to gesture, clever remarks, and theater.

Preparation

How you prepare will depend on which of the above formats you are in, the length of time allotted, and what you are trying to accomplish (e.g., educate, inspire, recruit). Also, find out about your audience. Who are they? What are their interests? Are they likely to be sympathetic? How much do they already know about the topic? Are there other speakers? What are their topics or perspectives?

What follows are ten suggested steps for preparing your talk.

1. Make all the random notes you can think of on a piece of paper. Read the basic material, becoming familiar with all arguments for and *against* your position. Continue making notes. In general, it's better to learn far more than you'll ever use.

2. Keeping in mind the particular audience you will be addressing, capsulize the main points you want to communicate to them. Don't try to make too many points (stick to two or three main ones). Present either new (to that audience) material or known facts from a clever or unexpected perspective.

3. Make an outline. Begin the speech with something that will get their attention. The "traditional" approach is to begin with an appropriate story or joke. But in some situations it might be better to start with a dramatic rhetorical question, or a reference to local incident or a current event (this tends to personalize the speech), or your common ground with the audience, or a compliment to the audience. An audience often makes up its mind about you very quickly, so it is important to start well. Next, if not already obvious to your audience, describe what the problem is. Follow with your proposed solution and how that will change conditions. Then, if appropriate, suggest actions the audience can take. If your allotted time is long enough, place your main points at the beginning and end, as well as the middle. Make sure your summation sounds like an ending, especially one which will produce applause.

4. Write a full draft following this outline, but without concern about length. Then adjust the speech for the time you have been allotted.

5. Put it away for a day or two, so you can get back to it fresh.

6. Reread it, but this time out loud to get the proper timing, allowing for breathing and pauses. More often than not, speeches run over. It takes longer to deliver a speech (100 words a minute is typical) than to read it in your head. Reading into a tape recorder can help this process. And if you have been given no hard limit on time, keep it to about twenty minutes, followed by a period for questions. An hour is about the limit an audience can listen comfortably. Remember, the question period often allows an opportunity to make additional points you didn't have time for in the main speech. When you have trimmed the speech to what appears to be an acceptable length, mark sections which could be dropped (at the time of actual delivery) if you find yourself running short on time.

7. Go over the talk thoroughly, memorize it point by point, *not* word for word. The best speakers are those who sound spontaneous. No audience likes to be read to, and would be dismayed to see a speaker methodically thumbing through a stack of notes.

8. Put your speech on cards, summarizing your main points. This will allow you to keep track of all you want

Don't try to make too many points in your speech.

Use a good story or humor when appropriate.

More often than not, speeches tend to run too long, so be prepared to drop some sections.

Be flexible enough to bring in current events and react with the audience.

to say without having it written word for word.

9. Develop and prepare support material—appropriate quotes from reliable sources, facts on cards (perhaps on charts or slides) to back up provocative statements you might make. Anticipate questions and important counter-arguments.

10. If you expect significant hostility and need support, have friends in the audience to ask good questions and applaud. Keep up to date on subject matter and revise your talk by incorporating new material where appropriate.

The Presentation

Listed below are some common points to keep in mind when making your presentation.

- Use simple, clear (and loud) language. Don't mumble.
- Make it short.
- Allow time for adequate audience participation through questions and answers.
- Stand, don't sit. This gives more energy to reach out to the audience. Find a place where everyone can see you. Make sure you have some place to put your notes.
- Don't worry about your appearance (except on TV).
- Go slow and pause. Mark pauses in your notes at appropriate points.
- If nervous, take long, deep breaths.
- Look at the audience. Picking out three or four sympathetic people in the audience to look at will help your confidence.
- Use inflection and emotion at appropriate points (don't talk in a monotone).
- Use humor or a story to keep the attention and interest of the audience. Don't make fun of a hostile questioner.
- Be flexible in presentation in order to play off of or react to the audience. Pull in current or local events.
- Take off your watch and place it in front of you, rather than looking at your wrist.
- Don't talk down to the audience.
- Don't get boxed in by details or facts which divert from your main points.

- If verbally abused, ignore the attack and mention your points. Appeal for non-interruption and freedom of speech.
- Get the audience involved (e.g., take a poll).

Getting Started

Accompanying someone else is a good way to get started into speaking gradually. Observe their presentation style, note which points cause favorable or unfavorable audience reaction. Aid in the collection of names or distribution of material after the talk. Make your first presentation in a workshop or before a class with a sympathetic audience.

Your group could also schedule a role play session. One or more people can prepare presentations of five to ten minutes. The rest can play the devil's advocate in asking provocative questions. Setting up street speaking situations for the group is a good way to learn "under fire" how to speak in public. Even an activity as simple as leafletting will often put you into situations where you need to be quick in dialogue and response.

To line up speaking engagements, check with radio talk shows, churches, civic organizations, schools (or teachers and students you know). If groups, such as high schools, are reluctant to have you for fear of showing bias, suggest a debate or forum. Always confirm the details of your talk—especially the length of time for the speech. It is not unusual to have your time cut at the last minute.

OUTSIDE SPEAKERS

By Jerry Coffin

One way for local radical and pacifist groups to spread our philosophy is through speakers. All of us should develop our skills in this area (see "Street Meetings" chapter). You can develop a regular program of sending members of your local group to schools, clubs, TV, and radio stations to speak on current issues and problems and how to create change. However, at some point you are no longer going to be "interesting" to local audiences. People will have heard you speak several times and no longer think you have anything new to offer. In addition, some clubs and media outlets won't even give us the opportunity to speak because you are local and therefore not "curious" or "special" enough to rate attention. It is at this point that you may wish to bring outside speakers into your community.

The outside speakers can spend one or several days in your community and, if you do the necessary advance work, make a real contribution to educating the community and recruiting folks for your organization.

The type of outside speaker this outline deals with is well-versed in a particular area of concern, or functions in her/his daily life in some kind of full-time "movement" capacity.

How to Get a Speaker

Virtually every national organization has some kind of formal or informal speakers program. Decide the subject you want your speakers to cover and contact the appropriate organization.

For illustration, here are some of the ways the national office of WRL sends out speakers:

- **National Tour.** Usually once a year a staff member of the League makes a 2- to 4-month tour of the country, traveling by car and speaking in dozens of communities. This is by far the least expensive way to provide a quality speaker.
- **Regional Tours.** Someone will fly into an area to promote a project and/or do some quick speaking engagements. The costs for air fare and other travel are split between the groups visited.
- **The One-Shot Speaker.** A League member travels to one town for a day or so to speak. All costs are borne by the sponsoring group.

Once you've decided what kind of speaker you want, and before you contact the appropriate organization, decide how much, if anything, you can afford. If you can't afford anything, the group may have a tour coming through your area and you can plug into it. If they want an honorarium (amount of money above the basic expenses), you're in a position to negotiate if you know how much you can afford. If a speaker comes to your area to fill a speaking engagement, you will usually be responsible for basic expenses (travel, housing, food) and an honorarium.

Using the Speaker

When you have a commitment for someone to come to your area to speak, use the person in other ways too. Most people who do movement speaking expect to be run ragged. You are wasting your time and your speaker's time if every hour between early morning and late night is not used.

Several weeks before your speaker arrives, start contacting possible places for her/him to speak and fill up the schedule. A good schedule would look something

Outside speakers who spend one or several days in your community can make a real contribution to educating the community and recruiting folks to your organization.

Most people who do movement speaking expect to be run ragged.

like this:

8-9 am	morning radio talk show
10-10:30	television interview show
12-1:30 pm	"Service Club" luncheon-speech
2-4	talk at high school or college
4-7	meeting with local movement people & dinner
7:30-9	speech at special meeting (large group)
9:30-10:30	evening radio talk show.

If you have a speaker for more than a couple of days, you'll need to schedule a day of rest. And regardless of how long you have the speaker, make sure she/he gets a good night's sleep every night.

How to Schedule a Radio or Television Interview

Get hold of the radio and television guide for your community. Draw up a list of all interview, general interest and talk shows on both radio and television. Don't forget the UHF, PBS, and cable stations. If you are not sure what the nature of a given program is, listen to it. Don't pass up things like "Alan's Afternoon Movies." Often morning and afternoon movies have a host who interviews people between movies. Your best chances are with talk shows which by their very nature are desperate for controversial guests. Next best are interview shows on both radio and TV, and this includes the so-called "women's morning television shows."

Once you have your list of prospective radio and television shows, look up the addresses and phone numbers and find out the name of the producer of each show. The producer is usually responsible for booking guests. In some smaller stations the host acts as her/his own producer. To get the name of the producer, call up the station and ask the name of the producer of "Sherrye Henry Show." As a last resort tune in the program and check out the credit lines for the producer.

Address a letter to the producer that says in effect "On February 3-5 Igal Roodenko, former Chairperson of the War Resisters League, will be in Asheville. He's available for an interview and to answer questions about the draft on 'The Sherrye Henry Show.' Enclosed is a photograph of Mr. Roodenko and a brief biography. I'll be calling you later this week to find out if you're interested in having Mr. Roodenko on the show."

Later in the week call the producer. When talking to her/him, convince her or him that your speaker is articulate, controversial (or soft spoken, depending on the show), interesting, has a lot to say and most of all is important. They like important people. In the minds of most producers, important people are the only folks of interest to her/his listeners.

Don't get discouraged if you're turned down repeatedly. Keep calling and eventually one of the shows will book your speaker. As you call the stations over a period of time with different speakers, the producer will get to know you and become more receptive to booking your speakers on the show. Once you get a good speaker on a show, the producer will come to regard you as a good source of guests and book many of the people you offer. The first time you try to get a speaker on radio and television, you'll have to scramble to get one or two bookings. After a while you'll know which shows are the best, develop personal contacts on the shows, and be able to pick and choose where you want your speaker to appear.

Scheduling Newspaper Interviews

Most local papers—especially small town papers—are hurting for local news of interest. They will run a special news item on your speaker if you set it up. Look in the paper for columnists who appear regularly and call them a couple of days before your speaker hits town. Tell them that your speaker will be available for an interview. Tie the speaker into something current like "Igal Roodenko, who's the former Chairperson of the War Resisters League, is in town for some speeches. He's available for an interview about the draft. When should we come by and see you?" Be positive and talk as if you assume the columnists will be climbing the walls for a chance to interview your speaker. Again, it helps if the newspaper person is convinced your speaker is "important." When you show up for the interview, bring a photograph of your speaker and a biography.

Don't neglect local high school and college newspapers. You can set up one interview with representatives from all area high schools and another meeting with folks from the college newspapers.

Once you get a good speaker on a show, the producer will come to regard you as a good source of guests.

Don't get discouraged if you're turned down repeatedly. Keep calling and eventually one of the shows will book your speaker.

Churches and Synagogues

Churches and synagogues are a natural for radical and pacifist speakers. Most religious bodies pay at least lip service to morality and because of this can usually be persuaded to invite your speaker to address the Wednesday morning prayer breakfast, the adult Bible class, or the social action committee. You can even get some religious groups to let your speaker give the weekly sermon.

When trying to book your speaker into churches, draw up a list of every religious body in town and the name of the pastor or rabbi. First call the ones you don't know. Remember the goal is to reach new people, but also consolidate friends. If you know the pastor or rabbi, you know he's at least a sympathizer. If you get turned down by all the pastors and rabbis you don't know, then call your friends.

When you make your call talk only to the pastor or rabbi, who has the power to make the decision. Others lack the power to say "yes," but they can say "no." When you make your pitch, emphasize the moral angle of your speaker's topic. Also be prepared to spell out in detail how your speaker's topic relates to religious concerns.

Service Clubs and Community Organizations

A "service club" is something like Rotary, Lion's, Elks, etc. Also Women's Clubs and League of Women Voters are good prospects. If your speaker also has a hobby or special interest, try to book her/him into that kind of interest club. For instance, Dave McReynolds of the WRL is a plant nut. You could book him into a garden club. Remember you want to reach new people. Garden club members are as open to our philosophy as anyone, but probably are never exposed to people who are anti-war, anti-capitalist, etc. Finally, the YMCA, YWCA, YMHA are all good prospects for a movement speaker.

Service clubs usually have a regular weekly luncheon in some restaurant. These meetings are filled with nonsense and trivia, and they usually have some kind of speaker. While these groups tend to be reactionary, sexist, and racist, inroads can be made. If we want to create change in this country, we need to reach out to everyone. The experience of the Dayton AFSC office can be instructive.

Over the years the Dayton AFSC has established a regular program of taking speakers to local service clubs. At first they couldn't get the clubs to book speakers. Finally they were booked into hostile meetings, then speakers were grudgingly given attention, and now speakers are welcomed and occasionally win people to their viewpoint.

As with all bookings, you need to draw up a list of clubs and find out who is the "speakers chairman" or whatever the club calls the person who sets up the speaking schedule. Call the Chamber of Commerce for a list of service clubs. They can also give you the name and number of the "speakers chairman." Also find out when the club meets.

Select those clubs who have meetings during the period your speaker is in town. Call the person responsible for speakers several weeks in advance and ask her/him to book your speaker. Make sure the "speakers chairman" understands that the speaker is from L.A. or New York or wherever, and will only be in town for a couple of days. This gives your speaker a sort of big city glamour (this is unfortunate, but true). If you've booked your speaker on a radio or television show, mention that your speaker "can talk to the Rotary Club before appearing on the Warner Wolf TV Show." This will put the touch of "celebrity" on your speaker and help you get a booking.

If you are not having any luck convincing the "speakers chairman" to book your speaker, try challenging her/him with something like "I know we have disagreements, but don't you think it is healthy in a democracy for an exchange of views? Besides, we think our speakers ought to get the thinking of groups like yours—education works both ways." Service clubs are a tough nut, so don't be discouraged if you're not able to book a speaker the first few times you call.

With YMCA, YWCA, League of Women Voters, and groups of this type, it's relatively easy to get them to invite your speakers to address their meetings.

High Schools and Colleges

Try to get your speaker into the schools. It's often pretty easy to find a sympathetic teacher to invite your speaker to talk to her/his classes. If you don't know any teachers, you can often succeed by writing letters and then calling the Social Studies teachers in high

If we want to create change in this country, we need to reach out to everyone. So try to book your speaker with groups which are not usually sympathetic with the movement, such as service clubs and community organizations.

schools and political science-type teachers in college. To find out the names of these folks, look in the local college catalogs and previous years' high school year books.

Special Meetings

The main talk your speaker will give should be the special meeting. This is a meeting that you organize which has as its purpose providing a forum for your speaker and giving your organization public exposure.

Most folks are pretty sloppy about their special meetings. They don't promote the meetings effectively, don't choose the right kind of room, or don't adequately prepare for the speech.

Choose the right space. You should be able to estimate pretty well the number of people who will show up to hear your speaker. Choose a room that will hold about that number of people. Your goal is to have a room that is slightly crowded. The reason for this is to give a sense of strength and togetherness to the audience. If there are twenty people in a room large enough for a hundred, they'll feel isolated and be nervous and fidgety. Your speaker will pick up the vibrations and not give a good talk. S/he will think that people don't really want to hear what s/he has to say if so few show up. On the other hand, that same twenty people in a room that barely holds them may lead to a successful meeting. The room is full so people feel that they are not alone, that they are part of something larger than themselves, and your speaker will be at her/his best since s/he "filled the hall."

However, some large auditoriums have a reputation of prestige, so if a speaker—no matter who—is booked there it may draw people simply because of the auditorium.

To find a room, contact the people you know at local churches, colleges (a student or faculty member can reserve a lecture hall or auditorium for no cost), or local YWCA or YMCA.

Promote the meeting. Use all of your standard promotion techniques. Get leaflets and posters where sympathetic folks gather. Put an announcement in the papers and in the "community billboard" of your local radio station. Make sure announcements appear in college and high school newspapers. Posters should be put up in record stores, restaurants in the student district, churches, coffee shops, etc. Be sure special mention of the meeting appears in all movement-type newsletters and the local alternative press. Call up local "talk shows" when they're on the air and in the course of commenting on the main topic, mention when and where your speaker will be appearing.

Have all your material ready. If you need a P.A. system, make sure it's set up and working well before the meeting. Same with projectors, etc. Have your literature set out for sale before people start arriving.

Debates, Forums, and Teach-ins

You may wish to set your speaker up for a debate, which often succeeds in providing drama and drawing a larger crowd. You could also involve several other speakers by scheduling a panel discussion or teach-in.

A debate is easier to organize, but be careful your speaker is consulted first. Debates are frequently more acceptable with high school authorities or where you are having trouble scheduling an engagement. For teach-ins you may wish to reserve and advertise smaller side rooms available for follow-up discussion with each speaker.

Select a moderator who can make announcements, do a fund pitch, introduce speakers, and field questions without bias.

General

Brief your speaker. When your speaker hits town, tell her/him everything you can think of about the people and past activities in town. Prior to each speech or interview, give your speaker a rundown on the composition and politics of the crowd or the politics and opinions and style of the interviewer.

Make arrangements to sell literature.

The main talk your speaker will give should be the special meeting you organize.

Generally, you should book your speaker in a room that will be slightly crowded to give a sense of strength and togetherness to the audience.

Many speakers will bring literature they want to sell. Whether or not they bring literature, you should sell your own. Try to have someone available to sell the literature and make sure each meeting has a table and place to sell the literature. Have some basic give-aways.

Take collections. At many meetings you'll be able to take a collection, and certainly you should take a collection at your own special meeting. Many broke folks are embarrassed to ask for money. This is a hard thing to overcome, but eventually you'll have to. Remember your speaker's time is valuable. People should pay whatever they can afford to hear your speaker. Too many people believe "you pay for capitalism but the movement is for free." If you're going to have a local radical and pacifist program of any consequence, you need money. Prior to every meeting ask the person in charge if you can take a collection. If the answer is yes, then get containers and one or more people to pass them around. You give the collection pitch. Don't expect your speaker to raise your money for you. Don't be embarrassed because it is the duty of people to support a people's movement. Tell people what the money is needed for (leaflets, office rent, speaker's travel expenses, etc.) and ask them to give the equivalent of what they spent that week on cigarettes, dope, records, movies, or gasoline or whatever is appropriate to the crowd.

Use your speaker as a resource. As much as possible, have your speaker meet with small informal groups of movement people. In these meetings really pick your speaker's brain. You'll learn a lot since, after all, you're bringing the speaker to town because s/he has something to offer.

Try to get honorariums. Every time you book your speaker, try to get an honorarium. Most clubs, organizations, and schools budget an amount for speakers. Always ask for what you think the group normally pays for a speaker. The standard amount is $25-100 for a small group. As you're booking your speaker, mention that you'll need an "x" dollar honorarium. If the person you're dealing with hesitates, then say the amount is negotiable. "What can you afford?" If the person says they cannot afford anything, ask if you can take a collection. If they say no, then go ahead and book the speaker for free. Any honorarium you collect should be split with the speaker. If you're paying the speaker an honorarium and/or travel expenses, then split honorariums you collect after you've covered your cost.

Get mailing lists. At every special meeting you have, pass around a sheet for names and addresses of attenders. This way you can follow up on people who drop by but aren't sure they really want to commit themselves.

Give people something to take home. At every place your speaker talks, hand out a free leaflet with a return coupon that tells briefly what your group does and why. The last paragraph should ask folks to join with you. The coupon should offer literature and an offer to send your newsletter.

Conclusion

Like all the chapters in this Manual, this one should be adjusted to meet local conditions. Try everything you can the first couple of times you bring in an outside speaker. After that, concentrate on what works best in your community. Remember above all that the goal is to reach new people. Too many of us are lazy and when we have a speaker coming to town simply bring out the same old people to hear her/him. It's work, hard work, to reach new people but it has to be done if we're ever to create fundamental change in this country.

Checklist

- [ ] RESERVE A ROOM for the main speaking engagement.
- [ ] BEGIN PUBLICITY EARLY (bulletin board, posters, leaflets all take time to produce/arrange).
- [ ] MAKE A LIST of all local TALK SHOWS on TV/radio.
- [ ] WRITE PRODUCERS OF SELECTED TALK SHOWS. Enclose an introduction to your speaker, brief biography and photograph. Mention you will follow-up with a phone call within the week.
- [ ] ARRANGE INTERVIEWS AND NEWS COVERAGE with local newspapers (community, college, high school).

ARRANGE MEETINGS IN THE COMMUNITY...
- [ ] religious community
- [ ] service organizations
- [ ] high school/college classes
- [ ] Try to get honorariums for your speaker. If you cannot, take a

Don't be embarrassed to take a collection at all possible meetings.

Every time you book your speaker, try to get an honorarium.

At every place your speaker talks, hand out a free leaflet with a return coupon.

collection at the meeting.

- [ ] ARRANGE MEETING WITH LOCAL ORGANIZERS.
- [ ] ARRANGE HOUSING AND CARE for your speaker. (Does s/he need a special diet? hard bed? etc.)
- [ ] MAKE ARRANGEMENTS TO SELL LITERATURE at speaker's events when appropriate (e.g., get permission if necessary, assign someone to bring literature and set up table).
- [ ] PREPARE BRIEFING FOR SPEAKER when s/he arrives. Run down activities, background on movement and local activities, politics of audiences, interviewers, etc.
- [ ] CHECK PUBLIC ADDRESS AND AUDIO/VISUAL EQUIPMENT.
- [ ] TAKE COLLECTIONS at all meetings.

Constituencies

WORKING WITH MINORITY COMMUNITIES

By William Douthard

A safe bet is many of you who will read and utilize the WRL *Organizer's Manual* will not be a member of the Black, Hispanic or Native American community. It will also be a safe bet your experience and involvement with programs and projects initiated by and within these minority communities will be limited at best. The statements and opinions which follow are to assist you in establishing the kinds of human inter-relationships required to organize effectively in minority communities.

Over 80% of minority populations in the United States are located in the large metropolitan areas of the country, from Boston to Miami, from Los Angeles to Seattle, and all of the major cities in between. As such, these constituencies, who are most often poor or working poor, are faced with the ever present increasing urban problems of unemployment or under-employment, inadequate housing, street crime, drug addiction, lack of adequate municipal services, substandard educational systems, and constant neglect from power centers. These minority communities are not monolithic in their approach to the resolution of their problems, nor are they all in motion to find solutions. Too many of them are faced with the day-to-day practicality of eking out an existence to be concerned with expanding the quality of their existence. Finding a job, paying the rent, getting a few clothes, and staying alive are the things which occupy their day-to-day thoughts, not the ecology, quality of elected officials, the arms race, or our country's foreign relations image. To work with them and to organize alongside them requires the realization that the majority of the poor and working poor of this country, and especially the minority poor and working poor, usually are not where you are in political or social consciousness and perspective. This does not mean they are stupid or they have failed to grasp the larger picture you have been able to understand, it simply means they have not had the luxury of time supported by advanced education and the absence of concerns about their economic future.

Important also to remember as you approach minority communities is that to offer your assistance, talents, and skills is useless—if they don't believe, trust, or accept you immediately. The working poor of this country have seen hundreds before you who have come in with the "plan" which would alleviate or end all of their woes and troubles. They noticed that when the going got rough, those with the plans got going. Consequently the community was left alone in its struggle. This built up suspicion will only evaporate when they get to know you personally and establish with you a brotherly and sisterly relationship. It is not an easy process. It requires the sublimation of your own working agenda until the time arises when your agenda and theirs naturally come together.

The following suggestions are intended to give you a basic understanding of your organizing potential within the non-white urban areas.

As you approach minority communities it is useless to offer your assistance, talents, and skills if they don't believe, trust, or accept you immediately.

The key is to let those in minority communities know you are there to assist them, not to usurp their energies and causes, nor attempt to impose your own agenda.

The white leadership of the anti-war movement made no real effort to become partners in struggles that the minority communities were daily involved in.

Church leaders play a very important role in the progressive leadership of the community.

- When you first approach this community offer your assistance in projects currently underway.

- Use the time while you are assisting to begin to point out the connections in what the community is doing and the larger picture you hold.

- Allow yourself to know them as individual human beings and for them to know you in a like fashion. Out of any struggle should come the awareness of their part and yours to share the same basic dream of an equal and just society and the desire to live in such a society.

- Encourage the members of your organization to be supportive of projects and actions of minority communities. This support process will help to establish the fellowship and camaraderie necessary for ongoing trust and struggle. Offer the use of special talents and skills you and your organization bring, such as specific knowledge of how governmental systems operate and how to use their grievance mechanisms, how to organize, demonstrate, run petition campaigns, do street theater, produce newsletters, conduct meetings, run training programs, etc.

The key then is to let them know you are there to assist them and to help them, not to usurp their energies and causes, nor attempt to impose your own agenda or your organization's agenda.

As this relationship develops, there should be regular visitations and representatives from your organization or group attending meetings in minority communities and representatives from the minority organizations attending meetings of your groups. Now joint discussions around mutual interests and concerns can begin. This process helps to raise the conscious level of the minority organizations so they come naturally ready to join in projects and actions the two of you plan and develop with common goals. The mistake the anti-war movement made in the 60's and 70's was first to assume the minority community commonly shared the peace movement's perspective of the war, and then to expect the minority community to participate in large numbers in projects and actions to bring the war to an end. This did not happen! The reason it didn't happen was the white leadership of the anti-war movement made no real effort to become partners in struggles that the minority communities were daily involved in. Without this groundwork, without this relationship, without this friendship, the minority communities would not respond to the anti-war calling. When the masses of anti-war organizations and people could not be found in the demonstration at a welfare center to protest the cut backs in welfare benefits, it could not be assumed the minority constituencies would join them at the draft boards.

There are other peculiar aspects of minority constituencies you should be aware of in understanding the human dynamics within those communities:

- Church and religious leaders play a very important role in the progressive leadership of the community. In fact, religious leadership is the most consistent form of leadership within the Black and Hispanic community. The

The Continental Walk in Louisiana, 1976. Photo by SCLC.

Native American community centers its leadership responsibility in its council of elders and this continues to be the longest established leadership forum.

- The leadership structure in the non-white community is dominated by men who are usually very chauvinistic in their views about the utilization of women in leadership roles.
- Financial resources required to sustain struggles are usually not present or available to minority constituencies. In addition, most minority communities are susceptible to economic pressures sometimes used to defeat their struggles. These pressures take the form of threatened job loss, loan denial, mortgage foreclosure, or a drying up of contributions by once friendly sources. An ancillary of this economic pressure or susceptibility is the experience these communities have acquired in maintaining struggles and movements with minimal financial resources. In essence, they have learned to make do with nothing and have developed indigenous organizing habits not always similar to more affluent struggles. Minority communities also developed a misconception about the financial resources available to non-minority struggles. They are prompted to believe anti-war groups or pacifist organizations are just loaded with bucks and may imply your only role in assisting them is to give them money. If you succumb to these misconceptions and pressures you will be doing neither community a service and in fact you will assist in the maintenance of the gaps that already exist.
- I say this next one in all candor. Though men in the non-white community picture themselves as the basic leaders and spokespersons of the struggle of those communities, it is the women and the students who do all the work and on whom you can depend the most. Part of this reason is they have more of the time and knowledge, while the men still tend to be the principal wage earner. Men also tend to have jobs that are not so easy to take off from as women might have. Nevertheless, a large part of this complex phenomenon still remains true. Young people and women tend to be the basic cadre of workers and are often less competitive.

After all I have said, if I can leave you with two basic thoughts, it might summarize most of this section. First, remember you are dealing with a community whose primary day-to-day concern is the bare existence of life itself with no time left to expound on the quality of that existence. Secondly, to organize with them and among them, the most important organizing tool you bring is yourself. Your friendship and your willingness to share your human qualities with them, to talk with them, to sing with them, to pray with them, to work alongside of them, to eat at their table, and to sit on the porch at night and ruminate about yourselves and your beliefs. Your appreciation of the many struggles they go through daily to live and your willingness to be yourself should be the basis for a long lasting relationship.

The leadership structure in the non-white community is dominated by men.

Financial resources required to sustain struggles are usually not present or available to minority constituencies.

PEACE ORGANIZING IN RELIGIOUS COMMUNITIES

By Dan Ebener

"I came to the conclusion long ago, after prayerful search and study and discussion with as many people as I could meet, that all religions were true, and also that all had some error in them, and whilst I hold my own, I should hold others as dear as Hinduism...So we can pray, if we are Hindus, that not a Christian should become a Hindu, or if we are Moslems, that not a Hindu or a Christian should become a Moslem, or should we even secretly pray that anyone should be converted, but our innermost prayer should be that a Hindu should be a better Hindu, a Moslem a better Moslem, and a Christian a better Christian...I broaden my Hinduism by loving other religions as my own....

"This implies the belief in the truth of all religions and respect for them...Religions are different roads to the same point. What does it matter that we take different roads so long as we reach the same goal? In reality, there are as many religions as there are individuals...All (religions) proceed from the same God, but all are imperfect because they come down to us through imperfect human instrumentality."

Mohandas Gandhi

The world's religions—Moslem, Christian, Jewish, Hindu, Buddhist, and most others—affirm the values of peace, justice, universalism, love and truth. In fact, almost everyone believes in "peace."

The fact that Jimmy Carter, Ronald Reagan, and John Anderson all proclaimed themselves to be "born-again Christians" during the 1980 Presidential campaign, is an example of how important religious beliefs can be in shaping political beliefs. It also indicates the extent to which religious principles have become distorted with a militaristic mentality which says that "to have peace, you must prepare for war."

This war mentality, which crosses religious, political, and ideological lines, is one of the most basic assumptions which needs to be challenged by today's pacifist. Many people find that they can do so most effectively by speaking from pacifist beliefs which are based on religious life and convictions.

To a "pacifist" (from the Latin, meaning *peacemaker*), peace cannot be achieved by war, nor the threat of war. This placing of trust in the ways of war is an old form of idolatry in the eyes of most religions, because trust should be placed foremost in God and the ways of God. "Some boast of chariot, some of horses, but we boast about the name of Yahweh, our God." (*Psalms 7-8.*) True peace grows out of nonviolent, loving means to resolve international, domestic, and personal conflicts.

The Old Testament prophets Isaiah and Micah speak of a time when "nations shall beat their swords into plowshares," and "study war no more." But such a time will come only when people of faith in that vision are willing to live disarmed lives and to work against the forces of war and militarism—to become peacemakers.

For many, this can begin in their community of worship, where a certain vulnerability allows some people to open up to further insights into the faith tradition they are grounded in.

Therefore, to enable religious people to be a more active force in the movement for peace, we must begin with an appeal to those *religious* values which call all the people of God to become peacemakers, instead of concentrating on the promotion of political arguments which may already divide us.

Approaching Your Local Religious Community

If you decide to try to organize in the religious communities for peace, you might begin by forming your own local worship/study/action group, or a small community within your congregation. Make a commitment to live out your religious principles. But don't expect to get quick support from the people you are trying to change! Most temples, synagogues, and churches are not prone to the political action you will be advocating. To create change, you will have to find your own spiritual base, as did Gandhi, Martin Luther King, and other figures in the nonviolent movement.

An effort within religious communities must also be grounded on familiarity and *respect* for the religious beliefs of that group. It is best if you, or at least one member of your group, is a committed member of the parish or temple you are trying to activate. Worship with them. Talk with them after their services. Attend their regular meetings and social gatherings if you can, and make sure your group's plans do not conflict with their schedule—especially in "keeping the Sabbath" or in celebrating holy days.

As you get to know members of the community, begin to raise some of the basic questions about the contradictions between the beliefs the congregation identifies with, and the actions (or lack of actions) they decide to take. Do this in a constructive way. Quote their scriptures and their leaders who speak for peace—such as the Pope, Billy Graham, and Rabbi Abraham Heschel. These questions may be raised at a "social concerns" committee meeting, or to the group of elders, or to the individual leaders of the religious community.*

Finally, develop a committee to plan regular activities to involve the congregation in peace work. Schedule speakers to preach on topics of peace and justice. Form study groups, roundtable discussions, or "Lenten classes" to meet in homes or in your synagogue/church hall. Celebrate "Peace Sabbath." Organize simple letter writing or petition campaigns after times of worship. Show films. Pray for your enemies. Announce the committee's efforts in your "bulletin" and publicize them to the outside community as well. For continued ideas and support, contact the organizations listed at the end of this chapter.

Working in the Long Haul

The suggested process above will vary from one experience to another. Most of us will tend to move into the action ideas very quickly, and sometimes these actions may help create an environment for setting up the first 3 points. However, this model is proposed to groups or individuals concerned about making a serious effort to empower religious peo-

ple to be active pacifists. Fundamental change cannot take place too quickly.

The power structures you will encounter will probably be hierarchial and male-dominated. Eventually these structures will need to be changed. But initially we need to tolerate the differences of speech or administration, as we try to correct them, especially through example. This may be particularly difficult if we are not used to having sexist language in our smaller communities.

Most religious communities have some kind of ministry to the poor, the handicapped, the young, or the elderly. Try to demonstrate the need for systemic change (justice) while remaining positive about their works of charity and social service.

Contact city-wide or regional Councils of Churches, Clergy Associations, or other interfaith groups to motivate them to become more active peacemakers. Also reach out to your own religious tradition's regional body. These groups may eventually help you fund and schedule outside speakers to your congregation, and to other seminaries, colleges, or religious communities in your area.

In January 1981 the Sojourners Fellowship, Pax Christi, World Peacemakers, Fellowship of Reconciliation, and others began a long-term mutual effort to mobilize religious support for a nuclear weapons moratorium, and other pacifist goals. The program called the New Abolitionist Covenant. For more information, contact one of the above groups.

An effort within religious communities must also be grounded on familiarity and respect for the religious beliefs of that group.

The power structures you will encounter will probably be hierarchial and male-dominated.

---

*For church statements, scriptural references and other background information for your particular religious tradition, contact the Fellowship of Reconciliation, Box 271, Nyack, NY 10960 for an address of a "peace fellowship" which they would have on these topics.

ORGANIZING OLD PEOPLE

By George and Ruth Dear

In organizing older people, take care not to "ghetto-ize" them.

"Senior citizen" is an establishment term which is used for powerless or poor old people; it manifests the ageism that is rife in our society.

Old age does not mean an automatic change of interests. The pacifist, the environmentalist, the women's liberation supporter do not lose interest in their causes because of additional years. In organizing older people, this must be kept in mind and care taken not to "ghetto-ize" old people. For example, it is a mistake to assume that a 66-year-old anti-war worker or environmentalist is interested only in social security, etc. We should rather draw on the experience and energy of the 66-year-old who has been in and out of movements, jail perhaps, and coped with many life-threatening situations.

One wide-spread "ghetto-izing" technique is the use of the term *senior citizen*. This is an establishment term which is used for powerless or poor old people. Supreme Court judges are not called "senior citizens"; they are called judges. Retired generals are not called "senior citizens"; they are called generals. The term "senior citizen" was coined by politicians who wanted, in our youth-oriented culture, to avoid using the word *old*. "Senior citizen" manifests the ageism that is rife in our society. It should be studiously avoided.

Bearing these things in mind, there are several issues an organizer should be aware of that are of increasing interest to old people simply because the society has turned its back on them.

Income

To people living on a fixed income, including a majority of old people, economic issues are primary—cost of food, medical care, changes in social security, compulsory retirement, and private pensions are matters of survival.

Housing

Old people who live alone may become depressed if they cannot cope as before, victims of the income squeeze, the *housing* squeeze, and social neglect. One answer is to organize intergenerational housing co-ops, shared living arrangements, etc. Another is to organize tenants' committees and committees to resist condominium conversion, etc.

Military Spending

Old people are particularly responsive to proposals to *decrease* military spending so that social services may be maintained and expanded. They are also concerned about sons and daughters, granddaughters and grandsons, being fed to the military.

Older Women

In organizing old people, it is important to be aware that a majority are women whose problems are often ignored (e.g., retirement is treated as a male syndrome). Many women do unpaid labor as housekeepers and/or child carers and thus are economically dependent on their husband's social security or pension in later life. Others reap the harvest of low wages in Social Security payments of about one half of what men receive. Only 20% of women over 65 get private pensions.

Health

In all people, deficiencies in hearing, weakness due to disease, problems with walking, etc., inhibit self-expression and creativity. These things are not caused by age but they are more frequently associated with age than with youth. Issues like health rip-offs and Medicare, the ageist prejudice of the medical establishment (for example, the medical establishment approaches menopause as a deficiency disease—lack of hormones, etc.— rather than a normal development), and the inattention to geriatrics become more interesting as one gets older.

Meetings

In organizing old people, perhaps the most important thing is sensitivity to ordinary details. For example, in calling people to a meeting, consideration of the following:

Time. Many retired people prefer afternoon meetings that permit them to get home before dark. If both afternoon and evening will be equally fruitful, afternoon is better.

Access. In the choice of a hall, the possible disabilities of those who are asked to attend must be kept in mind. Ideally, the hall should be on the first floor or in an elevator building with doors wide enough to admit wheelchairs.

Hearing and Sight. The meeting organizers at the beginning of the meeting should ask if everyone in the audience can hear. Adjustments can be made such as raising one's voice, tuning the loudspeaker system (if there is one), or asking those who are having difficulty to come to the front of the hall. The hall should be brightly lighted.

Volunteers

While old people, like any others in the movement, are willing to volunteer and many have the time, care should be taken to use their talents and experience and integrate them into the office, group, etc. Do not assume, as many agencies do, that shit work is all they can perform.

In conclusion, old people should be treated like everybody else. Chronological age should be down-played. Steps should be taken to counter disabilities (disabilities not necessarily peculiar to old people) which would inhibit participation.

Organizations Organized Around Older People's Issues

Gray Panthers, 3635 Chestnut Street, Philadelphia, PA 19104. An action, advocacy group. *Network*, monthly newsletter, covers all issues, not just those dealing with age.

Maggie Kuhn, Gray Panthers founder. Photo by The Witness.

American Association of Retired Persons, 1909 K Street NW, Washington, DC 20006. Very large, middle class group which focuses on consumer issues.

National Senior Citizens Law Center, 1424 16 Street NW, Washington, DC 20036. Excellent on current legislation.

National Council on Aging, 60 E. 42 Street, New York, NY 10017. Does research and educational conferences for the elderly.

While old people are willing to volunteer, do not assume that shit work is all they can perform.

Old people should be treated like everybody else; chronological age should be down-played.

ORGANIZING WITH LESBIAN AND GAY GROUPS

By Leslie Cagan

The differences between the sexes that exist throughout this society are reflected inside the gay community as well.

Being denied the right to express yourself and your sexuality freely is an experience that straight people do not have in this culture.

There is, on some level, no way for a heterosexual person to understand the reality of being gay in America.

Fact: over the past ten years a mass movement has developed in the lesbian and gay male communities of this country. In virtually every major city of America, as well as the small towns and in many rural settings, lesbian and/or gay groups are active and growing. Their work includes support for people coming out, health and counseling centers, the publication of newsletters and journals, legislative action either to pass gay civil rights bills or to stop anti-gay legislation from passing, demonstrations and actions demanding gay rights, etc. One indication of the vitality of this movement was the National March on Washington for Lesbian and Gay rights. On October 14, 1979, over 125,000 people from all over the country marched in Washington.

Fact: there is no such thing as the "typical gay person" or "THE gay community." To begin with, there are lesbians and gay men. The differences between the sexes that exist throughout this society are reflected inside the gay community as well. Beyond that are racism, class differences, various political perspectives, different religious attitudes and beliefs, and some very basic and deep differences in life style. Any attempt to organize the lesbian/gay community must be conscious of the great diversity that exists within this constituency.

Fact: it is estimated that 10% of the population is lesbian or gay...a low estimate would place us at something like 20,000,000 people inside the United States today. One of the effects of this is that we are to be found everywhere— including all of the social and political movements working for change. Being there and being visible as gays (let alone accepted) are often two different things. One of the great struggles of the past decade has been for visibility—both in the society generally and within social movements. That struggle is far from over.

Organizing Around Gay Issues

While support in various forms can and does come from heterosexual people, the backbone and core of organizing efforts around lesbian/gay issues comes from lesbians and gay men. Indeed, that is not only a statement of reality, it is also a political statement that makes the most sense. The experience of being denied the right to express yourself and your sexuality freely implies many things. It is an experience that straight people do not have in this culture. The reinforcements for heterosexuality, as well as the condemnations of lesbianism and homosexuality, are strong messages that we all get every day of our lives. There is, on some level, no way for a heterosexual person to understand the reality of being gay in America. Given this, it makes sense that the organizing around lesbian/gay issues will primarily be done by lesbians and gay men.

It may well be though, that you find yourself in a situation where there is no active or out-front lesbian/gay group and yet there is some vital gay issue that needs public attention. In that circumstance you should of course raise your voice. But probably your very first step should be to seek out those lesbians or gay men who might be willing to be public. They in turn might be able and willing to find other gay people to take up this work.

The issue of being out (or being public about your gayness) is complex. It does no good at all to say that all lesbians and gay men "should" be out of the closet. There are still too many real reasons for people to stay hidden; children are taken away from gay parents, people lose their jobs or are so isolated at work they are forced to quit; housing is denied gay couples; all sorts of ridicule and abuse takes place on the streets. Indeed, while it will be rare, there might still be times when it would be easier for a straight person to be the out-front spokesperson around some gay issue. But again, given the reality of the past decade and the existence of the gay movement throughout the country, this will be a very unique moment.

Organizing Gays in Other Movements

One of the interesting things to think about here is not so much how to activate gay involvement in other movements, but rather how to acknowledge the involvement that is already there. Lesbians and gay men are often still in the closet in peace, anti-draft, and other groups. Again, there is most probably a complex set of reasons for this. One is the fear of

Photo by Bill Wingell.

being ostracized...being told that it is all right to be gay but don't be public about it because people will be turned off and not relate to the issues. Nonsense! Our movements must be able to honestly say who we are. We must provide meaningful support to the people who work side by side with us. We must not hide from reality.

Beyond this, though, is the much more difficult issue of making connections between struggles. Are there ways both theoretically and practically to make links between the oppression and struggles of lesbians and gay men and the various other issues we are all hard at work on? There are, for instance, many lesbians exploring the connections between anti-gay attitudes and sexual repression generally with the pro-nuclear mentality. But to go further in our understanding will require an openness from these movements to having honest discussion. Still further, what is needed is a commitment to do some of the figuring out from the other end. It cannot always be the job of black people to raise issues of racism—white people must also take up that struggle. Women must not always be responsible for confronting sexism—men can do it too. And lesbians/gay men must know that there are straight people who will deal with homophobia (the fear of lesbians/gay men) whenever and wherever it comes up.

Summary

In some ways there is nothing special about organizing lesbians/gay men. Leaflets have to be written, money raised, press releases sent out, demonstrations planned, etc. And yet there are also some very unique and special concerns of the lesbian/gay community that must be kept in mind. Anyone, gay or straight, who is doing organizing with the lesbian/gay community has to be sensitive to the ways we experience our oppression and the risks we run when we do come out publicly.

If we are to build a movement that is strong enough to turn things around, then we must be sensitive to each individual in our ranks, as well as committed to the need for autonomous formations. Our strength will come from the respect we have for each other. In part that means confronting our own heterosexism and our own fears of lesbians and gay men, as well as confronting the attitudes and actions that seek to repress sexuality for all.

It does no good to say that all lesbians and gay men "should" be out of the closet.

Straight people must deal with homophobia whenever and wherever it comes up.

One excellent resource for responsible coverage of the gay and lesbian community is *Gay Community News* (167 Tremont Street, Boston, MA 02111). Send 50¢ for a sample copy.

LABOR OUTREACH

By Gail Daneker

The support or opposition of labor unions is a key factor in the success or failure of community-based and national conversion, arms control, and disarmament work.

The trade union movement is not politically monolithic.

Your local WRL is considering doing labor outreach. The first questions to ask are "What do we mean by labor, and why is it important to work with this constituency?"

It isn't possible to reach every working person. The labor force numbers 97 million Americans. Your efforts should probably focus on two groups: trade unions and those workers, organized and unorganized, who are employed by the military-industrial complex.

It is important to establish working relationships with trade unions. Although unions represent only 23% of the workforce, they are politically powerful organizations. In contrast to unorganized workers, unions have substantial lobbying ability, research capacity, and a constituency which can be mobilized. Their support or opposition is a key factor in the success or failure of community-based and national conversion, arms control, and disarmament work.

Unions represent not only military production workers, but also workers in civilian industry and services. The vast majority of American workers are not employed by the military-industrial complex. They work in education, retailing, construction, government, and in manufacturing non-military products. When military spending increases, jobs in these non-military sectors of the economy are lost because taxpayers have less take-home pay to spend.

Although military spending *decreases* total employment throughout the economy, it does create jobs in the military sector. Over 7 million men and women make their living working in the armed forces, in the civilian sector of the military, and in the production of weapons and military related equipment. Many of these workers are highly skilled. The salary levels in arms production are usually higher than in comparable civilian employment.

The millions of workers directly or indirectly employed in military production see their economic security and the welfare of their community as tied to military spending. They are caught by the Pentagon/corporate argument that military cutbacks and disarmament will cause massive unemployment. Nevertheless, several unions which represent these workers, including the International Association of Machinists & Aerospace Workers (IAM), the United Auto Workers (UAW), and United Electrical & Machine Workers of America (UE), already are working with peace activists on job protection proposals, conversion legislation, and community-based alternate use plans.

These proposals are intended to eliminate economic hardships for workers and their communities and to take the jobs issue away from the arms manufacturers. In addition, a growing number of activists within peace organizations and trade unions understand that mutual cooperation and support will be necessary to achieve the goals of each group—full employment, control of inflation, job protection, production to meet human needs, conversion, military spending cutbacks, ending the arms race.

Is It Possible To Work With Labor?

It is important to work with labor organizations, but is it possible? Members of your group probably remember the support of the AFL-CIO for the Vietnam War and the violence of some workers toward anti-war demonstrators.

The trade union movement is not politically monolithic. It comprises unions and members of various views.

While the late George Meany, the AFL-CIO, and most of the Building and Construction Trades unions supported the war, other union leaders and rank and file came out in opposition. In 1969, the UAW and the United Distributive workers supported the anti-war moratorium campaign. In 1970, the American Federation of State, County and Municipal Employees (AFSCME) and the Amalgamated Clothing Workers (ACTWU) passed resolutions condemning Nixon's war policies.

Five years ago, many people doubted that labor organizations would ever oppose nuclear power plant construction. Despite this view, a small group of environmentalists and trade unionists began organizing. Now international unions and locals across the country are passing resolutions in opposition to continued construction and for safe energy. Over 800 trade unionists who attended the first National Conference for Safe Energy and Full Employment in late 1980 dispelled the nuclear industry's claim that the trade union movement is solidly in support of nuclear power because of jobs. On the second anniversary of the Three Mile Island nuclear accident, 12 trade unions sponsored and participated in a mass demonstration to keep the plant shut down.

Of course, the struggle against nuclear weapons and the arms race is harder than anti-nuclear plant organizing for several reasons: military spending is more fully integrated through the economy; the military establishment is more powerful than the nuclear industry; the military-related workforce is larger than that in nuclear power; and, perhaps most important, there are problems in proposing what the American people will see as an alternative to weapons systems. Nevertheless, there still are unions and workers willing to listen and join the struggle.

Security and Economic Issues

Now that you know it is possible to work jointly with some labor organizations and workers, you may wonder what are the major arguments you'll come up against. You will immediately confront two issues: *national security* and the *state of the economy.*

Recent world events, including US dependence on oil imports, instability in the Persian Gulf, the taking of American hostages in Iran, and the Soviet occupation of Afghanistan, combined with the claims of military and civilian "experts" that our weapons are not being maintained or are obsolete and that the Soviets are surpassing us militarily, have elevated people's fears and enlarged public support for vastly increased military spending and development of new weapons systems. The important point here is that for most people, including workers and unions, these are very real fears and concerns.

It is crucial to consider these concerns sensitively and respond persuasively. You will need to inform yourself of the effects of foreign-policy and energy decisions on the economy and national security. But even if unions or workers do not accept a pacifist approach to national security and believe some degree of military preparedness is necessary, you can probably still work together on intermediate goals such as conversion and opposition to increased military spending and to new weapons systems.

Organizing on issues which people view as unrelated or detrimental to the economy during a recession is pretty tough going. You will need to explain the consequences of the arms race on employment and the economy. Official unemployment is over 7%. The consumer price index increased at an average of 11% a year in 1979 and 1980. Workers' real wages are falling. For many, job loss and rising prices are more immediate concerns than the threat of nuclear war. Indeed, in a tottering economy, the Pentagon/corporate argument that military spending creates jobs and is good for the economy seems pretty persuasive. This is particularly the case for those communities and businesses that are kept afloat by DOD contracts.

Several studies have disproven the argument that military spending is good for the economy, yet it persists in much the same way as the claim that economic growth requires energy growth. Both mythologies take two sets of circumstances and claim one causes the other. In the case of military spending, the fallacy is in the failure to acknowledge that it is not military spending *per se* which stimulates job creation and economic growth, but the billions of taxpayer dollars which if directed at almost anything would spur jobs and growth. In fact, if military money were redirected to non-military goods and services, through alternative government programs or even through tax reductions, more jobs and less inflation would be created, for several reasons:

- Civilian companies must compete with military contractors for skilled

International unions and locals across the country are passing resolutions in opposition to continued nuclear power construction and for safe energy.

Several studies have disproven the argument that military spending is good for the economy.

Trade unions were not organized solely for material gain—they were organized to defend the sense of dignity of the workers.

Pacifists should never hesitate to approach trade unions with moral concerns.

You will need to research the employment and economic status of your local community. This will help you determine your most effective types of outreach and projects.

workers and materials which currently are in short supply. This causes production bottlenecks and inefficiencies that lead to higher prices for both industrial materials and consumer goods.

• Military spending, unlike other investment, creates no new usable goods or services. It increases consumer demand (through salaries paid to military-related workers) without adding to useful production.

• The diversion of scientists and engineers away from civilian production into military research and development hampers technological innovations that could increase industrial productivity. "Spin-offs" from military production to civilian goods may appear to justify military R&D, but they are invariably fewer per dollar than innovations from non-military spending. (This is especially true in energy, where the atomic bomb gave rise to expensive, unsafe nuclear power rather than to renewable energy sources.)

You can see from these short responses that one of your first tasks is self-education. Listed at the end of this article are several publications to start you off. As you learn new information, establish a way of sharing it with all the members of your group—set aside time during meetings to report what you've learned, or organize a study group.

Moral Issues

In stressing the material needs of labor, the "real" world in which labor operates, a world where the paycheck, the hourly wage, the union, are related in instant ways to payments on the house, to medical care, etc., it is sometimes easy for those outside the labor movement to forget that labor also has a moral dimension. Trade unions were not organized solely for material gain—they were organized to defend the sense of dignity of the workers. Workers not only want a living wage, they want meaningful work. Workers not only want working conditions which are decent, they want to feel themselves whole and useful persons. The trade union movement *must* be concerned with bread and butter issues. But trade unionists *are also* concerned with the environment, with their children, with the *quality* of life. When Sam Gompers spoke of labor seeking the full lunch pail he was only half right and he spoke for only part of labor.

Labor does want bread—and who doesn't? But the slogan of the International Ladies Garment Workers Union caught the deeper hopes of labor with the phrase "Bread and Roses." Pacifists should never hesitate to approach trade unionists with moral concerns. They are dealing with a movement which, at its best, has fought racism, defended women's rights, opposed militarism, and sometimes has suffered empty lunch pails for long periods of time rather than yield on some basic moral issue.

Basic Research

In addition to understanding the consequences of military spending on the general economy, you will also need to know the employment and economic status of your local community. You should begin collecting the following information:

1. *Community Employment Profile.* The number of people employed, the kinds of employment, the major employers and what they produce, the local unemployment rate, who is unemployed (age, skills, race). This information is obtainable from your local and state governments. Also useful is the U.S. Handbook of Vital Statistics, available in your local library.

2. *Military Firms or Facilities in Your Community.* The percent of your local workforce employed at the companies, the types of employment (managerial, scientists, engineers, skilled labor, unskilled labor, clerical), and the unions involved. The "Peace Conversion Organizing Guide" in *WIN's* special issue on "Peace Conversion" (see Bibliography) explains how to track down local firms receiving military contracts. Although it may be difficult to gather employment information on military firms, workers in these companies with whom you develop contacts can help.

3. *Union Profile.* Names of unions in your community. Most unions will be listed in the Yellow Pages under "labor organizations."

Although putting together this material may seem time-consuming and difficult, it will help you determine your most effective types of outreach and projects. For example, outreach in a community with exclusively civilian employment will differ from working in a community with military firms. Or suppose you discover there are several firms in your community receiving military contracts. By comparing the number of workers in these firms and their skills with your community employment profile, you will have some idea of whether the local economy can absorb these workers in the event of military cutbacks. If the answer is No, you should think about developing a local conversion project.

Approaching Labor Organizations

Obtaining local employment and economic information, and learning about conversion and job protection measures is vital to establishing your credibility with unions and workers. At a conversion workship held by the Puget Sound Conversion Project, machinist Gerald Dargitz noted "Many groups continue to talk 'peace' in a manner which workers see as putting them out of work." Having hard information when you approach trade unions and other workers will help convince them you take the jobs issue seriously. Your pamphlets and public distribution materials should include sections on the employment impacts of military spending on your community and the economy. Also, if at all possible, have your material printed by a union printer, and be sure it includes the "union bug."

Before approaching trade unions you should understand they are not structured like most peace organizations. Unions are hierarchical organizations in which decisions are made by majority rule and protocol is important. Unions are made up of locals whose independence from the national union varies. In some unions it may be very difficult for locals to pass resolutions which are contrary to the positions of the national union. In other unions this is possible. For example, Local 1010 and District 31 of the United Steelworkers of America have adopted resolutions opposing nuclear plant construction while the national organization is on record in support of nuclear power.

Before approaching a local, write to the national union's office of public relations and inquire if the national has adopted any resolutions on the issues you are working on. (The IAM prefers you contact the national union before attempting to contact your local.) If you find they have passed a favorable resolu-

tion, write back requesting the name of a local official you can meet with. This is one way of discovering potentially sympathetic contacts. Don't give up if you find the national has an unfavorable position, but understand that your work with the local may be difficult.

It is important to understand how unions work, and what their main goals are. One way to do this and develop labor contacts at the same time is to invite local trade unionists to speak at your meetings. If there are several peace organizations in your community you may want to organize a "Labor Education Meeting for Peace Activists." Environmentalists for Full Employment successfully organized similar meetings for environmentalists. If you do not have any labor contacts, write a letter to the president or top officers of your local unions requesting a speaker. (The IAM, UAW, UE, AFSCME, ACTWU, and the Hospital Workers Local 1199 are most likely to respond to such a request.) Follow-up the letter with a phone call. Remember that the objective of the meeting is principally to educate yourselves.

It is always difficult to begin working with a new constituency. If you do not know any trade unionists in your community, write to national organizations doing labor outreach for possible names before making your initial contact. Another source of names and information about your local labor community is the locally based committees on occupational safety and health (see resource list). If you are unable to obtain any names, Paul Milne's excellent article, "How To Do Labor Outreach," explains how to contact a local (see bibliography).

> "Many groups continue to talk 'peace' in a manner which workers see as putting them out of work."

> Your pamphlets and public distribution materials should include sections on the employment impacts of military spending on your community and the economy.

> Before approaching a local, write the national union to inquire their position on the issue you are working on.

Labor march for J.P. Stevens boycott. Photo by Karl Bissinger.

Invite local trade unionists to speak at your meetings.

When developing materials for labor outreach, include statements made by trade unionists.

It also briefly describes how labor unions are structured and how they function.

An important principle to remember is that constituencies listen to and trust their own members more than they do outsiders. When developing materials for labor outreach, include or refer to statements made by trade unionists. Work toward having your projects, conferences, and written material co-sponsored or endorsed by individual trade unionists or preferably by unions. Include union members on any advisory boards you set up. One of your principal strategies is to identify sympathetic union members who are willing to work with their co-workers to gain formal union support on issues. Also remember that constituency organizing involves reciprocal support. You should be ready to work on issues which unions and workers consider important.

Follow-up

The Political Economy of Arms Reduction: Reversing Economic Decay, edited by Lloyd Dumas, Westview Press, 1982.

Military Expansion: Economic Decline, DeGrasse, MacGuiness, Ragen, Council on Economic Priorities, 1983.

The Freeze Economy, edited by Dave McFadden and Jim Wake, Nuclear Weapons Freeze Campaign, 1983.

The Economic Consequences of a Nuclear Freeze, William Hartung, Council on Economic Priorities, 1984.

"Briefings on Peace and the Economy," video series by Seymour Melman, SANE, 1985.

"The Impact of Military Spending on the Machinists Union," Marian Anderson, IAM Public Relations Department, Washington, DC, 1979.

The Permanent War Economy, Seymour Melman, Simon & Schuster, 1974.

The following articles and newsletters deal with conversion of the military industry:

Economic Conversion: Revitalizing America's Economy, edited by Suzanne Gordon and Dave McFadden, Ballinger, 1985.

"International Economic Conversion Conference: Transforming the Economy for Jobs, Peace &
Justice," 1984 Conference Proceedings, available from 45 Pine Street, Arlington, MA 02174.

The Lucas Plan: A New Trade Unionism in the Making, Hilary Wainwright and Dave Elliot, Allson and Busby, London, 1982.

Economic Adjustment/Conversion, President's Economic Adjustment Committee and the Office of Economic Adjustment, Office of the Assistant Secretary of Defense, The Pentagon, Washington, DC, July 1985. Contains a superb annotated bibliography.

"Swords Into Ploughshares," Niven, Topham, Benn, END Papers, Norringham, England, 1983.

The Arms Drain: Job Risk and Industrial Decline, a trade union analysis by Tim Webb, available from the Campaign for Nuclear Disarmament, London, 1982.

Directory of National Unions and Employee Associations, U.S. Department of Labor, Bureau of Labor Statistics, Superintendent of Documents, GPO. Washington, DC.

The following list of organizations can provide valuable information on working with organized labor:

The International Economic Conversion Conference, 45 Pine Street, Arlington, MA 02174.

The Center for Economic Conversion, 222C View St., Mountain View, CA 94041.

Jobs With Peace Campaign, 76 Summer St., Boston, MA 02110.

Nuclear Weapons Freeze Campaign, 220 I Street NE, #130, Washington, DC 20002.

Sane, 711 G Street SE, Washington, DC 20003.

Center on Budget Priorities, 236 Massachusetts Ave. NE, Washington, DC 20002.

Council on Economic Priorities, 30 Irving Place, New York, NY 10003.

National Action/Research on the Military-Industrial Complex (NARMIC), 1501 Cherry St., Philadelphia, PA 19102.

International Association of Machinists, 1300 Connecticut Ave., NW, Washington, DC 20036.

United Electrical Workers, 1411 K Street, NW, Room 410, Washington, DC 20005.

HIGH SCHOOL ORGANIZING

High school organizing can be approached from two directions: high school students organizing themselves, and "outside" people trying to communicate with high school students and help them organize. The emphasis of this chapter will be the former, though ways of "getting inside" high schools will be suggested.

The three basic goals of a high school group are:

1. to make the students within the school aware of the issue;

2. to make the surrounding community equally aware; experience has shown that once people—especially students are made aware of the issue, they can generally be organized to get the facts to the people;

3. to mobilize students into action.

Developing strategies to achieve these goals requires careful evaluation of your local situation. Is there enough interest in your issue so that you can just work with the "already convinced," or will you first need to begin an educational campaign to develop interest? Is there enough time to do the groundwork necessary to move ahead quickly with an ad hoc committee of concerned individuals? Who will you need to reach and what kind of support will you need? As you answer these questions, you will find some suggestions in the following sections more useful to your own strategy than others.

The high school organizing issues tend to be either those which relate specificly to the school or those which also pertain to the community and beyond (e.g., the draft, day care centers, disarmament, South Africa). Grievances that high school students have are genuine. For the most part they have few rights within the school. Dress regulations are decided for them, curricula are made by administrators and faculty, the school newspaper is censored by the advisor, speakers at assemblies are chosen by the administration. The constitutional rights that are supposedly assured for everyone in this country are not being protected for students. Unfair teachers, overly stiff disciplinary measures, and other inequities have been challenged by students all over the country.

Some Cultural Considerations

Years of socialization in homes, churches and schools have shaped the attitudes of high schoolers regarding war and military service. Many young men feel that war and killing are expressions of masculinity and as such are vehicles for them to achieve a measure of self-esteem. Similarly, many feel that the US should conduct its foreign policy as they conduct their street lives—with swift, devastating retaliation for even slight insults regardless of moral considerations.

A further consequence of this "rugged individualism" is a serious aversion of joining formal groups; the operant philosophy seems to be, "You're not a man if you need to join some organization to deal with your problems." These manifestations of the macho mentality usually mean that anti-draft workers in high schools are predominantly female. Male or female, organizers must early on confront the prejudice that those who are anti-war, etc., are unmanly or cowardly.

Male students have an aversion to joining groups.

Grievances that high school students have are genuine. For the most part they have few rights within the school.

Years of socialization in homes, churches and schools have shaped the attitudes of high schoolers regarding war and military service.

School decision-making is governed by a near religious reverence for the "proper channels."

Organizers should avoid any unnecessary non-issue-related alienation of central figures, such as principals.

If administrators are not sympathetic, they may tell you certain acts are not permitted when in fact you have a legal right to do them.

It's wise to aim for the endorsement of the usual student leaders.

Dealing with the School Administration

Public school administrators and staff want to maintain the appearance of objectivity. Most are reluctant to be associated with one or another side of a current political issue, which means that forums or debates are always preferred to speakers who espouse one particular viewpoint.

School decision-making is governed by a near religious reverence for the "proper channels." The normal line of authority is—from the bottom up— teacher, department head, principal, superintendent, school committee. Community groups seeking approval for an activity can be stalled, often interminably, simply for not going through channels. Although the process is painfully slow, it can also serve upon occasion as a means of gathering allies. It is important to understand the special place the principal has in this picture.

Principals feel personally responsible for what happens in their schools. Organizers should recognize this and avoid any unnecessary non-issue-related alienation of these central figures. If possible sit down with the principal and talk to her or him about your aims and planned projects. Stress the fact that you want to deal honestly and openly. Although administrators must remain neutral, yards of bureaucratic red tape will magically fall away if you have a good relationship with them. Clear all advertisements with them and ask permission for all activities that are to be held on school grounds. Teachers are often more amenable to the requests of a group if they know that the group's activities have the OK of the principal. In general, the administration doesn't like to be surprised, so everything will move more smoothly if it's kept on top of the table.

If administrators are not sympathetic, or are feeling pressure from above, they may tell you certain acts are not permitted when in fact you do have a legal right to do them. Leafletting outside the school, or wearing armbands or buttons in school may fall in this category. Consult your local civil liberties group—ask if they have a pamphlet on students' rights.

Getting People Together

When it comes to getting people inter-ested in and involved with your efforts, high school organizers have a big advantage: the people they want to reach are confined to a relatively small area, the school building, for a long period of time each weekday. This makes advertising much easier (e.g., fewer posters are needed to reach 1000 students than to reach 1000 members of the general public). On the other hand, students are constantly bombarded by announcements and posters, and many ignore ads totally. Therefore it will help your campaign if your advertising approach is fresh, innovative, or unusual.

For many actions within your school, it's wise to aim for the endorsement and active support of students already accepted by other students as leaders. If the student body president and the school paper editor can be persuaded to endorse your actions, they can be powerful allies. When just beginning to organize, it is sometimes useful to keep the politics of the organizing body general rather than specific in order to attract the most people. Invite leaders of all student clubs and organizations to strategy meetings to get as many viewpoints as possible, and of course to get them to press their constituencies into action.

Listed below are some suggestions for advertising:

- announce your first meeting as part of a letter to the editor of the school paper
- ask your teachers for permission to stand up in class and announce the meeting
- advertise with posters, short messages in daily bulletins, leave messages on lunch tables, place in each teacher's mailbox with a note to read to their first class
- get class lists for your classes and call each member
- get permission to stage a short, informal skit in the lunchroom, and follow the skit with an announcement of the meeting
- call local churches for the phone numbers of students in their youth groups
- contact other local groups; they may get you in touch with students they know are organizing.

Getting Inside

Non-student organizers trying to reach high school students will find schools are tightly controlled and guarded institutions. Some creative thought must be given to getting inside to inform, educate and organize secondary school students.

The best vehicle of entry into a school is the students themselves. It has long been established that students cannot be prevented from distributing flyers, collecting signatures or posting signs in school so long as it does not interfere with the educational process. Non-students do not have such freedom to use school facilities to disseminate information.

Another avenue of approach can be through sympathetic teachers, who have a great deal of autonomy over events in their classrooms, and can invite guest speakers who fit into the class curriculum (be creative). In addition, a group of 8 to 12 volunteers can effectively leaflet students on their way *to school* in the morning (better than leafletting after school). Leafletting must be done off school grounds. Also, leaflet related events such as sports activities or cultural programs. In particular, take the opportunity to distribute counter-recruiting information when military recruiters are present. School officials may be reluctant to stop it for fear of appearing biased. Consider approaching school clubs. Forums or debates before large groups of students are good ways to attract potential activists. However securing approval and making all the necessary preparations will usually take from six to eight weeks.

Show politically appropriate movies at the school; have a rally after school or during lunch period and invite musicians, jugglers, et al., to attract attention; make a political skit part of the annual variety show; place an ad in your school paper; take an unbiased survey and issue a press release with the tabulated results.

Each opportunity for contact with students should be used to attract others into subsequent activities. Therefore any materials distributed should include some mechanism, such as a coupon or phone number, through which students may indicate further interest or address questions.

Unfortunately, student groups may have to spend a great deal of time initially struggling over issues that should not have to preoccupy them, such as securing the right for students to pass out flyers on school grounds. Although such efforts are time-consuming, they can give the students a sense of shared struggle and provide useful political experience.

Finally, in its initial stages of growth, the group should be allowed to develop independently from other, non-student community efforts. Students need to feel that it is their organization working in their best interests and not on someone else's agenda. Once a student group has developed a history of activity and success, it can come together with anti-draft community groups or similar groups from other high schools and, while continuing to organize within their own school, become involved in the broader efforts to make our society peaceful and just.

Resources

For more information, see the *High School Organizing Packet,* available from the War Resisters League for $5 (plus a dollar postage). This packet contains extensive suggestions on high school organizing as well as numerous case histories of successful organizing efforts among high school students.

You might also want to contact Student/Teacher Organization To Prevent Nuclear War (S/TOP), 11 Garden Street, Cambridge, MA 02138. S/TOP is a nationwide organization of high school students and teachers committed to informing their local communities of the dangers of nuclear war.

This chapter draws heavily from an article by Alan Brickman in *Peacework* (February 1981) and the Stanford Against Conscription "A Guide to Organizing an Anti-Draft Group in your High School."

Sympathetic students are the best way to get inside the school.

Always leaflet in opposition to recruiters.

Struggling together is important for growth and experience of your group.

OUTREACH TO WOMEN'S MOVEMENT

By Helen Michalowski

We should not go to the women's community with the attitude that we will organize it.

All too often, peace groups have a lot of work to do putting their own house in order.

Integrate a feminist perspective in your newsletter and other public statements.

Assumptions

1. In many areas of the country, the women's community is already fairly well organized with women's centers, a feminist press or newsletters, women's cultural groups, self-help centers, etc.

2. Many women, organized or unorganized, already have some sympathy with anti-militarist and anti-war issues. Often women already have some sense of the connections between a militarized society and violence against women, and some sense of the connections between military spending and the lack of resources to take care of the problems which concern women, e.g., health care, public transportation, childcare, job training.

3. We should not go to the women's community with the attitude that we will organize it. We should not go with the attitude that women should work on peace issues when we have little understanding of or involvement in the work women are already doing on issues they have identified as important.

4. All too often, peace groups have a lot of work to do putting their own house in order. Are there women in leadership positions who are committed to addressing women's concerns? Do these women represent the group in public—for example, by speaking or writing? Do the men in the groups do their share of the day-to-day detail work (e.g., sweeping, mailing list maintenance)? Does the group process encourage participation by everyone in discussion and decision making? Do the men in the group relate to the women as respected co-workers and not as sources of ego-gratification and/or potential bed-mates? These things are important if women are to feel comfortable working with the group.

5. Doing this work takes time and perseverance. More often than not it takes a year or two to build up the personal and working relationships, and to establish your group's reputation as being seriously concerned about the problems which face women. Take joy in small accomplishments and learn from "false starts."

Internal Organization

1. Provide the opportunity for women in your group to get together for mutual support and encouragement (e.g., women's pot-luck brunches, a feminism & nonviolence study group, etc.)

2. Integrate a feminist perspective in your newsletter and other public statements. Examine everything for sexist and/or heterosexist bias. Don't use "he" to mean everyone. In writing or speaking about any particular issue ask if there is any way it especially concerns women, and then make sure that that concern is addressed. Acknowledge the contributions women have made to the group.

New York pro-choice march, May 16, 1981. Photo by Grace Hedemann.

3. Make sure that women are involved in planning any event or program your group sponsors, and make sure that there are women speakers, cultural workers, etc.

4. In planning meetings and events, remember that many women do not like traveling alone at night. Encourage ride-sharing and encourage people to wait together for public transportation.

5. Always be sensitive to the possible need for free, quality childcare. Arrange childcare for all your programs/events. Make it possible for children to be brought to meetings, which means that everyone in the group should share in taking care of and entertaining the child(ren), even if this means missing part of the meeting. This makes it more possible for people with children to participate and communicates to the parent(s) that the group supports them.

6. Women tend to have less money than men. Keep all your events low-cost or allow for a sliding scale.

7. Because of the society we are brought up in, women often are not fully confident of their ability to speak in public, to facilitate a meeting, to influence a decision. In a group discussion, ask the quiet ones if they have anything they'd like to say before moving on. Rotate the role of facilitator. In making any decision ask if there is any dissent or other concern, and allow time for an answer and discussion. Try to take everyone's remarks seriously. Don't assume that quiet means agreement. Have the group consciously affirm that the decision "made" has been made before moving on.

If possible, conduct a skills workshop in public speaking, and encourage women to speak for the group when the opportunity arises. No single press conference, rally, or event is going to be the end-all, be-all of our work. In the long run it is as important for new people to gain experience as it is to put forward the most complete and correct statement.

8. The men in the group should be supportive of each other and offer criticism to each other as to how they interrelate with women as co-workers so that the women do not carry this burden alone.

Building Organizational Connections

1. Announce your programs and events in the local feminist press and make sure that your flyers get to local women's groups, health clinics, child-care centers, etc. Follow the local women's press. While taking flyers around to local women's groups, use the opportunity to learn what women in these groups are doing and what they think about what you are doing.

2. Sponsor events ranging from women's brunches to forums to women's conferences which will provide an opportunity for women working on peace, nuclear, and women's issues to meet each other and share information and views.

3. Rather than trying to get women to work on peace issues, go to women working on other issues and try to make the connections.

Encourage women to speak for the group when the opportunity arises.

Learn what issues the women's community is involved in and find out what they think about what you are doing.

In doing peace movement work, make sure that women's particular concerns are addressed.

Learn about the philosophical connections between feminism and nonviolence from the autonomous women's movement.

Any man making pronouncements about matters affecting women's lives is highly suspect.

- Offer nonviolence training to women organizing "Take Back the Night Marches" or working to stop violence against lesbians.

- Work with women working to stop battery/rape and raise the matter of military basic training and how this shapes the male attitude.

- Work with women concerned with health and safety issues and make the connections between the dangers of radiation, nuclear power and nuclear weapons.

- Work with women concerned about funding for social services, job training, etc., and point up the impact military spending has on the availability of resources.

4. Announce pertinent events sponsored by the women's community in your newsletter and at your meetings and encourage support and participation. Take the opportunity to learn more about the issues and views women are raising by doing these events. Ask permission to come with banners, literature, etc. Be visible without seeming to "take over the show."

5. As appropriate, ask to do a workshop on militarism as a women's issue, or on feminism & nonviolence at women's conferences and gatherings.

6. In doing peace movement work, make sure that women's particular concerns are addressed, and that women are supported to take positions of responsibility and decison making. In doing anti-draft work, make a special effort to find and nurture the participation of women veterans. Address yourself to the recruitment of women. In working against nuclear weapons make it also an issue of reproductive rights, being careful not to stereotype women's motherhood role. In working against conventional arms sales, stress the impact this has on the women in developing countries.

7. Simply addressing the specific ramifications of our concerns on women without bringing a feminist perspective both to the way we work and the philosophy we espouse can be seen by skeptical feminists as a recruitment strategy, which could threaten to divert attention away from their issues. Learn about the philosophical connections between feminism and nonviolence not only from peace activists but through direct exposure to the feminist thinking of the autonomous women's movement, then use what you've learned to address the philosophical as well as strategic con-

nections between the two movements.

Unresolved Things that Might Cause Confusion &/or Hard Feelings

1. Allow time and space for lesbians and straight women to discuss with each other differences in experiences, expectations, and sensibilities.

2. Is there any problem with your group sponsoring "women only" or "lesbians only" events/gatherings?

3. What is your group's position concerning nonviolence and the question of abortion/reproductive rights?

4. Any man making pronouncements about matters affecting women's lives is highly suspect. Thus, men who come to support women's events need to be sensitive as to what they say, and how they conduct themselves. In most instances it is not appropriate to have a man represent your group at a women's meeting. And, to have only a man do a workshop on anything to do with feminism, even in a mixed group, is at best a delicate matter.

Conclusion

Both feminism and nonviolence cover vast ground, so don't try to do everything. You will probably be more effective if you concentrate on one or two priorities. As time goes on and your work develops, people will start looking to you for your particular perspective, experience and network of people.

It is easier to talk about, than it is to practice, nonviolence and feminism in a consistent, integrated way. All we can do is keep on working to bring into reality the way of being that nonviolence and feminism describe.

ORGANIZING IN A RURAL AREA

By Randy Kehler

FRANKLIN COUNTY—26 towns in NW Massachusetts; population: 63,000; county seat: Greenfield; major rivers: Connecticut, Deerfield, Millers; terrain: mostly hilly, 80% wooded; principal occupations: services and education (large and growing), manufacturing (large but shrinking), agriculture (small but steady); character: predominantly rural Yankee increasingly influenced by progressive urban refugees.

Though I'm still regarded as a newcomer by the Franklin County natives, and probably always will be, I feel as though I've been here for a long time. I arrived in Franklin county eight years ago, quite by chance, and almost immediately I knew that I wanted to make it my home for many years to come. Five years ago I married Betsy Corner, a suburban immigrant like myself who had fallen in love with the area a decade earlier. Two years ago we finally scraped together the money to buy a little farmhouse and proceeded to have our first child. Now we are indeed settled.

To some extent, organizing is organizing. Wherever you are it involves finding out what people's concerns are, trying to persuade people that they should be concerned about things they may not be concerned about, convincing people that collective action *can* bring about change, getting people to follow through on tasks they have taken on, helping people see the underlying causes of the problems they are confronting, and so on.

Yet *where* you are—and your relationship to that place and to the people there—does make a huge difference. Because every place, every community is different, is unique. Organizing in Franklin County is definitely not the same as organizing in low-income neighborhoods of Boston, where I helped set up a black school and a tenants organization; or in the San Francisco Bay Area, where I was a draft resistance organizer during the late '60s; or in federal prisons in the Southwest, where I helped organized protests and boycotts among Chicano and poor white convicts; or in northern New Jersey, where I was a coordinator of a Dump Nixon/End the War campaign.

Four characteristics of Franklin County which affect community organizing come to mind: distance from the city, population density, local traditions, and rural issues. These same characteristics probably apply to many other rural areas, particularly in New England.

Distance From the City

With some exceptions—for example, some rural college and university towns—political ferment, at least since World War II, has usually begun in the major cities and metropolitan areas. The winds of unrest and change, whether related to political thought or styles of dress, often reach the rural areas years after they have swept through the cities. The nearest major city to Franklin County is Boston, 100 miles to the east. Sometimes Boston seems like light-years away.

While anti-War protests raged in Boston and in other cities throughout the late '60's, back editions of the *Greenfield Recorder* make it clear that

Distance from the city, population density, and local traditions all make rural organizing distinctly different from urban organizing.

only a very small handful of local citizens publicly opposed the War. In 1972, Franklin County, the most rural in the state, was the only county in Massachusetts that did *not* vote for McGovern over Nixon.

Traditionally, there has been much less political organizing in Franklin County than in Boston. Tenants organizations have been almost non-existent, active left political groups are no where to be found, and the percentage of unionized workers in the overall workforce has been very small. This situation is definitely changing—as more and more newcomers with some kind of political experience move into the area—but it's changing slowly.

As a result, there seems to be less expectation of social or political change, and therefore greater reluctance to participate in change-oriented groups and efforts—particularly among poor people. A couple of us recently did a door-to-door survey in two low-income neighborhoods of Greenfield to find out people's attitudes towards local banks and landlords. Many more people than we expected expressed total resignation with respect to their acknowledged exploitation by the local monied interests. Most couldn't imagine doing anything, individually or collectively, to change the situation.

Population Density

When you enter the village of Conway, whose population couldn't be more than a couple hundred, you are greeted by a road sign that reads, "THICKLY SETTLED." Most of Conway's resident's, the other 800 or so, live scattered over the 38-square-mile township. No doubt they are "thinly settled." Conway is a typical Franklin County town.

For me to drive to Conway from my home in Colrain takes a good half hour. If a resident of Charlemont, at the western end of the county, wants to attend a meeting in Orange, at the eastern end of the county, it takes a full hour—and that's traveling *via* Route 2, one of the straightest, fastest roads in the county. If the meeting were somewhere up in the hills of North Orange, add another twenty minutes. Public transportation in Franklin County is practically nonexistent.

Rural distances make organizing difficult, particularly during the winter when roads are icy and sometimes unplowed. If you were just organizing in Greenfield, which has a population of 18,000, or in downtown Orange or Turners Falls, it wouldn't be so bad. But 20 of our 26 towns have populations of less than 2,000 and virtually no "downtown" centers. Because of the distances and the low population density, it is harder to get people to come to meetings and harder for organizers to go door-to-door.

The low population density also means that such standard urban organizing tactics as street speaking, street theater, leafletting at lunch hour or rush hours, sidewalk picketing and vigiling, and marches along Main Street are usually not appropriate. There just isn't enough pedestrian or vehicular traffic to make it worthwhile.

Local Traditions

To an outsider most of Franklin county's 26 towns, particularly the smaller, more rural ones, may seem nearly alike—typical New England towns. But once you have lived here awhile you find that each one regards itself—and, in fact, *is*—unlike any other. After all, each has had two or three hundred years during which to evolve its own traditions and institutions. Most towns have already celebrated their bicentennials, and Deerfield had its tercentenary eight years ago.

What differentiates these little towns? In most cases it is a combination of geography, traditions, and people (or politics). Whately has its rich river bottomland, Warwick boasts the beauty of Mt. Grace. Conway's annual "Festival of the Hills" is known far and wide, as is Charlemont's "Yankee Doodle Days." The Streeter family has dominated town politics in Bernardston for generations, while Greenfield is run by a handful of downtown merchants, bankers, and lawyers.

Most people in Franklin County, including most of us newcomers, seem to identify to an extraordinary degree with the town we live in. This feeling sometimes expresses itself in a friendly yet fierce rivalry between towns. This is not to say, of course, that within any given town there isn't a fair amount of squabbling among factions, families, and ethnic groups. As an aside, I should mention that ethnic groups do exist in this seemingly homogenous environment. Most of the towns in the valley, as opposed to the "hilltowns," are split

Rural distance make organizing difficult.

Such tactics as street speaking, picketing, marches, and leafletting are usually not appropriate in rural areas.

down the middle between Poles and Yanks, and there's considerable racism lingering just below the surface of these towns' politics. There are also pockets of other Eastern European peoples, as well as a sizeable number of people of French Canadian extraction spread throughout the County.

Most of my organizing ventures in Franklin County involved more than one town, usually the County as a whole. But organizing on a town-by-town basis—that is, within each town separately—has proven to be the most effective approach. This means finding allies in each town who are willing to contact their fellow townspeople. Though some people are timid about becoming associated with a possibly unpopular cause, we have found that most people are far more willing to collect signatures, or distribute information, or hold a meeting in their homes if they are asked to do it just within their own towns and not all over the County.

People seem to know, or soon discover, that if you are on a political mission and you need to call or visit someone you don't know, your effectiveness is much greater when you can introduce yourself as someone who lives "over on the Shelburne Line Road, just up from Scranton's farm." The likely response: "Oh, sure, I know where you live. You must be in the old Bruso house. So what can I do for you?" Of course, it's even easier when you know the person to begin with—your neighbor, mail carrier, the bus driver, the parents of the kids your kid plays with.

One institution that most towns (nearly every town in New England, for that matter) have in common is the Annual Town Meeting. In all but the three largest towns in the County, any registered voter who is a resident of the town can attend, speak, and vote. In Greenfield, Montague, and Orange, only elected town meeting members can vote. Though often poorly attended—largely due to the State's steady whittling away of the towns' authority—the Annual Town Meeting is usually the biggest event all year, with the possible exception of the town fair.

Articles, which have the effect of local law, and resolutions, considered expressions of public sentiment, can be placed on the agenda ("warrant") of the town meeting simply by submitting the signatures of ten registered voters to the town Board of Selectmen. In this way, over the past few years we have managed to persuade several towns to prohibit the transportation of nuclear waste through the town (though the feds don't recognize town authority in this matter). One year we also got most of the affected towns to oppose the installation in their towns of a large Tenneco pipeline which would have carried Algerian natural gas from Canada to Pennsylvania. And another year we succeeded in getting the majority of towns to set up Town Energy Conservation Commissions (the foundation of Franklin County's nationally-touted local energy planning), and almost every town passed our resolution against state control over county budgets.

In a similar vein, though with less dramatic effect, the annual town fairs—often called "Old Home Days"—have provided wonderful organizing opportunities. Nearly everyone in town attends these gala events, to watch the horse- and ox-pulling contests, listen to the fiddle music, look over the flea market tables, or just see all one's neighbors. We have used these occasions to set up tables and exhibits, hand out leaflets, conduct local surveys, and recruit local volunteers. No matter how unpopular our cause may be, few people get upset with us: we're just part of the show.

Rural Issues

Most people in Franklin County love it here. They love the relative peacefulness of this area as compared to more urban ones. They appreciate the clean air and the pure water, the acres and acres of woods and forests surrounding well-tended fields of corn and hay, potatoes and onions. They also cherish the feeling of good old Yankee independence and self-reliance that is part of the area's heritage, if less a part of its present-day life.

The problem is hanging on to these things. Exploitation and encroachment by the state and federal governments, the power companies, and large outside corporations have defined all the major issues in recent years. It would not be far-fetched to say that many people in Franklin County feel colonized. In some ways not much has changed since local hero Daniel Shays led the Shay's Rebellion nearly two hundred years ago.

These days the most charged issue of them all is nuclear power. Everyone knows you don't put nuclear power plants near large population centers. Thus, thinly-settled Franklin County is just a few miles downwind of the Ver-

Your effectiveness is greater when you can introduce yourself as someone who lives "over on the Shelburne Line Road, just up from Scranton's Farm."

The annual town meeting is usually the biggest event all year, with the possible exception of the town fair.

The annual town fairs have provided wonderful organizing opportunities.

The most charged issue of them all is nuclear power.

non, Vermont plant, we are the home of the relatively small Rowe plant, one of the first built anywhere in the country, and it was only this past year that Northeast Utilities postponed indefinitely its plans for twin reactors on the Montague Plains in the center of the County. The battle over Montague was ferocious, though nonviolent, and there are rapidly growing campaigns calling for the decommissioning of Vernon and the conversion of Rowe. As I write, a clamor is also being raised over rumors that Franklin County is a possible site for the storage of all six New England states' low-level radioactive waste.

Preserving our rivers is another volatile subject around which there has been much organizing. The water levels in the Connecticut and Deerfield Rivers already go up and down due to the operation of the utilities' pumped storage projects in Northfield and Rowe. Now Boston wants to divert huge quantities of the Connecticut's waters to provide drinking water for Boston's ever-more-thirsty metropolitan population. The opposition from Western Massachusetts is loud and unanimous. It was only ten years ago that local residents had to defeat a similar plan whereby Boston wanted to turn the ecologically-delicate Montague Plains into one vast municipal garbage dump—for the City of Boston.

Other successful battles include keeping a Wendy's Hamburger store out of a residential neighborhood, preventing an LNG tank from going up in another residential area, and thus far, stalling off the unnecessary widening of Route 2 between Orange and Greenfield.

On the unsuccessful side, Interstate 91 did get built, as did Greenfield's Cherry Rum Shopping Plaza, neighboring Hadley's Pyramid Mall, and the tract homes that destroyed prime farmland in Deerfield. Then there was the Ingersoll-Rand heist of a couple years ago when they moved the Millers Falls Tool Company from Greenfield to Deerfield by legally extorting subsidies from local and state governments and the equivalent of a wage cut from the union.

There are other issues, of course, such as low-income housing and the retention or expansion of government services to the poor and the elderly. But until recently, prior to Reagan's "velvet cleaver," and the passage of Massachusetts' version of California's Proposition 13, organizing efforts in these areas have been limited.

Any conclusions from all of this? Just one. Before plunging ahead as a community organizer, *get to know your community*. Get to know it and then be sensitive to it. This means understanding how it operates, economically, politically and culturally. It means finding out what's important to people, how they view the world *they* live in, how they express themselves, what institutions and traditions they maintain and respect. I know of no better way of doing this than by becoming part of the community yourself.

Before plunging ahead as a community organizer, get to know your community; and then be sensitive to it.

Literature Production

RESEARCHING CORPORATIONS

By Mike Clark and Valerie Heinonen

In the work that we all do on a wide range of issues, it is usually quite obvious who is being hurt or threatened or imprisoned or starved or discriminated against or impoverished or killed or oppressed or laid off. The victims of war and injustice are many and obvious. War and injustice are crimes with victims. As with other crimes, if one looks for the perpetrators, one most usefully begins by asking *cui bono*—who benefits? The primary purpose of corporate research is to find out *cui bono*.

In doing so, we isolate the most formidable obstacles to our work. In some cases, this is a handful of individuals, in most cases, an iron-clad interlock between individuals and organizations whose interest is in maintaining the *status quo*.

We do so, not because we expect immediate management conversions when corporations are put on notice, but as one effort to sensitize and organize people against whose interests the corporations function and without whose acceptance and support that functioning cannot continue.

The power of the transnational corporation surpasses any accumulation of economic power in previous history. There is scarcely an issue, domestic or international, in which there is not a corporate role. For this reason it is important for organizers to know how to find information about transnationals, the organizations that work on corporate issues, the history of the corporate responsibility movement, print and media resources, and some current issues in corporate responsibility.

Having a corporate component to our ongoing campaigns is important for a number of reasons:

- *It concretizes the issues*. Injustice is not something that results from implacable fate or impotent deity. It results from decisions made by individuals within institutions. When 5,000 people are laid off and a plant closed down, that is not "just the way things are," that is the way that some people defend and extend their interests at the expense of other people.

- *It localizes the issues*. The apartheid system and the human suffering that it creates are 5,000 miles away. It is difficult sometimes to feel close to the struggle of the Black majority there. It becomes easier when one realizes that banks and corporations with branch offices in one's own community are involved in supporting racism in South Africa.

- *It familiarizes the issues*. Through advertising, the corporate mentality and its varied product lines are numbingly pervasive. We need to help people see that the company which manufactures components for nuclear warheads at Oak Ridge, Tennessee, (Union Carbide) also makes Eveready batteries, Glad bags, Prestone anti-freeze and Simoniz car wax.

Highlighting the role that private corporations play in fostering militarism and injustice also makes possible a new dimension to principles that we would be struggling for in other aspects of our common work:

- *Democratizing decision-making*—The management of transnational corpora-

The power of the transnational corporation surpasses any accumulation of economic power in previous history.

Injustice is not something that results from implacable fate or impotent deity.

The bottom line of the transnational corporation is sacrificing people to the maximization of profit.

We cannot expect _major_ changes in corporate practices without major changes in the US political and economic system.

There is a great deal of information readily available in certain magazines, newspapers, books, and from some organizations, and the companies themselves.

Peg Averill

tions makes decisions that affect the lives of millions, even billions, of people. These decisions are made by a small group of individuals with the goal of maximizing profit. Corporate work seeks to break open that decision making process to shareholders, employees, immediate community residents, and especially those on the negative side of such corporate decisions.

- *Linking domestic and international injustice*—The policies and practices of transnationals show an amazing consistency in how they affect people in this country and abroad. Overseas oppression is usually more blatant, but there are common elements of manipulation, intimidation, insensitivity and, of course, the bottom-line sacrificing of people to the maximization of profit.

- *Holding unjust institutions accountable*—Corporate campaigns have been successful, e.g., J.P. Stevens, infant formula manufacturers, bank loans to South Africa. There will be more successful campaigns in the future. But, at the very least, we need to be unmasking and publicizing the ways in which these massive concentrations of economic power are working against the best interests of everyone but themselves.

We will have victories along the way, but we cannot expect *major* changes in corporate practices without major changes in the US political and economic system. As a modest counterweight to present injustice, we will have to learn from our victories and our defeats as we educate and organize for the long haul.

Information Sources

While much the transnationals decide to do is done behind the closed doors of corporate boardrooms, there is a great deal of information readily available.

Magazines and Newspapers

The first place to look is the business press. Become a regular reader of the following:

The Wall Street Journal—the daily which covers the corporate world

Barron's—the weekend equivalent

Business Week—the *Time* of the business world

Fortune—the organ of philosophy and ideology

Forbes—which advertises itself as "the capitalist tool"

The Multinational Monitor—tracks big business across the globe, offering a citizens perspective on corporate power in the international arena; can be ordered from P.O. Box 19405, Washington, D.C. 20036

The Corporate Examiner—provides information on the social performance of major US corporations; it's available from the ICCR, Room 566, 475 Riverside Drive, New York, NY 10115.

Business and Society Review—the liberal critique of business ethics and practices; available from Warren, Gorham & Lamont, Inc., 870 Seventh Avenue, New York, NY 10019.

Most of the above are available from public or university libraries. They present the way the business community thinks about itself.

Books

While you are in the library, check out these books in the reference section

Standard and Poor's—this directory has every major corporation in the US, its annual sales, its product lines, the address of the corporate headquarters and the names of the Board of Directors

Moody's Manuals—provide basic financial business information, together with historical data, location, management and security descriptions

Who's Who in America—once you've isolated a particular company's directors, look in this volume to find where they live, what their families are like, the schools they attended, the companies they are involved with, and so forth.

The Companies

From the companies themselves you can get additional information by writing to the corporate headquarters directly. Also, every company publishes an *Annual Report,* which is the company's way of letting shareholders know the good things about the company's performance over the last year. Furthermore, each year a company must file a detailed report with the Securities and Exchange Commission in Washington, DC, called *10-K.* This report contains detailed additional information but is usually only available to shareholders.

Organizations

It is important to learn what the corporate community thinks about itself, how they articulate their ideology, how they package it for public consumption. When you are interested in analyses and critiques of the corporate role there are a number of organizations waiting to help you.

The Council on Economic Priorities. CEP does basic research on a variety of corporate issues. They publish a monthly newsletter, periodic reports and at least one major study each year. CEP is well respected, and can be relied upon for accurate information. Of special interest to organizers is their Corporate Information Center, which can help with data on military corporations, and their impact in your own community. CEP's address is 30 Irving Place, New York, NY 10003.

The Corporate Data Exchange. CDE does a specific task of research into the ownership of US corporations, the interlocking network of institutions that actually hold the power. Their studies are expensive and can best be found in public or university libraries. For more information about their work write 198 Broadway, New York, NY 10038.

The Interfaith Center on Corporate Responsibility. ICCR is a coalition of church agencies who use stock holdings to pressure transnational corporations to change their policies. ICCR does research on corporations which it publishes in its monthly newsletter, *The Corporate Examiner.* ICCR can also respond to questions about particular corporations involved in abusive practices. You may write ICCR at Room 566, 475 Riverside Drive, New York, NY 10115. ICCR continues to be the main actor in the corporate responsibility movement and will be the primary organization that local organizers will be relating to. For that reason it is important to sketch out the scope of its work. For ten years church agencies have been using their investments to obtain change by challenging policies and practices of US-based transnational corporations. ICCR began with a concern for US investment in southern Africa. It soon became clear that while investment in apartheid presented a serious moral challenge to the West, the activities of transnational corporations in other countries followed similar patterns of exploitation and domination. The next step in ICCR's development was to appreciate that the transnational behavior elsewhere was rehearsed first in the United States. Churches began to see that nearly all aspects of life (and death) are touched by transnational power. Because of this, ICCR's current agenda now reads: southern Africa, Guatemala, plant closings, community reinvestment, dumping of prescription drugs in Third World countries, affirmative action, nuclear weapons facilities, economic conversion of military factories, OSHA, nuclear energy, infant formula, genetic engineering, chemical dumping and agribusiness.

National Action/Research on the Military-Industrial Complex. NARMIC developed as a project of the American Friends Service Committee to explore the connections between the Indochina War and US corporations. NARMIC has produced a number of excellent slide shows; the latest two deal with nuclear power/weapons, and US corporate involvement in the Third World. NARMIC's address is 1501 Cherry Street, Philadelphia, PA 19102.

Stockholders Resolutions

ICCR has developed a method for raising issues, engaging in discussion, filing of shareholder resolutions and presenting the corporation with its demands. The instrument which churches have chosen is the shareholder resolution. Any person or group owning one or more shares of common stock can bring a resolution before the annual shareholder meeting of the company. A resolution must not be longer than 300 words, but it can be on any significant aspect of the company business. It can be a simple request for information, to be made available to all shareholders, or

ICCR continues to be the main actor in the corporate responsibility movement.

The shareholder resolution is an effective instrument to raise issues and engage in discussion.

There are handles for local organizers to be involved in this work. Once you've done your homework and plugged into a particular organization or campaign, you can do any one of the following:

- write letters to management
- buy a share of stock and attend the annual shareholder meeting
- hold an action in your own community at the time of the annual meeting in another city
- boycott the company's products
- pressure institutions of which you are a part to vote their stock in favor of church-sponsored resolutions
- take any action which helps build the climate in which one day the transnational corporations will be controlled.

Current campaigns which are of special interest to War Resisters League organizers would include: 1) the campaign which would get universities to sell their South Africa related stock; 2) efforts to get nuclear weapons manufacturers to stop their production (there are a lot of local campaigns on this issue); 3) attempts to get military corporations to consider economic conversion of particular facilities; 4) a boycott of General Electric products because of their involvement in the nuclear industry and "Star Wars" contracting; and 5) generally a campaign focused on all corporate contractors doing the "Star

it can be a strong demand for some policy to be halted or changed.

If the shareholder resolution is debated at the annual meeting and receives more than 3% of the vote, it can be brought back a second year. Three percent is no mean achievement, and, in fact, shows a significant level of shareholder interest. If 6% is achieved the second year, the same resolution can be brought back yet a third time. And if 10% is achieved that year it can be brought back indefinitely. The goal of ICCR is severalfold: to reach sympathetic management and shareholders, to educate the public about corporate issues, to get the minimum vote necessary to continue to raise an issue, to make a media event of the annual meeting, and to achieve change in corporate policy. ICCR members over the last 10 years have played an important role in challenging corporate practices.

Three percent vote of the shareholders shows a significant level of shareholder interest.

Demonstration in front of ITT headquarters in Manhattan, May 10, 1972. Photo by Karl Bissinger.

Wars'' (Strategic Defense Initiative) work. Inquiries to ICCR can get you information on the current campaign and how you can plug into them.

Audio-Visual Aids

Obviously, when taking on the power of the transnationals, we are at a lethal disadvantage so long as we are few. The most useful thing to do in your own community is to educate people about the role of corporations in determining their lives and the lives of billions of other people. Audio-visual resources are helpful in this effort. Some of the best are:

Controlling Interest. A 60-minute film linking the overthrow of the Allende regime in Chile with plant closings in Massachusetts. It demonstrates the ability of the multinational to create havoc domestically and internationally, and suggests the potential alliance of all those whom the transnationals threaten.

Weapons in Space: The Next Arms Race. An excellent 25-minute slide show available from Union of Concerned Scientists, 26 Church Street, Cambridge, MA 02238.

Weapons in Space: An Overview. A 7-minute animated video narrated by James Earl Jones (Darth Vader's voice in the ''Star Wars'' movies) is available from Union of Concerned Scientists, 26 Church Street, Cambridge, MA 02238.

As with most aspects of working for peace and justice, no single act is going to be enough. Tackling the power of the transnational corporation is not easy. We must not match their budgets dollar for dollar or their staffs, person for person. We must get our facts straight and help people to see why exploiting others is, in the final analysis, not in their interest either. In reseaching and organizing around the corporate role and the problems we address, Gandhi's advice to his followers is still appropriate: ''Never let them rest.''

The most useful thing to do in your own community is to educate people about the role of corporations in their lives.

We must not match their budgets dollar for dollar or their staffs, person for person.

''Never let them rest.''

LEAFLETS AND POSTERS

By Ed Hedemann*

There are two types of leaflets: the call leaflet and the education leaflet.

To be effective, design is the most important element of the call.

For the education leaflet, the text is the dominant element.

All too often, the movement has turned out some rather pathetic excuses for leaflets and posters. The purpose of this chapter is to offer a few suggestions on how they can be improved.

Leaflets and posters are probably the cheapest and most common forms of communication for the movement. The *effectiveness* of this medium depends directly on content, design, and distribution—and that is what this chapter will focus on.

Content of the Leaflet

There are basically two types of leaflets: the *call* leaflet and the *education* (or analysis) leaflet. The call is an announcement of a meeting, demonstration, or other event to which you are inviting mass participation. The key elements of the call are when, where, subject, demands (if appropriate), something the reader can do (e.g., boycott), why attendance is important, and a contact for further information. These leaflets should have a minimum of words (no text), since they are not meant to argue or convert anyone, but simply to announce your event and get "the already concerned" to it. To be effective, design is the most important element of the call leaflet. The poster is essentially a larger version of a call leaflet, although posters are often done to communicate a message graphically, rather than announce an event.

*Drawn from material by Jerry Coffin, David McReynolds, Charles Walker, Nancy Brigham, and Artworks.

The education leaflet seeks to present new facts or a different analysis of commonly accepted facts, refute establishment propaganda, communicate a message using the collective wisdom of a specific constituency, respond to an immediate news event, explain an action which is occuring (e.g., a sit-in at an armed forces recruiting station), or convert the reader.

For this type of leaflet, the text becomes the dominant element. Writing a good, effective leaflet is difficult. Complex concepts and politics must be presented in clear, concise, and simple language. Generalities must be avoided. Unstated facts and ideas must be commonly accepted.

Because our society is made up of many different cultures and other groupings, leaflets handed out *on the street* must aim at the lowest common denominator. This does *not* mean writing "down" to people because you feel they are stupid. But it does mean that poorly educated people, for example, are able to understand complex ideas if the words are simple. Therefore, never overestimate the vocabulary of the person in the street, and never underestimate people's ability to grasp ideas if you use words they are familiar with.

It is often easier to sit down and write a leaflet after you've had a good, two-hour political discussion with a few people. So schedule a writers' session to develop ideas for the leaflet or poster. If you have people talented at drawing, include them so they can be thinking of graphic and design ideas during the session.

Develop a file of material from which pertinent quotes and statistics can be

ONLY SOCIALIST REVOLUTION CAN END NUCLEAR POLLUTION!

(text of a densely printed leaflet; section headings include:) "Developing Workers' Power: The Transitional Approach to Socialist Revolution"; "Some Transitional Tactics in Progress to Socialist Revolution: Put Real Material Pressure on the Capitalists and Exhaust Illusions of Progress, Reform, etc., under Capitalism and Exhaust Illusions of Helplessness Against Capitalists!"; "But What About the USSR and its Nukes?"

A typical terrible leaflet, circa 1979.

drawn. Easy access to such a file can facilitate the writing of your leaflet. Movement periodicals, newspapers, and fact sheets on various subjects can constitute the basis of your research material.

The education leaflet is commonly made up of a title, text, graphic or photo (to grab attention and illustrate the message), and follow-up information. The design—the way in which these elements are presented—will be covered in the next section.

The Title. The purpose of a title is to catch the attention of the reader. So generally, leaflets need big bold titles, which reflect the text. The shorter the title, the better. Sometimes a photo or graphic is used in conjuction with the title. A few suggestions for the title are the use of catchy phrasing, bold type, different color, a provocative question, or a generally accepted fact (e.g., "Taxes Are Too Damn High").

The Text. As a general rule, the text should be *short*. Some people write leaflets as if Americans are starved for words. Unfortunately, it is not unusual to find leaflets with a small title followed by solid text on *both* sides of a legal-sized sheet with narrow margins, and no graphics or subheads to break the text; and more often than not, it's been printed on a 30-year-old mimeograph machine, long in need of ink and repairs.

The text can be broken into four parts: the introduction, the background, the argument, and the summation. The first paragraph—and more often the first line—is what will determine whether or not your leaflet is read. So the *introduction* needs to attract attention, create curiosity, or cause identification. The title *alerts* the passerby, and the introduction *hooks* the reader. A startling revelation, a question, or a common grievance make good lead sentences. When you hand out leaflets, watch the reaction of those who receive them. Are they read immediately? Or are they thrown away or stuffed in a back pocket? Don't just write leaflets, evaluate them. *If a leaflet isn't read immediately after it's received, chances are it will never be read.*

For the introduction and the title, you need to relate to what is in the mind of your audience. A leaflet that might be considered absolutely "correct" ideologically, and "great" in wording—if it was being judged by a pacifist group—can go over like a stale peanut butter sandwich when handed out on the streets. Never fall so in love with your own ideas, words, and concerns that you think everyone you meet will share them or even appreciate them. For example, "Nukes Are Capital Intensive" as a title will be less effective on the street than "Why Are Our Electric Bills So High?" In the sixties, Dutch anti-war activists leafletted American tourists to express opposition to the Vietnam War. To make sure the leaflets were not thrown away, they listed good dating spots and interesting night clubs in Amsterdam.

The Background of the leaflet text demonstrates why the reader should be concerned. Here you are attempting to have the reader identify with you, the leaflet, and ultimately the issue and cause. For example, in a leaflet on disarmament, the background might be to bring attention to the high taxes, unemployment, inflation, and increase in military spending. Use of common grievances is good, as is the use of the all-inclusive "we" or "us."

The argument is the heart of the text, where you make your case. In a disarmament leaflet, for example, you could establish that military spending is a prime cause of inflation, etc. You buttress this section with quotes by famous people and statistics to lend legitimacy.

In *the summation,* you draw conclusions from your argument, tie together loose ends, restate issues, and in one sentence try to gain agreement from the reader. In the disarmament leaflet suggested above, a conclusion could be that

Some people write leaflets as if Americans are starved for words.

If a leaflet isn't read immediately after its received, chances are it will never be read.

Never fall so in love with your own ideas that you think everyone you meet will appreciate them.

"in order to stop inflation, lower taxes, create employment, and provide *more* security, we must begin to disarm."

The Follow-Up. Where possible always include something the reader who is in agreement with you, can do: return a coupon, get more information, send a contribution, come to a meeting, boycott a product, write a government official, join your organization, etc. Be specific, make sure it relates directly to the text, and make it something that a reader can reasonably be expected to do. *Always,* include the name and address of your group. If you use a coupon, don't expect a tremendous rate of return—7% is a good return from a membership mailing and 1% is an incredible return for a leaflet distributed to the general public.

Again, the leaflet text as a general rule should be as short as possible and still make your point. Short paragraphs make reading easier. Also, the leaflet should confine itself to one issue and try to make one argument. It should end with a call for some kind of action.

Other. Other parts of a leaflet such as photos, graphics, subheads, "sandwich quotes," and highlighted boxes help break up the text and reinforce the content. These elements are discussed in the next section.

Design

There are three basic purposes to leaflet and poster design: get the attention of the passerby, communicate or emphasize key parts of the message, and improve the ease of reading.

The first step in the design process, after determining the role of your leaflet (or poster), is to figure out how much copy you have and what size your finished product will be. This will often dictate what room you have for a photo or graphic, the type size, margins, whether or not you can have a border, the size of your title, if you must use both sides of the leaflet, and so forth. Usually, you will find it necessary to shorten the text. If you can communicate the same message with fewer words, you'll be more effective.

Sometimes it is appropriate to have the front side of a leaflet designed like a call or poster and the back side designed like an education leaflet. Though the cost of printing on both sides is higher, it may save money by having one leaflet instead of two.

Although design is pretty much a per-sonal decision and there is no *one* correct design, there are many mistakes that can be made. This section is an attempt to help you avoid those mistakes and make suggestions for improvements.

Just as a research file is helpful for writing a leaflet, it may prove valuable to have a design file. Make a collection of the best leaflets you get on the street or at a demonstration, no matter what the subject. Clip out newspaper or magazine ads which are the most striking. Then analyze those designs. What about them caught your attention? Can you adopt any of those design ideas for your own material? Experiment with different styles. Madison Avenue isn't paid millions of dollars a year to turn out ineffective ads. There's a lot to learn from their propaganda techniques.

In addition, a file of "clip art" can prove useful, especially if you don't have the time to collar an artist and need a graphic right away. Check movement publications, especially foreign ones (because they are less likely to have been seen here), for clear and strong graphics. But only use graphics (or photos) if they enhance the leaflet message. Gratuitous graphics detract from your message.

Sometimes the best designs are those which are unusual or different, but not to the extent to which clarity and neatness are sacrificed. In the unusual situation of a leaflet having a lot of blank space, there is a tendency in the movement to fill that space with more words. Often blank space, through wide margins or space around the title, will improve the design. An extreme example is a virtually blank—except for a few words in the dead center—full page ad

A typical "Call" leaflet, 1980.

Where possible always include something the reader can do.

Use good design ideas you see in newspapers and magazines.

Use graphics if they enhance the leaflet message. Gratuitious graphics distract from your message.

(costing $40,000) which runs in the *New York Times* once in awhile. This may appear wasteful, but you can bet it will be seen by a high percentage of the readers.

Even if you get someone to take your leaflet, chances are they won't read the whole thing. So to communicate your message to those people, you will find the following design techniques helpful: subheads; "sandwich quotes," which extract and enlarge key phrases or sentences from the text, sandwiching them between 2 bold lines; boxes or shaded boxes (e.g., which highlight the leaflet's demands); the use of italics, bold, caps, or a second color ink for key sections of the text; illustrations, charts, or photo which communicate your message clearly.

Though the letter size sheet (8½ " × 11") is standard, using a smaller sheet, such as half the letter size (5½ " × 8½ "), may prove to be more effective because of its unusual size. And it will probably be cheaper. The best size for a poster depends largely on where they are to be put up. A 17" × 22" poster is not useful for telephone poles or many bulletin boards. A smaller poster may not be noticed in a store window or in a subway station.

A frequently neglected possibility for leaflets or posters is the border. A simple 1/16" black border will sometimes do wonders to a leaflet. Art stores carry all kinds of borders on rolls of tape or transfer type sheets. For example, a "barbed wire" border might be appropriate on a leaflet concerned with political prisoners. Again, look at professional ads for ideas.

Typesetting the text will increase the number of words and improve readability of a leaflet. Typesetting produces letters which are solid black, sharp, neat, and take up only the space each needs (rather than the equal spacing of most office typewriters). In addition, the size, style, and spacing between lines can be easily varied to suit your needs. And the columns of type can be justified (flush on both the left and right hand margins). If you have little time or money to pay for typesetting, at least use a typewriter with a carbon ribbon. If faint, fuzzy, and irregular type makes a leaflet hard to read, then it probably won't be read.

To have your copy typeset, you must determine the width of each column of type (usually measured in picas; there are 6 picas per inch), the style of type (typesetters will show you the styles they

GIVE EARTH A CHANCE

The front side of WRL's most successful leaflet, used November 13-15, 1969, Washington, D.C.

carry; a serif face is perferable if you have a lot of copy), type size (measured in points; there are 12 points to a pica or 72 to an inch), which for the text is often 10 points and much larger for the title; *leading* or spacing between lines of type (also measured in points and usually one point more than the type size, so leading for 10 point type is 11 points); and whether it is justified (left and right sides straight), flush right, or centered. When these specifications are made (called speccing), it is possible to get a rough estimate from the typed copy of how long the typeset copy will be. Then you can determine how much room you have for photos, graphics, title, etc.—or how much copy you must cut before it is typeset.

To estimate the length of the typeset copy, you need to count characters. First, determine how many characters are on your typewritten page: multiply the number of characters (plus space) per inch (e.g., an elite typewriter has 12 characters per inch and a pica has 10) times the average length of a line (in inches) times the number of lines on a page of copy to be typeset times the number of pages. Next, determine the number of *typeset* characters per column-inch: multiply the number of characters per pica (ask the typesetter) times the column width in picas times the number of lines per inch. Therefore, to get the total number of column-inches of typeset copy divide the total number of characters in your copy by the number of typeset characters per column-inch.

There is a tendency in the movement to think every blank space on a leaflet must be filled.

A frequently neglected possibility for leaflets or posters is the border.

Typesetting the text will increase the number of words and improve readibility.

A messy leaflet implies a subtle lack of respect for your audience and your message.

The advantage of photos and graphics for fitting copy is their size flexibility.

In paste-up, neatness is essential.

Paste-Up

The final step in preparing your leaflet or poster for the printer is the paste-up, also refered to as *the mechanicals.* Neatness in this part of the process is essential if you don't wish to detract from your message. A messy leaflet implies a subtle lack of respect for your audience and your message. No matter what color you will print in, the mechanicals should always be black on white.

Equipment. The following tools are necessary for straight and neat mechanicals:

- *table* with solid, straight edge (on left hand side for right handed people)
- *T-square* to draw horizontal lines
- *right triangle* to draw vertical lines (in conjunction with the T-square)
- *ruler* (with inch and pica/point scale)
- *light blue pencil* to draw guidelines, which will not reproduce photographically
- *black pen* for marks and lines you wish to show up after printing (e.g., cut lines for trimming)
- *layout sheets* (should be larger than the image area of your leaflet)
- *rubber cement or wax* to adhere the copy and graphics to the layout sheets
- *X-acto knife* for precision cutting of copy and aid in moving small pieces of type
- *masking tape* to hold down layout sheet on table.

Other helpful equipment include a light table or box (particularly useful for stripping in corrections), "burnisher" to firmly press down copy and aid in transferring press type, "proportional wheel" to calculate enlargements or reductions of photos, white correction fluid to eliminate spurious black marks, eraser, "registration marks" to position overlays, acetate for overlays, border tapes, transfer type, and so forth.

Basic Paste Up Techniques. The first step in pasting up copy is to tape down a clean white layout sheet, using the T-square to make sure the sheet is square with the table. Then measure and mark the height and width of your leaflet. Now draw the perimeter of the leaflet, using the blue pencil with the T-square and triangle. Next, measure and draw in where the columns of copy are to fall. Leave 3 picas (or half an inch) margin all around. Don't forget to allow space for borders, if any.

To determine placement and size for the title, any graphics, photos, and borders, sometimes requires a little experimenting. The advantage of photos and graphics for fitting copy is their flexibility. If there is little space, they can be cropped or reduced—within reason, of course—more easily than type. Using the proportional wheel and knowing where to crop, you can calculate the percentage reduction or enlargement to fill desired space.

Unless you are using a waxer (and can pre-wax all your copy), cut out the columns of copy and position on the layout sheet, then apply a few brush strokes of rubber cement and place into position. while the rubber cement is drying, place the T-square along the base of a line of type to square it up. Then using a burnisher (or other flat rigid edge) rub down the copy to fix it securely in place. When connecting another section of type, use the T-square to level it, the triangle to line it up with the section above, and the ruler to make sure the sections are the proper distance apart.

For graphics with shades of gray and for photos, a half-tone (a photo which has been converted to a pattern of dots, giving the illusion of tone) has to be made. Therefore, clearly mark the position and size of where the halftone is to go, but do not paste in on to the mechanicals. The printer will take care of that. A photo which touches the edge of the paper (no margin) is called a "bleed." If you do this, you have to plan for it to be printed 1/8" or so over the edge of your leaflet. After it is printed, the printer will trim the sheet to its final size. Be sure to number and indicate which photo/graphic goes where.

Titles can be typeset, handlettered with a dark black pen, or you can use transfer type (which can be purchased in an incredible variety of styles and sizes at an art supply or stationery store). Borders and rules (lines which separate articles or columns of type) can be drawn with a good pen, such as a Rapidograph, but evenness may be difficult to achieve; placed down with line tape, but this has a tendency to be less than straight; or rubbed on from sheets of transfer type.

Overlays. If you wish to have more than one color (black is considered a color, in printing), then you will need to attach one overlay for each additional color to your mechanicals. Each color requires a separate inking operation on the press. Overlays are usually a sheet of clear acetate (flexible transparent piece of plastic)

BUTTONS AND STICKERS

By Clay Colt

Not only are buttons and stickers good ways to propagandize your group's political views or advertise an event, they are effective fundraisers, if managed properly.

If your group is organizing a special event or mass demonstration, it may be of value to custom print buttons not only to advertise the event, but also to "commemorate" it—a button to sell to those who participated in the activity.

In any case, it is seldom worthwhile having your own button made in a run less than 500 to 1000. In those quantities a button will cost about 10¢ to make, and sell for 50¢. Allow three weeks for manufacture and delivery of the custom-made buttons, after the mechanicals are sent in. Rush service available in 48 hours, but not worth the extra cost.

Preparation of mechanicals for buttons or stickers proceeds the same way as anything else which is to be made "camera-ready" for an offset printer. You can prepare your design any size you wish, since the printer can reduce (or enlarge) it to the size of the button. However, you may wish to prepare the design the same size you want it printed, so you won't be surprised at how tiny it is once it is reduced.

Camera-ready copy should be black on white paper or card stock. If you wish more than one color, each additional color must be "separated"—meaning a clear acetate overlay for every extra color. You could have a one color job done on colored paper to give the effect of two colors.

Buttons commonly come in the following diameters: 1″, 1¼″, 1½″, 1¾″, 2-1/8″, 2¼″, 2½″, 3″, 3½″, and 4″. The most popular sizes are 1½″, 1¾″, and 2-1/8″. There are three types of fasteners on buttons: straight pins (which are a little dangerous and often fall apart), lock pins (which hook under a clasp), and safety pins. Lock pins are good up to 1¾″. After that safety pins are preferable.

You should instruct the manufacturer to put your group's name, address, and phone on the rim. A union label can be printed on the rim or front of the button.

For pressure-sensitive bumperstickers, the art work is done the same way, except usually not within a circle. There are four standard sizes: 3″ x 11½″, 2¾″ x 15″, 3¾″ x 15″, and 3¾″ x 7½″. Though the minimum order is 125, it is best to order 500 to 1000 or more, to reduce the unit cost. You can also have information printed on the backing paper at the same cost as an extra color (about 20% extra). Stickers usually come printed on paper or vinyl. Vinyl will last longer. Whichever kind you get, always apply it to a dry, clean, smooth non-porous surface for best adhesion.

Now you have the buttons, but they won't do anyone much good until you have a means of distributing them. The most common ways are on literature tables, and mounted on aprons or a piece of cardboard and carried through crowds at rallies or other mass events. Make your prices clearly visible wherever the buttons are displayed. The more variety you have in buttons and bumperstickers, the more likely you will attract people to buy them.

If you cannot find a place to buy buttons in quantity or have them custom made in your area, contact Donnelly/Colt, Box 188, Hampton, CT 06247, 203-455-9621. The WRL national office has a limited supply of certain buttons and stickers.

If you have a program for regular leafletting, then you can develop a following by giving out leaflets at a regular time and place.

taped to the layout sheet. Three or four "registration marks" (which come on a role of transparent tape) on the layout sheet and on the overlay make sure the printer will properly line up all the colors.

For a shade effect (a light even gray or other tone), you need an amberlith or rubylith overlay. These are transparent films made up of one clear layer and a very thin colored (but black to a camera) layer. Carefully make a cut into the colored layer with your X-acto knife, peel away and throw out that part of the colored layer which you don't want to be part of the shade. Then indicate to the printer the percentage of shade, usually 10% or 20% (100% is solid).

To give the effect of white letters on a black (or dark) background, you can do a "drop out." Place what you want to be dropped out on an overlay so that it falls in a black area of the mechanicals. Then indicate on the overlay that the letters are to be dropped out.

The Printing Process. Once your mechanicals are ready ("camera ready"), then they are sent to the printer. For an offset press, the first thing a printer does is to make negatives of the mechanicals—one negative for each color and a halftone for each photo. The negatives are then "stripped": mounted on a goldenrod masking sheet the same size as the press plate, windows cut out of the masking sheet to expose the image areas, and any unwanted spots or shadow lines opaqued. Next the stripped negatives are placed on top of a (usually) metal plate and exposed in a platemaker. The exposed plates (one for each color) are developed, then mounted on the press. A separate run is made for each color, unless the press can handle more than one plate at a time.

Leaflet Distribution

Obviously, with few people, you need to focus your leafletting in those areas and times of high traffic, such as work shifts and lunch hours at entrances of office buildings, exits, at the end of sports events, key shopping times at department stores. If you have a program for regular leafleting, then you can build up a following by giving out leaflets at a regular time and place.

The following are some basic suggestions for effective leafleting:

- station 2 or 3 people at each entrance and a couple on each corner
- leafleters should be within an arms length of pedestrians, but not such that they block traffic
- hold the leaflet so the title can be clearly seen, and lead people with it as they walk by
- hand people leaflets; don't wait for them to come to take them
- establish eye contact
- smile and be friendly, but not aggressive

Leaflet and tag distribution, May 6, 1979. Photo by Grace Hedemann.

WALLPASTING

By Kate Donnelly

Anything can be posted from an 8½" x 11" flyer to a 4' x 8' large poster, though a 17" x 22" format poster is used for most events. This is about the best size for easy posting and visibility. If you do a large run of a poster, you can afford to wallpaste. But it may be worth your while to do a run on newsprint, black and white. Minimum run is usually 3000 at any web offset press. The thinner the paper the easier the paste absorbs and the longer it'll stay up.

The equipment you'll need, besides the posters, include two wallpasting brushes, one small bucket filled with wallpaste and water. Follow instructions on the box for mixing, and don't let the paste sit around before you go out or it'll get stiff. Wear old clothes—a rain parka works well—and bring a few rags to wipe off the paste. Always wash out the bucket and brushes before you go out for a beer afterwards.

Most cities and towns have laws against wallpasting. It will be easier not to get caught in cities. Check your local ordinances. In most cases it's a misdemeanor—but it is important to plead First Amendment rights while pointing out such laws discriminate against people with little money. However, if caught be prepared for a fine; in New York City it's $5-10, and in Asbury Park, NJ, it's $100.

Some towns will only bother you if you deface property or nature, like storefront windows and trees. Common sense will tell you where your message is best placed without alienating the people you are trying to reach. Sometimes storefront windows are appropriate, e.g., army recruiting stations. The best place to paste are boarded-up windows, train stations, mail boxes, construction sites. But sometimes those places which are easiest to put up posters (e.g., abandoned buildings) are not the most effective in reaching many people, for lack of visibility.

Once you have the equipment together, divide people into teams of two or three and assign each team to a different area. Depending on available transportation, teams can be dropped off along the perimeter of the area to be covered and work inward, so that all the teams can easily reunite.

One person in the group should slap the paste onto the surface, the other should slap up the poster, then the poster should be pasted over again. Pasting over will make it harder to pull off. They're easy to get down when wet, but impossible when they dry. Every inch of the poster should be saturated. A third person can be preparing a new surface while the last poster is getting pasted over. Also, the third person has the important job of watching for cops. Nothing beats the effect of 5 to 10 posters all in a row. The first few posters you do may be clumsy. But after a few you become adept and agile. It's an artful sport and can be fun.

Though wallpasting has to be done at night, small pressure-sensitive stickers have become popular for plastering up anytime. The normal size is 4" x 6"; they can come on rolls, often with a minimum order of 3000. Everyone loves to put these up, including people who would never wallpaste. They can be used anywhere and are especially good on subways, buses, phone booths, and so forth.

Postering is also a good activity for people newly involved in your group. It requires little time and builds solidarity. But everyone should poster—it takes organizers who spend long hours in offices and at meetings off the phone and into the streets. Walking past a well-posted area can be one of the most rewarding and satisfying feelings associated with the shit work of putting together a campaign.

- say something like
    "This tells why we're here. Hope you think about it."
    "This is for you."
    "You ought to read this."
- be prepared with brief answers to questions such as "What's this all about?" "Who's doing this?" etc.

If someone wants to talk to the extent that it interferes with leafleting, talk briefly, then offer to send additional material or make an appointment, or have someone else take over the conversation or the leafleting. If someone is abusive, or grabs the leaflets and throws them away, don't panic—react non-violently and creatively. Say something if you think it will help. Have plastic bags available in case of rain. Pick up discarded leaflets, even though people who discarded them are legally responsible, not you.

For blanket leafleting, use a map to determine the key spots to be covered: shopping centers, campuses, factories, and office buildings. After deciding how many people you need for each location, get firm commitments from people to leaflet (contact 20% more than needed, to cover last minute dropouts). Ask them to meet the morning of the blanket leafleting, where they will be given leaflets and leafleting assignments. Or tables can be set up at mass demonstrations, where people can pick up leaflets and their assignments after hearing announcements from the stage.

For blanket leafletting, use a map to determine the key spots to be covered.

Poster Distribution

The usual way the establishment distributes its posters is by paying for space on public transportation, billboards, etc. Since free space for posters is very limited and since movement groups do not have the money needed to buy space, creativity must be employed.

The most common places used for movement posters are in stores, offices (e.g., bulletin boards), designated areas of campuses, apartment building lobbies, dorms, and on the street—anywhere there would be a significant flow of pedestrian traffic. For all but the last, it's best to ask permission to ensure the poster will remain up a little longer.

As with blanket leafleting, it is valuable to begin your postering strategy with a map to determine the key locations you wish to send postering teams. Since posters are frequently ripped down, it is important to do periodic spot checks

Since free space for posters is very limited and movement groups do not have the money needed to buy space, creativity must be employed.

to replace those removed.

Depending on the event, how many posters you have, and the number of volunteers, posters should be put up two weeks in advance, and then again several days before. For a *major* event it may be of value to have posters up two or more months ahead.

Of the various means used to poster on the street—pasting, stapling, tying, taping—wallpasting is the best in terms of speed and longevity of the poster. See the box on "Wallpasting" for an effective method.

Follow-up

How To Do Leaflets, Newsletters, and Newspapers, Nancy Brigham, The Boston Community School, 1976.

For the Could-Be Artist—A Graphic Arts Manual, Josely Carvalho, et al., Artworks/The Silkscreen Project, 1980. Emphasizes paste-ups and silkscreening.

Pocket Pal, International Paper Company, 1983. A handy summary of the entire graphic arts process from paste-up through binding. Emphasis is on offset printing. Has a nice glossary.

In addition, there are many fine textbooks on graphic arts available in bookstores and libraries if you would like more in-depth references.

PRINTING

By Ed Hedemann

There are a number of ways to communicate one's message: public speaking, use of mass media, demonstrations, canvassing, films, and printed literature. But, it is only through the last medium that an organizer has complete control over the content of a message which remains with the recipient.

Organizers who wish to be effective must be able to use a variety of printing processes to disseminate their information. Improper choices can result in a waste of money, unsightly and confusing literature, untimely materials, or some combination of these problems.

The factors to consider in selecting a printing process are expense, appearance, accuracy in reproduction, availability or convenience, and speed. See the Chart below for a comparison of the printing processes.

Types of Printing Processes

What follows is a brief description of the types and uses of the various printing processes.

Spirit Duplication. Often referred to as "ditto," this process uses a clear (or "spirit") fluid to dissolve a dye onto paper fed through the machine. The gelatin/dye mixture is adhered onto the master sheet by typewriter pressure or pen. Ditto machines usually can be found in schools, churches, and business offices. They are quick and cheap for small, straight copy runs (about 100 or less). Their chief disadvantages are the short run and poor quality.

Screen—*Silk Screen.* The basic process is the passage of ink through a screen, which holds the stencil. Before being adhered to the screen, the stencil is cut photographically or by hand. Besides holding the stencil, the screen allows for an even distribution of ink. The chief advantages of the silk screen process are its versatility, creativity, and the fact that it can easily be made by anyone. Not only is it used to print on posters and T-shirts, but it can print on bottles and other unconventional printing surfaces. The disadvantages are its awkwardness and short run (usually less than several hundred).

Screen—*Mimeograph.* This movement workhorse operates on the same principle as the silk screen, but it is constructed in a rotary fashion with automatic inking. Masters are prepared by typewriter or pen pressure displacing a thick wax layer on a screen mesh, or automatic cutting by an electrostencil machine. The greatest advantage of a mimeo is to provide leaflets quickly, and cheap printing of limited distribution analyses and position papers. Besides being quick and cheap, mimeos are very accessible. The primary disadvantage is its poor quality (compared to offset).

Offset. Also known as photo offset or lithography, this process works from the basic principle that grease and water do not mix. The image on the offset plate is a hardened, grease-based substance. A thin film of water is applied to the plate, which adheres to the non-image areas. Then the plate is inked. But the ink, not mixing with the watery non-image areas, only adheres to the image areas. The plate then offsets the image onto a rubber blanket cylinder, which in turn transfers the image onto the paper. Movement use of offset printing is usually for leaflets, newsletters, posters, and anything requiring a long run (several thousand on up). The chief advantages of offset printing are its quality (with moderate price) and long run. The primary dis-

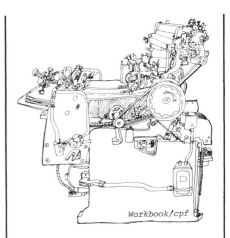

Workbook/cpf

advantages lie with the cost and slower turn around.

Xerography. This process, often referred to as xeroxing, is rapidly displacing the spirit duplicator and mimeograph for short runs (a few hundred and less). Xerography is a electrostatic process which bonds graphite to paper. In the last few years the quality has improved dramatically as the price has gone down. A number of companies have machines that not only do solids and decent reproductions of photographs, but are able to do reductions, enlargements, 4-color prints, and transfer color slides to paper. The main disadvantage (expense for long runs—1000 or more) is also a main advantage (cheap for very short runs). Because of its speed and availability, many offices are getting rid of their mimeograph machine and carbon paper.

Letterpress. This process, which used to dominate all fields of printing up until a couple of decades ago, is based on raised (relief) images transferring ink directly from the type face to the paper. Letterpress, which is characterized by high quality and long runs, is rarely used by the movement because of its expense and lack of availability.

Gravure. This process is used a lot for magazine sections of newspapers. The originals are screened. A negative of the screen is exposed to a plate which, when treated with chemicals, etches tiny cup-shaped cavities in the plate. Ink is applied to the plate, retained by the cavities, and transferred to the paper. Though it produces literature of high quality and is convenient for copy with lots of photos, the gravure process is rarely used in the movement because of its high expense.

Plate Engraving. This process is similar to gravure but instead of etching patterns of dots into the plate, letters and images are carved into a copper or steel plate. The plate engraving process is used in the movement in a similar way to the silk screen: to make posters and print on T-shirts. However, instead of metal, other surfaces such as wood, linoleum, and even potatoes are used. Though such a process can easily be built and used, it is somewhat awkward and is limited to relatively small runs (less than a few hundred).

COMPARISON CHART OF PRINTING PROCESSES

printing process	type of job	cost	speed	quantity	quality	solids	photos	colors	accessibility
spirit duplication	straight copy (e.g., minutes)	cheap	quick	100 (maybe 500)	poor	poor	limited	usually not	moderately
screen: silk‡	posters, T-shirts, & all kinds of odd jobs	moderate	†	1000	good	good	limited	yes	limited
mimeo	leaflets, simple newsletters, copy for mailings	cheap	quick	2000—10,000	limited	poor	very poor	usually not	very
xerography	straight copy, some graphics, etc.*	cheap for small run	very quick	unlimited	poor to moderate	*	*	usually not	very
offset	brochures, leaflets, posters, books, magazines, etc.	moderate	slow	50,000—100,000 with metal plates	moderate to excellent	good	good	yes	very
letterpress	(same as offset)	expensive	slow	100,000—500,000	excellent	good	good	yes	moderately
gravure	(same as offset)	expensive	slow	100,000—500,000	very good	good	good	yes	limited
plate engraving‡	posters and T-shirts	moderate	†	1000	good	good	*	yes	limited

‡ assumes done by organizer
* depends on machine
† labor intensive

SILKSCREENING

By Ed Hedemann and Kate Donnelly

A silk screen printer is a device that allows a person to do mass printing on unusual objects (e.g., large posters, thick boards, banners, irregular surfaces, T-shirts). It is also a cheap way to print up a small run of posters. And it can be a very satisfying and creative way to express yourself.

Basic Operation

A silk (or other material, such as polyester) piece of cloth is tightly stretched over a wood frame. A stencil with the design you want transferred to your poster (or whatever) is adhered to the bottom of the silkscreen. The stencil and the silkscreen is placed flat over a blank poster. Ink is put on the silkscreen and spread over the area where the poster is positioned with a squeegee. The ink passes through the areas where the stencil allows, in a very uniform way.

Constructing the Printer

Cut up a 2″ x 2″ piece of wood, such that when you nail together the frame your inside dimensions match those of your poster (e.g., 17″ x 22″). Next take a piece of 10xx silk mesh (e.g., 25″ x 30″), which can be purchased at an art supply store, and stretch it very tightly over the frame with the help of one or two other people. Then tack down one side (a tack every inch or two), then the opposite side, then the other two sides—making sure the screen is well-stretched and tight. The screen should overlap around the edge of the frame to better hold the screen (otherwise it may tear away from the tacks).

Then cover the frame with paper tape to further secure the screen on the frame.

This also strengthens the frame and minimizes snags. Cover the wood completely. Shellac the frame and allow the shellac to extend about ¼″ onto the screen—making sure the frame is completely sealed from any liquids (paint or solvent). Allow to dry overnight.

Attach two hinges (with removable pins) to the frame and a piece of wood (e.g., ½″ plywood). The bottom of the screen must be flush with the board. The removable pins allow silkscreening on thick items such as boards. The part of the plywood touching the screen should be very smooth to prevent snagging—which would be disastrous.

Making the Stencil

There are several ways to make stencils. The simplest is cutting out a stencil on a piece of paper. However, this stencil is only good for two or three dozen posters. Another method involves painting directly on the screen with a screen filler (which can be obtained in an art supply store). Wherever you apply the filler, ink will not flow, since in both these methods you are creating a "negative."

You can also paint on the screen in a "positive" sense by first drawing your design with a lithographic tusche or crayon. Next cover the screen with the screen filler (it won't mix with the lithographic tusche). Then dissolve the lithographic tusche with turpentine, which leaves only the screen filler.

You can also use a hand cut screen printing film (e.g., Ulano S3S-Stasharp). This film is composed of two layers: a colored (e.g., green), very thin layer and a thicker (e.g., 3 mil) clear plastic backing sheet. To the stencil, tape the film—colored side up—on top of your

Silkscreening is an inexpensive way to create attractive and effective posters, T-shirts, etc.

design. Then, using an X-acto knife with a swivel blade, cut along the design. Caution: do not bear down with the knife—just drag it along the surface ever so lightly. You just want to cut the colored layer without denting the clear backing sheet, which may cause problems in adhering the film later. Remember, you are creating a negative. So once you have finished cutting, peel off and throw away that part of the colored layer you wish to have ink flow through and print. As with any of the handcut methods, detail—especially small print—is difficult to cut.

To adhere this stencil to the silk screen, place the film on the plywood board, colored layer up. Then place the screen directly on top. Next, with a cloth lightly soaked in the adhering liquid (e.g., lacquer thinner for the Ulano S3S-Stasharp) lightly rub over the entire screen to try to adhere the thin colored layer to the lower side of the silk screen. Careful: if you rub too hard or with too much adhering liquid the stencil will dissolve, but if you don't put on enough liquid the stencil will not adhere. Since the adhering liquid is also a solvent of the stencil, you want to dissolve *just enough* so that the stencil blends somewhat with the silk mesh. Later, the adhering liquid will be used to dissolve and remove the stencil from the screen.

Now lift up the screen and *carefully* attempt to peel off the heavy clear backing from the underside. This should leave on the thin colored layer. If the peeling process seems to be pulling off the colored layer as well, put it down and rub some more with the adhering liquid.

The best method—particularly for detailed work and half-tones—is to create a stencil photographically. With this method you need to prepare your art work in camera ready form, as for an offset press. There are places which will create a photo stencil on a silk screen for about $30. If you wish to do it yourself, any library has a number of books on silk screening, or send $3 to The Silkscreen Project, St. Mark's Church in-the-Bowery, Second Avenue and 10th Street, New York, NY 10003, to get a copy of *For the Could-Be Artist,* which gives a simple explanation of this and other methods.

Printing

Now that your stencil is made, you are ready to print. But first you must mask off (with newspaper and masking tape) the edges of the stencil and other areas on the underside of the screen you don't wish to print. Use screen filler to fill in pin holes and other small areas. Now glue or tape cardboard guides on the plywood base so you can position each poster exactly where you wish to print. Then lower the screen on the blank poster, spoon the ink (which can be purchased in any art supply store, usually by the quart) along one edge of the screen, and spread the ink evenly across the screen, pulling the squeegee firmly towards you. As one poster is taken out to dry, another blank one can be put in its place to repeat the process. Do not stack posters until *thoroughly* dry. If you have

Positioning blank poster before lowering screen. Photo by Karl Bissinger.

Using the squeege to spread the ink. Photo by Karl Bissinger.

a lot of posters, pinning them to a clothes line is best.

When you have finished, clean the screen immediately with paint thinner. If the paint were allowed to dry, the screen would be ruined. Besides paint thinner, come prepared with lots of rags. Make sure all the paint is removed from the holes of the mesh. However, it is OK if the strands of the silk are no longer white, but colored by the ink. To remove the stencil, again use lots of rags but with the adhering liquid (often lacquer thinner). Rub both sides of the screen simultaneously to completely remove the stencil.

For multicolor jobs, each additional color requires a separate run through the printer. Depending on the job, you may have to have separate stencils (and maybe more than one screen) for each color. Or you could print several colors with one stencil by masking off appropriate areas for each run.

T-Shirts

Silkscreening T-shirts is pretty much the same process. However, you need textile ink, and mineral spirits to clean up. There are two kinds of textile ink: plastic, which sits on top of a shirt like a decal, and the other is like a dye. The former, once heat-cured, will never come off even if the shirt falls apart. While the latter will fade with time and washing. Beware of ink bought in art stores; some brands such as "Speedball" are awful. "Naz Dar" is an example of a good brand. A quart of ink will last for around

20 dozen shirts.

When you are ready to print, place cardboard or newspaper inside the shirt to prevent ink from leaking onto the back of the shirt. Make sure the shirts are laid out flat with no creases in the shirt or newspaper. Practice on scrap cloth, since each shirt is a big investment. You can have someone bring each stuffed shirt to the silk screen printer, or you can spread your shirts around the room, and take the unhinged screen around to each shirt. Sell rejects at cost to minimize the expense of mistakes.

One common problem occurs when the ink dries on the screen. This will cause some part of the image not to come out. Once you start to screen, keep going at a steady pace. If it gets too dry you may have to clean the screen and start over. If you must *pause* in the screening process, leave a thick layer of ink on the screen (a thin layer would dry more quickly). But never leave ink on a screen very long when not using it. To heat-cure the shirts, iron on both sides for 3 minutes or put in the dryer for 30 minutes.

T-shirts can be bought blank, but only in dozens of each size. Union-made T-shirts are next to impossible to find, and do not come in 100% cotton (they are available in 50% cotton and 50% polyester). Jim Yocum of Yocum Knitting (Stowe, PA 19464) has a union made 50/50 shirt with a union label. If you have trouble finding wholesale T-shirts locally, Eisner Brothers (72 Orchard Street, New York, NY 10002) will ship anywhere and has only a one dozen (same size and color) minimum order.

When you have finished, clean the screen immediately with the paint thinner. Otherwise, the screen will be permanently ruined.

Silkscreening T-shirts is pretty much the same process, except you need to use textile ink, and shirts are more expensive than posterboard.

BLOCK PRINTING

By Peg Averill

FOR T-SHIRTS, ARM-BANDS — ANYTHING!

ANY ART SUPPLY STORE WILL HAVE WHAT YOU NEED — LINOLEUM BLOCK (IT COMES IN ALL SIZES), INK, CARVING TOOLS, AND A ROLLER (TO APPLY THE INK TO THE BLOCK).

THE EASIEST WAY TO PUT YOUR DESIGN ON THE BLOCK IS BY DRAWING IT OUT ON TRACING PAPER, THEN FLIPPING IT OVER (FACE DOWN) ON THE BLOCK WITH A SHEET OF CARBON PAPER. THEN RE-TRACE ONTO THE BLOCK. WHAT YOU WANT TO PRINT, LEAVE. WHAT YOU DON'T WANT TO PRINT, CARVE AWAY. AND BE CAREFUL — THE TOOLS ARE SHARP. TRY TO CARVE AWAY RATHER THAN TOWARDS YOU.

THE TOOLS CAN ALSO BE USED TO MAKE TEXTURED AREAS, BY GOUGING OUT LITTLE HOLES ≣≣≣, OR LINES ≡≡≡, ETC. THE LARGER YOU WORK, THE EASIER IT IS. POSTERS CAN BE DONE ON LINOLEUM BLOCK TOO. THE BIGGEST DRAWBACK IS THE LABOR-TIME USED IN CARVING THE BLOCK AND IN PRINTING, SO BE SURE TO ALLOW YOURSELF PLENTY OF TIME TO DO IT RIGHT. WASH THE BLOCK UP AFTER USE, AND RE-USE LATER, IF YOU LIKE. OH, AND IRON PRINTS MADE ON FABRIC, AND THEY'LL STAY BRIGHTER LONGER.

Action

CAMPAIGNS

By Ed Hedemann

Most movement programs revolve around organizing single, unrelated events—demonstrations, forums, whatever. Were these activities strung together in an integrated fashion—building on one another—the impact and potential for success would be magnified dramatically. Such is the advantage of campaign organizing.

The campaign provides an escalating series of actions over a period of time focused on a target in order to achieve specific goals. Persistence and a systematic approach are key ingredients of a campaign.

All this is not to say demonstrations should not be organized on individual dates like Hiroshima Day (August 6), Tax Day (April 15), and so forth. But, when possible, actions which are part of campaigns can make a stronger statement.

Planning a Campaign

While a demonstration takes a good deal of careful planning, a campaign requires considerably more attention.

The first step is to do the basic groundwork of self-education on the issues and problems to be combated. This can be accomplished through research, study groups, workshops, and conferences.

The next step is to decide *where* to focus our initial efforts. What you need to find are weak points in the opponent's "armour," which will provide levers or handles to focus criticism and action.

During one phase of the Indian campaign for independence from Britain, Gandhi selected the British monopoly on salt as the focus for a campaign. At first this appeared to be an insignificant issue to worry about, compared with independence itself. But because salt affected everyone on this rather hot sub-continent, because its cost was a hardship on the masses, and because it was relatively easy to manufacture (and thereby violate the salt laws), it became an ideal symbol of why independence was being sought. The British viewed the Salt Campaign as "nothing less than to cause a complete paralysis of the administrative machinery." In retrospect, the year-long campaign was the most spectacular effort in the 28-year struggle for independence.*

The United Farm Workers grape boycott is another example of a well chosen campaign in the struggle to win union recognition and better conditions for farm workers.

One of the most important steps in a campaign, after determining the target or focus, is to choose the *short range goals*. Long range goals are easy, e.g., world peace or no military. But sometimes if short range goals are not clearly defined, then the campaign could be stalled. Short range goals should be *winnable* within the near future (providing a boost and the encouragement needed to keep your group moving toward the longer range goals), *measurable* (you ought to be able to tell when you have accomplished them), set on a *timetable* to allow for periods of evaluation, be a *significant step* towards the long range goal(s).

For example, in opposing the establishment of a Junior ROTC unit in a local high school, your medium (or short) range goal might be to prevent the unit from setting up. A short range goal could be getting the local paper (or student body) to come out against the unit. An example of something which is *not* a short range goal would be the holding of a forum or having a picket. These repre-

*See *Conquest of Violence* by Joan Bondurant (pp. 88-102) for an analysis of the campaign.

The first step in a campaign is self-education.

Choose your target or focus carefully.

Clearly defined short range goals are essential to the success of a campaign.

Establish a bottom line.

Determine who the campaign needs in order to succeed.

Who are your opponents and how can their supporters be won over?

sent vehicles toward your goals, rather than goals themselves. Saying that a short range goal is "to educate the student body" has little value as a goal unless it is measurable (e.g., a poll or vote).

In setting goals, you might consider establishing a *bottom line* on what is acceptable, to guard against being coopted into ending the campaign without making any fundamental change.

Analysis

After the goals have been set, an analysis should be made to see who the participants in the campaign are and how they can aid the campaign. Who do you need to participate if the campaign is likely to succeed? Who is on your side now? How are those people reached? Write, call, or visit the community groups which are likely to be sympathetic: cooperatives, clinics, *some* veterans groups, women's groups, Third World groups, student groups, religious organizations, men's groups, and so forth.

Who are the opponents? How can they or their supporters be won over or neutralized. In the example above, the opponents might be the school board or principal. The supporters of the opponents might be the community, PTA, local paper, or clergy.

After this analysis, a plan of action set on a timetable is needed. This plan of action should be in a step-by-step escalation. Escalation is necessary if the pres-

sure on opponents needs to be increased. This does not necessarily mean the previous level of activity is abandoned, but simply that an escalated stage of activity is added to the previous stages. For example, education should be a constant and complementary component of every campaign—never being abandoned. In the campaign above, the first level of action is to approach the school board and ask them to turn down the JROTC application. Should that fail, set up study commissions to analyze the value of a JROTC unit; solicit outside opinions; hold public forums; write letters to the editor; etc.

Should an escalation be necessary, picketing, leafleting, or boycotts might be next. Beyond that, demonstrations, marches, and rallies could be organized. Then perhaps, a student strike, and maybe carefully chosen civil disobedience actions.

Organizers should not lightly go from one level of a campaign to the next. Each stage should be evaluated and considered seriously. Remember, shifting to the next stage does not mean activities at earlier levels should always be forgotten (e.g., going from picketing to a sit-in does not necessarily mean picketing should be discontinued).

Step by Step Escalation in a Nonviolent Campaign

investigation and research
   checking facts and allegations; build-

B-1 Bomber campaign vigil in Senator Alan Cranston's San Francisco office, May 10, 1976. Photo by J.C. Stockwell/Celebrations.

ing an airtight case against opponents and preparing for countercharges

negotiation and arbitration
meeting with opponents to settle conflict before going public; ultimatum issued before moving to next level

public forums, letters to editor, etc.
basic public education on issues

picketing, leafleting, etc.
public contact with opponents

demonstrations, rallies, marches
show of strength by maximizing numbers

Martin Luther King, Ralph Abernathy, and marchers during the Voting Rights campaign in Selma, Alabama, 1965. Photo by UPI.

limited strike
involving those immediately affected

boycott
against company or product in question, if appropriate

limited noncooperation
by those most immediately affected

massive illegal actions
noncooperation, civil disobedience, direct action

general strike

establishing a parallel government

Analyzing a Campaign

This outline is an expansion of an outline used by Joan Bondurant in her analysis of Gandhian campaigns. It can be used either in evaluation of a campaign or in preparation for a campaign.

1. **Dates of the Campaign**

2. **Goals**
   long range
   What were the ultimate goals being sought?
   short range
   What goals were set?
   Were they achievable?
   Were they measurable? Can you tell if they've been accomplished? Would reaching them have brought the campaign measurably closer to the long range goals?
   timetable
   Was a timetable set to allow for periodic measurement of progress of the campaign? What was it?
   bottom line
   Were there any minimum acceptable goals set in advance, so as to avoid being compromised or coopted?

3. **Participants**
   Who was on "our side" at the beginning?
   Who was needed if the campaign was likely to succeed?
   How could those people we needed have been reached?
   Was there a core of people organized and prepared to stay with a sustained campaign so as to provide continuity?

4. **Opponents**
   Who were the opponents?
   Who was calling the shots in opposition to the campaign?
   Was it necessary to win over or neutralize supporters of the opponents in order for the campaign to succeed?
   How were supporters of the opposition won over or neutralized?

5. **Organization and Constructive Work**
   What was the organizational structure to carry out the campaign?
   How were decisions made?
   How was the campaign funded?
   Were there parallel institutions to replace those being opposed or any constructive work done during the campaign?

6. **Preparation for Action**
   What research and investigation was done?
   Education? Public forums? Mass media?
   Training for the main actions?

A campaign must be prepared to escalate in its tactics in order to increase pressure on the opponent.

Each step in escalation must be done with care and deliberation.

A proper analysis of your campaign is useful not only for evaluation, but also for preparation.

Was there adequate preparation for anticipated repression (jail, levies, violence)?

7. **Preliminary Action**

Were approaches made to opponents? Negotiation and arbitration? Petitions or letters?

Was an ultimatum issued? If so, what was the response?

8. **Action**

What forms of action were used: picketing, leafleting, marches, etc.? Was it necessary to escalate to a higher level of struggle? Why and when? Were there strikes, boycotts, or limited noncooperation?

Did the campaign escalate to civil disobedience, mass noncooperation or some form of mass direct action? Why?

Why did the action end when and where it did?

9. **Reaction of Opponents**

Were participants jailed? Beaten? Repressed?

Property seized?

Lies spread? Media blackout?

Intimidation? Ridicule?

Concessions or coopting attempted?

Was campaign basically ignored?

10. **Results**

Were the short range goals achieved?

Any progress made towards the long range goals?

What happened to jailed or injured people?

Was property returned? Amnesty?

Did any of the opponents lose support?

Any property destruction by participants?

11. **Analysis**

Were appropriate tactics used at appropriate times?

Was the best target chosen?

Was the timetable realistic?

Did the campaign meet the timetable? If not, why not?

Was consciousness raised among the general public?

Did the actions clearly communicate the myths, secrets, and realities of the issues and society?

If short range goals were not achieved, why not?

How could the campaign have been improved?

If there was property destruction, did it help or hinder the campaign?

Was the organizational structure adequate to conduct the campaign?

Was the decision making responsive

to participants?

Were there problems in making decisions or a lack of decisiveness?

Who had the initiative during the campaign?

Were there any surprises which hurt or helped the campaign?

Resources on Campaigns

Conquest of Violence, Joan Bondurant, see pp. 45-104, 1965. Analysis of five Gandhian campaigns.

Strategy Manual, Carl Zietlow, 21 pp., 1971. Tactics, dynamics, strategy of campaigns.

A Nonviolent Action Manual, William Moyer, 20 pp., 1977. Organizing demonstrations and campaigns.

Resources Manual for a Living Revolution, Virginia Coover, et al., see pp. 221-232, 1977. Outline of campaign organizing.

Shoulder to Shoulder, Midge Mackenzie, 333 pp., 1975. A history of the militant British campaign for women's suffrage.

Why We Can't Wait, Martin Luther King, Jr., 159 pp., 1964. An account of the 1963 campaign to desegregate Birmingham.

RALLIES AND MARCHES

— a check list —

By Ed Hedemann

The primary purpose of a rally is to gather as many people as possible to show how much support a particular issue has. Ideally, this will in turn generate publicity through the mass media, depending on the numbers, the issue, who is speaking, etc.

Rallies also educate, stimulate further action, raise money, energize supporters, serve notice on the opposition, and help build coalitions. Compared to many other types of actions, rallies involve little risk, have high visibility, and are often fun.

However, rallies involve a number of potential problems. They are particularly weather sensitive—bad weather can lower the turnout precipitously. Because numbers are important, a poor turnout can be disastrous politically (it may appear the cause has little support, thereby encouraging your opponents), financially (collections and sales at the rally are critical in overcoming the debt mounted in organizing), and emotionally (organizers and supporters who do show may be demoralized). Even a good turnout does not guarantee mass media coverage.

In addition, rallies are often long, usually have too many speakers and not enough music, the speakers frequently say nothing new, and the whole event is passive and evokes a party-image atmosphere to many onlookers.

Recognizing that there are different considerations for different rallies, some items in the checklist below will not be appropriate or feasible for some events.

Preliminary Logistics

Initial Meeting

- [ ] develop structure for overall coordination
- [ ] select date with minimal conflicts and a lot of symbolism (e.g., March 28, April 15, August 6)
- [ ] set a time which will avoid darkness and allow people to arrive and return

Location

- [ ] Is it accessible? For the handicapped?
- [ ] Sufficient parking? Shuttling necessary?
- [ ] Any problems with sound?
- [ ] Is it too big or too small?
- [ ] What permits are necessary?
- [ ] Are exits adequate for dispersal?

Timetable

- [ ] brainstorm tasks which need to be done, and put on timeline
- [ ] set up task forces for specific areas needing coordination (e.g., program, logistics, housing, finances, peacekeepers, media, outreach, sales)
- [ ] recruit staff

The Office

- [ ] open an office
- [ ] select a staff
- [ ] put in phones
- [ ] print up stationery
- [ ] find rooms for meetings and training

The purpose of a rally is to make a visible show of strength by turning out the maximum number of people.

Though rallies are particularly weather sensitive and usually rife with too many boring speakers, they can be an energizing experience for the participants.

Advertising

- [ ] leaflets, posters, buttons, stickers, ads, camera-ready materials for organizers
- [ ] articles in newsletters; mailings to sympathetic lists
- [ ] leaflet other events
- [ ] traveling organizer

Buses

- [ ] Is it necessary to rent buses to get people there?
- [ ] Reserve buses and print bus tickets
- [ ] Where will buses unload people and park?

Endorsements

- [ ] prominent individuals to "legitimize" the rally and attract people
- [ ] organizations—coalition building to secure material, political, staff, and monetary support

Fund Raising

- [ ] get loans and contributions to front money for event
- [ ] prepare for a post-rally fund appeal

Media

- [ ] initial press release/conference
- [ ] ongoing work: contacts, releases, interview programs

Site Logistics

Stage

- [ ] locate or build suitable stage
- [ ] chairs for speakers/entertainers
- [ ] podium
- [ ] rain and sun protection
- [ ] establish press area near stage
- [ ] sound system—sufficient microphones for musicians
- [ ] a security system to limit access to stage

Permits

- [ ] obtain permits well in advance
- [ ] Are insurance or clean-up deposits necessary?

Toilets

- [ ] if long rally with a lot of people, you need to rent toilets

Medical

- [ ] nurse/doctor and first aid equipment (ambulance for very large rally)

Food Vendors

- [ ] set up booths for food and drinks—good way to raise money

Directions

- [ ] if location not obvious, put up signs or station people to direct participants

Stage Decorations

- [ ] make banner(s) for stage with official slogans/name

Clean Up

- [ ] have trash cans available at site
- [ ] bring bags and brooms to help col-

A.J. Muste speaking to anti-Vietnam War rally in Central Park, 1966.

lect trash

☐ have a crew (e.g., peacekeepers) who will stay to help clean up

Legal

☐ have legal team/observers assembled if expecting any trouble from authorities or counter-demonstrators

Transportation

☐ have vehicles available for speakers, money, material transportation

Program

Speakers

☐ moderators
☐ line up speakers well in advance, especially celebrities
☐ determine how long program is to be, how many speakers, how long they are to speak (1 minute to 10 minutes, usually)
☐ get proper balances: female/male, minorities, labor, scientists, sponsoring groups, dramatic speakers, organizational speakers
☐ plan for problem of speakers running over schedule
☐ sign language interpreters/foreign language interpreters

Entertainers

☐ line up well in advance; could be key attraction to rally

Fund Appeal

☐ have person near middle of program give pitch, after a particularly moving speech; make several appeals
☐ have volunteers with properly marked buckets cover the crowd thoroughly, more than once

Emergency Decisions

☐ determine mechanism to make last minute decisions (e.g., someone, who is not scheduled, demands to speak)

Crowd Control

For large rallies, organizers must be prepared to deal with the usual problems of crowds: guiding people to and from the site, providing information (medical, buses, etc.), minimize crowding, secure press and stage areas, and minimize impact of hostile folks and counter-demonstrators.

☐ peacekeepers or even small affinity groups could be used
☐ set up training sessions for peacekeepers

Literature and Money

Literature Tables

☐ buttons, posters, T-shirts, follow-up leaflet, stickers, cheap or popular booklets
☐ have at key and visible locations
☐ get tables, chairs, signs, tape, string in advance (rent to others)
☐ make up special commemorative buttons

New York City anti-Vietnam War march. Photo by Harvey Lloyd.

Button Sellers

- [ ] establish system to cover crowd adequately
- [ ] recruit people in advance to sell buttons
- [ ] aprons to make change
- [ ] buttons on apron or on cardboard with price clearly visible

Money Collectors

- [ ] get buckets (or bags) and trusted people to cover the audience during the fund appeal
- [ ] provide a safe place to hold, count, and transport money

Marches

Marches give participants something to do rather than just standing around listening to speeches. Marches expose your views to more of the general public. Marches also have the distinct advantage of being able to link sites. The items listed below are in addition to the considerations above.

The Route

- [ ] decide plan, make up charts, and go over route (by walking)
  check for...
- [ ] rest stops (if a long march)
- [ ] breaks because of traffic signals
- [ ] roads that become narrow, sidewalks that vanish, etc.
- [ ] how long it takes; don't make it too long or you'll lose people

Miscellaneous Points

- [ ] street permits (if not walking on sidewalks) and sound permits
- [ ] vehicles to carry medical equipment, sound equipment, and leaflets
- [ ] people to leaflet during march
- [ ] publicize route and timetable (noting breaks for people to join late)
- [ ] line of march—if arranging march by constituency, issue, organization, etc., have signs and people to mark off each segment
- [ ] money collection—barrels across line of march
- [ ] assembly—allow a half hour to assemble; for large march, allow 1 hour
- [ ] legal observers can be recruited from a nearby law school, or can be simply volunteers with arm bands, placed along the march
- [ ] peacekeepers are needed to aid in directing march, helping pace it, and distracting any hostile onlookers away from march

- [ ] communications system is desirable so line of march can operate smoothly (e.g., using runners, bicyclists, roller skates, walkie talkies)
- [ ] rallies at both ends of march may require 2 sound systems, 2 stages, 2 sets of toilets, etc.
- [ ] finale—every march should have an ending, other than simply dispersing, e.g., rally, sit-in, rousing speech, or song

Follow Up

- [ ] clean up site
- [ ] clean up debts, deposit money from sales and collections
- [ ] thank yous to speakers, big contributors, volunteers, et al.
- [ ] gather mailing list for fund appeals and future actions
- [ ] evaluation

Resources

There is very little in the way of organizer's books on putting together rallies or marches. And what exists is either hard to get or out or print.

An Organizers' Manual for the May 6th Anti-Nuclear March on Washington, edited by Tim Massad, New York Public Interest Research Group, 1979.

Washington Action Nov. 13-15, 1969, Bradford Lyttle, New York, NY, 1970.

Continental Walk Organizer's Manual, The Continental Walk, New York, NY, 1976.

We Come with Naked Hands, Bradford Lyttle, 1964. An account of the San Francisco to Moscow Peace Walk of 1961.

We Walked to Moscow, Jerry Lehman, 1966.

The Continental Walk, ed. Vickie Leonard and Tom MacLean, The Continental Walk, 1977. A picture book account of the Continental Walk for Disarmament and Social Justice.

Manual for Peace Walks, Paul Salstrom, 1967.

CIVIL DISOBEDIENCE ORGANIZING

By Ed Hedemann

Sit-ins, occupations, blockades, and other forms of civil disobedience are confrontational actions characterized chiefly by their illegality. Therein lies their strength—they *cannot* be ignored. While most other actions can be dismissed if they do not involve massive numbers (rallies, voting, etc.) or incredible persistence (longstanding vigils, boycotts, constant education), illegal actions generally force the authorities to deal directly with the demonstrators or risk disruption of their activities.

This chapter is meant not so much as a political or philosophical discussion of civil disobedience as it is an organizing guide. For the former, there are numerous books available (see the references at the end of this chapter). This chapter does not pretend to be a complete prescription for every possible form of civil disobedience. Because of differences in police reactions, issues involved, needs of organizers, there will be a good deal of variation around the country. So I hope this will provide an outline of suggestions for those organizers who are considering the use of civil disobedience.

What Is Civil Disobedience?

There is some confusion about what civil disobedience is or is not. So what follows is a brief definition and description of how civil disobedience is used here.

Henry David Thoreau coined the term through the title of his 1848 essay, "On the Duty of Civil Disobedience." Its use since then has been to attribute all *open and deliberate (usually nonviolent) violation of law for political or social reasons* to civil* disobedience. These violations have been of either "neutral" laws (e.g., blocking induction centers) to demonstrate opposition to the policies of those people or institutions protected by law, or objectionable (such as racist or draft) laws.

Some people use "nonviolent direct action" interchangeably with "civil disobedience," while others claim civil disobedience and direct action are mutually exclusive. The diagram schematically illustrates that direct action can be legal or illegal (civil disobedience), and civil disobedience can be either symbolic or direct action.

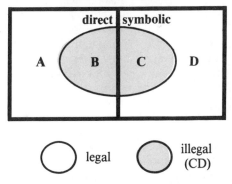

Nonviolent Action

*"Civil" as in a civil "manner" and as in civil "law"

"Disobedience to be civil has to be open and nonviolent."
—**Mohandas Gandhi**

Anti-nuclear examples:
- A: a boycott; or construction of windmill for power
- B: blocking construction of power plant
- C: occupation which does not inhibit construction
- D: vigil at the nuclear power plant

Generally, civil disobedience is best used as an escalating step in a campaign, but there are those times when any other response would be too little and too late.

The knee-jerk use of civil disobedience to solve every problem can lead to a boredom which will inhibit the creativity necessary to achieve success.

"Nonviolent direct action seeks to create a crisis and foster such a tension that a community which has constantly refused to negotiate is forced to confront the issue. It seeks so to dramatize the issue that it can no longer be ignored."
—Martin Luther King, 1963

While the distinction between direct and symbolic action is often blurred, direct action (legal or illegal) generally refers to activities which seek to *directly* alter the situation being protested, rather than appealing to a third party (e.g., Congress or the general public) to make the changes desired. A direct action which is not sustained or uses too few people to realistically accomplish its goals tends to be more symbolic in effect, though direct in intention and style.

Purposes and Timing

Civil disobedience can serve a variety of purposes including

- dramatizing, publicizing, and perhaps winning demands (e.g., Birmingham in 1963)

- shutting down a facility or stopping production (Flint sit-down strike at GM body plant in 1937; May Day demonstration in Washington, D.C. 1971)

- confront opponents who wish to ignore the issues/demands (Wall Street 1979 and Sit-in For Survival at the U.S. Mission to the UN 1978)

- maximizing exposure by presence in jail (Seabrook 1977) or airing views during trial (Chicago conspiracy trial 1969)

- symbolizing human concerns above "private property" (draft card and draft file burnings in the 1960's)

- energize supporters and stimulate other actions (Gandhi Salt March 1930).

None of the above is meant to imply that illegal actions are a substitute for other forms of action, when and where appropriate; or that civil disobedience cannot be done in sequence or conjunction with legal actions.

Generally, civil disobedience is best used as an *escalating step* in a campaign which seeks to increase pressure on the opponents (see "Campaign" chapter). But there are times when it is appropriate in an emergency situation (for example, if the crippled Three Mile Island nuclear power plant is to be restarted), which cannot wait for progress through a normal campaign. Or civil disobedience may be used as a means to express a strong personal protest to injustice, such as Thoreau's nonpayment of a tax to protest the Mexican War and slavery, and Rosa Parks' refusal to leave the "white" section of a

Birmingham bus in 1955.

Dangers

As with any action, civil disobedience can be misused or overused. It can also be underused. A nonviolent movement which seeks to change fundamentally the social or political order must be prepared to employ civil disobedience, if necessary. The powers-that-be depend on the *fear* of arrest and jail to maintain the status quo. A serious movement must seek to break that fear and communicate a sense of fearlessness to their opponents, or else risk running aground should the adversary call their bluff.

Because of the high personal risk, civil disobedience requires careful planning to avoid "sacrificing" people where little is gained. Also, is the major part of the suffering on the shoulders of the demonstrators or on innocent bystanders? Are the people inconvenienced really those involved in the injustice?

Among the dangers involved in illegal actions is the possibility that the participants are not properly prepared for arrest, rough handling, or jail. Also, arrests may not occur, demonstrators may not be able to stick it out, supplies may be blocked, or the action coopted into ending before any gain is made. Furthermore, time, energy, and money could be tied up and drained by legal proceedings which provide little progress. Without adequate groundwork, the "target" may not be clear to the public or the action may be misinterpreted by the media. And finally, civil disobedience may be employed *too early*. Attempts should be made to solve problems, before employing civil disobedience, to minimize potential alienation from a seemingly uncalled for escalation of tactics. The knee-jerk use of civil disobedience to solve every problem can lead to a boredom which will inhibit the creativity necessary to achieve success.

Planning Civil Disobedience

Because of the illegality of these actions, civil disobedience demonstrations will always carry a number of uncertainties: Will the police or employees react violently? Will demonstrators or supporters break nonviolent discipline? Will there be provocateurs? Will the police try to prevent the demonstrators from reaching the target? Will they play a waiting game by refusing to arrest so that demonstrators and media dribble away frustrated? Is the timing such that the action will happen before (or after) supporters and media reach the site?

So planning for the action must be done with great care once the decision has been made that civil disobedience is desirable. Listed below are the steps which might be used and some questions to be answered in planning for a civil disobedience action.

1. Set up a meeting to determine the politics of the event (issues to be focused on) and the scenario to be employed.

2. Select the target that is clearly related to the issue and will allow a chance of direct confrontation between the campaign and the opponents.

3. Determine when the action should occur, figuring how long it will take to organize and when it will be most effective.

4. Length of time. Decide whether the event is to last for a specified length of time (if so, make early announcement to that effect), or until demands are met or demonstrators are arrested.

5. Will there be a role for people not risking arrest?

6. Is the action to be announced, encouraging mass participation? Or will it be an unannounced activity with a small number of people? Secrecy is sometimes crucial for the success of an action, but can create distorted information, fear, mistrust, elitism, and police spying.

7. Will affinity groups (see below) be used?

8. Will the action be preceeded by a march or several marches converging on the site?

9. Do guidelines (e.g., asking that all demonstrators agree to nonviolent tactics) need to be drawn up for participants to agree to? If so, then circulate a draft of guidelines for approval.

10. Will the police be contacted in advance?

11. Will the action be largely symbolic, or will it be a sustained mass action?*

_____
*Of course, small, limited events can be effective direct actions.

12. What are the contingencies if the scenario doesn't go as planned?

13. Under what circumstances should the demonstration be postponed or called off? This is an important consideration to avoid the temptation of coopting the action under the inevitable pressures of last minute maneuvering by the authorities.

14. Prepare a detailed timeline from the present to the time of the event, listing all the work which needs to be done and when it must be accomplished.

15. Form subcommittees (e.g., media, logistics, materials, recruitment/ outreach, finances, training, support)—with convenors to guarantee they will meet—to carry out the preparation for action. Set the time for another general meeting to review the progress of the preparation.

Preparation for Civil Disobedience

Much of the preparation for civil disobedience is similar to that for marches and rallies (e.g., office, fund raising, media, advertising, housing, permits). So to avoid repetition, this section will emphasize the parts of preparation which are different for civil disobedience. It will be assumed that the organizer is familiar with the "Marches and Rallies" chapter.

Materials. If the action is to be announced in advance, then one of the first tasks is to produce a "Call to Action" in order to notify and recruit participants. Later, posters, stickers, buttons, and a "handbook for participants" might be developed. Handbooks for mass civil disobedience actions have proven useful in simplifying the necessary training and educating about legal materials, etc.

Recruitment. In conjunction with the "Call to Action," existing affinity groups and participants in past actions should be alerted about this event. Recruit through all the normal channels—fliers in organizational mailings, articles in newsletters, visits to meetings of sympathetic organizations, and so forth.

Check Out Target. Make map and take photos of entrances, possible barriers, and access roads. Go over routes to target(s). Check the flow of pedestrian and vehicular traffic at key times. How

To avoid cooptation, determine in advance, under what cirumstance the action should be called off.

Carefully check out the target site of the action in advance.

Two affinity groups during Wall Street Action, 1979. Photo by Steve Jackson.

Decision making, legal consequences, training, and a support mechanism should all be worked out or determined well in advance.

can entrances be blocked (if that is part of the plan)? Are there security guards who might disrupt the plan? If there is more than one entrance or site, how should demonstrators be apportioned to cover them? If in summer, are there shady spots for demonstrators?

Decision Making. If something unexpected occurs during the action or just before, what emergency decision making will be employed? A coordinator? Affinity groups? Fall back plans? Postponement?

Legal. Investigate all appropriate laws that may be violated, and possible as well as likely penalties. Form a committee of lawyers and legal observers. Prepare to deal with questions of bail solidarity, noncooperation, minors, and trial.

Training. Training sessions, besides being valuable in preparing and educating potential participants, are useful to recruit uncertain people. Training sessions usually are key times to form affinity groups. Set up a schedule of training sessions, find locations, advertise the sessions, develop a pool of trainers with a coordinator, and put together a packet of materials for each trainer.

Police. This is often controversial, and usually put in terms of "whether or not to negotiate with the police." If the action is announced with the expectation of being large (100 or more risking arrest), it may be of value to contact the police—not to negotiate, but reassure them that the demonstrators are nonviolent (to minimize police violence or erratic behavior) and to discover as much as possible about their planned reaction. The police will always have

two primary questions "What are you going to do?" and "How many?"

Peacekeeping. Needed primarily for those not risking arrest but who will be at the action. They may accidently get mixed in with those being arrested or play an unhelpful role, such as egging on the authorities.

Support. Any successful civil disobedience requires people (who will not be arrested) to provide support for media contact, take photographs, bail (if necessary), establish identification, look after cars, contact relatives and employers, communicate with opponents, bring in supplies, and provide a communications network among those jailed if in separate facilities. Each affinity group needs to have at least one support person who is plugged into the support network early.

Affinity Groups. Depending on the nature and size of the action, the use of affinity groups may be warranted. If so, they should be formed well before the action takes place. These are usually groups of 8 to 15 people (ideally, friends) who operate as a unit within a large civil disobedience action. At best, members of affinity groups provide personal support for each other during times of stress, are able to isolate provocateurs (especially if all participants are part of affinity groups), and provide a basis for decision making.

Personal Supplies. If the action involves an overnight stay (e.g., nuclear power plant occupation), then supplies will have to be brought in: food, water, sleeping bag, flashlight, shovel and toilet paper, medical, salt tablets, weather protection, toiletries, tooth brush, change, hard protective case for glasses, extra pairs of underwear (cushions body during dragging and allows one to be washed while other is worn), note paper and pen, coat (jails are often cold, and a coat can also act as a pillow). Don't drink a lot of liquids before the action and use the toilet just before departure; it may be a long time before you have access to a toilet again. Don't wear high heels, dresses, sharp objects, necklaces, earrings, loose shoes (can come off during dragging), nylon underwear (reacts with tear gas).

Demonstration Paraphernalia. Signs and banners would be desirable for any march to site, on site, or to hang out of a building. Chains for the entrances, if part of the scenario. Costumes, leaflets to explain the action to passersby and employees.

Contact Employees. Establish contact with employees and union at the protest site. Generally, they are not the target of the action, so any friendly contact with them is a step closer to success. Leaflet at shift changes. Also, there are always sympathetic employees who are willing to pass along memos or other information (to demonstrators) on the planned counter-actions by authorities.

Ultimatum. Gandhi felt it was important to issue an ultimatum to opponents giving them a last chance to agree to the demands. He also wanted to make it clear to supporters and the general public that all reasonable channels of communication and resolution were tried.

The Check-in. In large actions, a check-in of affinity groups is important for purposes of an accurate count, proper distribution/coordination of demonstrators, and last minute update.

The Night Before. The night before the action should be low key, allowing sufficient sleep, and no heavy last minute decision making. Perhaps a gathering for pot luck supper, singing, etc.

The Staging Area. A staging area (which might also be a communications area) should be designated for participants to gather before marching to the target or committing civil disobedience. This is important to minimize demonstrators simply drifting into the action at various times in an uncoordinated fashion. Also, is there transportation to and from the site?

The Action

Since it is not possible to go through every possible form of civil disobedience,* I will focus on the organizing of three common types: 1) sit-ins, 2) blockades, and 3) mass occupations. In all of these cases, try to initiate the action as deliberately and steadily as possible. If moving to or from more than one location, try to make the action simultaneous to maximize the impact.

Sit-ins

The sit-in usually occurs in an office, normally involves a small (say, 5 to 50) number of people (tough to get more in most offices), and is often unannounced (or else the chances of getting in would

*See *The Politics of Nonviolent Action*, volume 2, Gene Sharp.

To facilitate timing and coordination, be sure a staging area for the action is set up.

Sit-ins are often unannounced, usually small in number, and frequently occur in offices.

Sit-in for affirmative action hiring on San Francisco's "Auto Row," 1964. Photo by Haword Harawitz.

Blockade of school bus to protest school conditions, Georgia 1968. Photo by UPI.

If the sit-in might be an overnight venture, take care of logistical considerations, such as food and communications.

be reduced). The group can enter as a delegation and refuse to leave if demands are not met. Or, normal operations can be disrupted by occupying places for customers, such as the civil rights lunch counter sit-ins in 1960.

Orderly conduct is critical, if you wish to minimize adverse publicity and increase sympathy. Don't hassle secretaries or other workers. Generally, act with discipline and restraint. Don't destroy property except under very special and limited circumstances (e.g., draft files or blueprints for weapons manufacture).

If it appears to be a long stay, be sure you have the necessary supplies, such as food, water, toilet facilities, a way to communicate to supporters, signs to put up on doors or hang out windows, etc. Organize sleeping shifts, so at least two people are awake at all times. If outside contacts are limited, make certain media is updated by supporters. Try to get a public statement on demands from opposition. Any negotiation should involve approval of both sit-iners and supporters. Amnesty should be part of any agreement to leave. When leaving, make that a demonstration as well, even if demands are not met.

Because a sit-in is sometimes isolated from the public, there is a greater chance of rough handling by the police or even the use of tear gas. Be aware of and prepared to use all possible emergency exits.

Blockades of all types of vehicles—cars, trucks, trains, ships, airplanes—as well as entrances to buildings and even whole cities have occurred with varying success.

Blockades

There are a whole variety of blockade types: entrances to buildings or offices

(Wall Street 1979), roads or highways (protesting lack of stop sign), waterways (arms shipments to Pakistan 1971), railroads (Vietnam troop train blockades in Berkeley 1965), airport runways (new Tokyo airport 1978), construction sites (nuclear power plants), cities (May Day actions in Washington, DC, 1971). Successful blockades have involved anywhere from one person to thousands.

If the number is small then it is sometimes useful to consider chains or handcuffs to help keep an entrance shut. Such small actions means it is essential to keep the action unannounced. With large numbers clogging a small entrance, chains are not as important; except as a means of slowing down removal or arrest by having bunches of people chained together (Trident action, Groton, Connecticut, 1979).

Road and especially railway blockades carry the added danger of being run over. Trains cannot swerve and their breaking distance is long. The road blockade of the Seabrook reactor pressure vessel (1978) was less of a risk because it moved so slowly.

Surprisingly, sea blockades can be very effective. With enough rowboats, canoes, or sailboats even very large ships have been stopped. For example, the 1971 blockade of the Pakistani ships, trying to load arms in US ports for use in the Bangledesh war, was successful (see *Blockade* by Richard Taylor).

The massive blockades of the New York Stock Exchange in 1979 (where 1000 were arrested) and the 1971 May Day action in Washington, DC (where 13,000 were arrested) announced their goal as stopping the Exchange from opening and shutting down the city, respectively. Though these failed in their ultimate goal, they succeeded marvelously in disrupting business as usual and calling attention *most dramatically* to the issues.

If a blockade is announced in advance, the authorities will usually try to prevent demonstrators from getting to their target. For example, during the Wall Street action most demonstrators never got to the entrances, because police set up five blockade check points. But demonstrators, viewing the check points simply as extensions of the entrances, blocked the check points.

Other common police counter-tactics (in blockades and especially occupations) include tear gas: CN (a mild gas which disperses rapidly), CS (more severe, causes nausea and stinging), DM (extreme nausea, vomiting, and diarrhea, rarely used in demonstrations). There are a number of preventive measures that can be taken, but in any case *do not panic and run*, that only exaggerates the effects of these "gases." Make sure demonstrators are familiar with how to deal with these techniques. Elaborate paraphernalia such as gas masks are often counterproductive since they encourage strong police reaction, inhibit communication, and sometimes don't work.

Police dogs and horses are used more for their psychological effect on demonstrators. Dogs are trained to hold, not bite, but yanking a leg out of their mouths will cause lacerations. Police can more easily control demonstrators if they are standing, so faced with a physical confrontation, sit together. Never run. Running may create panic as well as result in over-reaction by the police.

Fire hoses may be withstood if you hold on to each other in a human chain, lie flat, or duck behind a stationary object (e.g., a lamp post or tree).

If the blockade involves moving targets, intelligence becomes crucial.

When will the shipment be made? The best way to get such information is through sympathetic employees, but beware of planted false information. Often, the planning must involve a reliable telephone tree which can spring demonstrators into action at a moment's notice. Also, key observation points have proven essential to alerting demonstrators.

Occupations

Loosely speaking, the term occupation is being used here to represent a sit-in on a mass scale. Examples of occupations would include the 1964 Free Speech Movement occupation of the Sproul Hall administration building on the University of California at Berkeley campus (801 were arrested after a night's stay) and the 1977 Seabrook (New Hampshire) nuclear power plant occupation (1415 were arrested after a day's stay). In both cases there was no blocking of entrances or construction, but business as usual was disrupted until the demonstrators were removed.

Occupations, being mass events, are difficult to pull off without being announced in advance. But spontaneous ones have occurred at the urging of a speaker following a mass rally outside the protest site. For most occupations, however, the prior announcement has given authorities time to devise countermeasures. Sometimes these countermeasures are fences hastily put up. So the question arises on how to "cross the fences." Demonstrators should be prepared to either climb, cut, or dig under the fences after thorough discussion well in advance of the action, since this has caused a good deal of debate in the movement.

Occupations are often appropriate times to attempt symbolic conversion of the facilities involved. Also, should the occupation appear to be a long scale event, it will be desirable to leave a core of people on site (assuming there is ac-

Loosely speaking, occupations are sit-ins carried out on a mass scale.

Occupations are often appropriate times to attempt symbolic conversion of the facilities involved.

Occupation of Seabrook nuclear power plant, 1977. Photo by Grace Hedemann.

Arrest at Pentagon during Continental Walk, 1976. Photo by Dorothy Marder.

A mass event, by nature being of short duration, must be planned with a logical conclusion or it will end through attrition.

Though the decision on cooperation with arrest is an individual matter, it helps to role play and discuss in advance.

cess to and from), which can be periodically rotated. And a communications network to alert nearby supporters, should authorities decide to evict them. This was done successfully at the Wyhl (West Germany) nuclear power plant site occupation in 1975. A large number of people cannot hold out for a long period of time without such provisions. Too often, poorly planned mass events end through attrition, allowing police to crack down on the exhausted core group which remains.

Arrest

In any of these forms of civil disobedience, thought should be given in advance to how to react to arrest—cooperate, go limp, link arms, sing, avoid arrest. The latter, often referred to as "mobile tactics," can become a teasing tactic to avoid arrest. More often than not it will encourage stronger police reaction out of frustration. Linking arms can also create overreaction by the police. Singing precludes verbal communication with the police to explain the noncooperation. A rigid body makes dragging by the police much easier than a totally limp body. In either case, the police may try to force a person to walk by twisting a hand or arm in an unnatural way. A person who does not cooperate, should be prepared to follow through; because walking after an arm twist is applied may encourage the police to try the same tactic on demonstrators who will never walk—hurting them seriously. Being dragged by the feet, may endanger the head. Police have been known to use stretchers, but don't count

on it. The problem with cooperating is it helps end the demonstration sooner. In blockades, cooperation makes less sense. In any case, though the decision on cooperation with arrest is an individual matter, it helps to role play and discuss it in advance.

During arrest, every demonstrator should note the name, number, and type of police officer making the arrest. Write it down as soon as possible.

Thought should also be given to post-arrest processing: name, address, fingerprints, mug shot, strip search, and a variety of other information (driver's license, mother's maiden name, job, education, drug use, previous arrests, etc.) can be asked for. Refusal to give some or any of this or a refusal to walk *may* result in additional charges, in a night court appearance for arraignment (rather than being released and a later date set for arraignment), bail being set (rather than release on recognizance), or even forcible finger printing or strip search.

A policy should be adopted on "bail solidarity"—no one accepts bail or release until everyone can (aside from those who must bail out). Part of the problem with this is that it is sometimes hard to be sure that the authorities will not change their policies midprocessing or will process differently at different locations. A way to communicate, such as through sympathetic laywers who have access to the jails, needs to be established.

Court and Lawyers

The first time you are likely to see a

judge is during the arraignment, where you will be asked to plead, should the judge decide there is enough evidence to warrant a trial. There are five possible options for plea: guilty, not guilty, nolo contendere (unwilling to contest), "creative" plea (e.g., "I plead for humanity"), or standing mute. The latter three are *usually* interpreted as "not guilty" by the judge. A guilty plea normally results in immediate sentencing. A trial date is set at arraignment, but could be preceeded by a date for "motions."

Considerations after arraignment are whether to accept representation by a lawyer or go "pro se" (represent yourself); whether the trial will be based on a *technical defense* ("I wasn't warned that I was about to be arrested"), a *Constitutional defense* ("It was my First Amendment right to be on that military base distributing leaflets"), a *competing harms defense* ("I had to break the trespass law in order to warn about the greater danger of the arms race"), or an *offense* (that is, instead of defending what you did, attempt to turn the trial around by accusing the authorities of crimes against humanity); whether to pay a fine, do "community work," or agree to supervised probation if found guilty; or whether to accept guilt on a lesser charge if a stiffer one is thrown out (plea bargaining).

If you choose to be represented by a lawyer, it is best to have one who understands your organization, action, defense. Work with sympathetic lawyers in advance so they can be familiar with your needs.

Jail

Whether awaiting processing, arraignment, trial, or serving time, one of the first things you'll notice about jail is that it is *monotonous*. Ways to break the boredom and routine are sleep, singing, reading, writing, and sharing and learning with other prisoners. Care should be taken before launching into a campaign to organize the prisoners. Other prisoners will be suspicious of short timers and may even be psyched up against you as "unpatriotic commies," etc. Common forms of organizing have included noisemaking, singing, helping prisoners with their cases, sitdowns or work strikes, and hunger strikes. But that is all another subject.

References

On the Duty of Civil Disobedience, Henry David Thoreau, 21pp., 1848. The classic.

Civil Disobedience: Theory and Practice, Christian Bay and Charles Walker, 60 pp, 1975. Read pages 32-46 for good outline on organizing for civil disobedience.

Power of the People, ed. Robert Cooney and Helen Michalowksi, 240 pp, 1977. Many examples in 20th century America.

Politics of Nonviolent Action, Gene Sharp, 1973. See chapter 8 and pp. 315-319, in particular.

A Manual for Direct Action, Martin Oppenheimer and George Lakey, 138 pp, 1965. An excellent how-to-do-it manual.

Blockade, Richard Taylor, 174 pp, 1977. An account of the successful action against the Pakistani arms ships.

Do It!, Jerry Rubin, 1970. See pages 33-36 for account of Berkeley troop train blockade.

Handbook for the Land and Sea Blockade of the Seabrook Reactor Pressure Vessel, Clamshell Alliance, 39 pp, 1978. A manual for blockade participants.

See various **Occupation Handbooks** by Clamshell, Coalition for a Non-Nuclear World, Wall Street Action, Abalone, SHAD, Rocky Flats, Livermore Action, Blockade the Bombmakers, etc., 1977–1982.

"Modern justification for civil disobedience . . . is frequently based on a conviction that obedience would make one an accomplice to an immoral or unjust act or one which is seen to be . . . illegal."
—Gene Sharp, 1973

NONVIOLENCE TRAINING

By Grace Hedemann

Training is part of a teaching process. Training prepares people in planning and organizing for nonviolent social and structural change. Training can cover such general areas as philosophy, personal behavior, organization development, decision making, specific skills, and campaign development. Training begins the process of unlearning much about the attitudes and behaviors taught in general society.

Training begins the process of unlearning much about the attitudes and behaviors taught in general society.

Training Purposes

In preparing for action, nonviolence training

- raises philosophical issues of nonviolence, and sets the tone and style of a demonstration, campaign and movement
- develops confidence, solidarity, and cooperation, helping people to develop confidence to be in action situations, confidence in companions, and confidence in the organization
- provides a communication link between organizers and participants
- can develop discipline
- facilitates a more democratic decision making process
- clarifies goals
- analyzes and tests tactics and strategies by developing new alternatives through experimentation
- enables skills to be learned quickly
- is an organizing and recruiting tool
- prepares particpants to train others.

Training sessions can vary from an hour in length to several years.

Gandhi made nonviolence training an integral part of the Indian movement for independence from Britian.

Training Session Length

Training sessions vary in length depending on the purpose. A session lasting several hours prepares participants for a particular demonstration or as peacekeepers for a rally, march or action. One day sessions prepare participants for a particular demonstration, covers one aspect of a campaign, or introduces a number of tactics. A weekend session usually covers the above, in addition to strategy and campaign development, philosophy and its application to a particular project or strategy, or introduces a national campaign. Sessions lasting from a week to several years are more comprehensive, include an action project or campaign, extensive skills training, and experimentation with the applications of nonviolence.

History

Gandhi made nonviolence training an integral part of the Indian movement for independence from Britain. In the beginning of that struggle the training was rudimentary: "pep talks" by Gandhi followed by participants pledging themselves to nonviolence.

Later, a day-long fast for self-purification before each action was added. Training emphasized discipline, songs, prayers, and mass meetings. Skills taught included crowd control as well as thieves control, medical aid, and yoga. Rigid discipline meant a successful campaign. Discipline meant faith in God, obedience to a leader, an ability to work cooperatively in "army units," daily prayer, keeping a personal diary, and spinning as a constructive program.

Three writers influenced the early nonviolence training movement in the United States: Richard Gregg, Aldous Huxley, and Shridharami. Richard Gregg (*The Power of Nonviolence* [1934] and *Training for Peace*]1937]) emphasized the importance and unique contributions of training in the Gandhian movement. Aldous Huxley (*Ends and Means* [1937]) stressed that new forms of education and psychophysical re-education were necessary for effective social change. Shridharami's *War Without Violence* (1939) served as the basic study book out of which grew the Congress of Racial Equality (CORE).

In the early 1940's the cell group and the workshop were the vehicles for nonviolence training. Today, the closest thing to a cell is the affinity group, although the cell put a lot of stress on study as well as action. These cell groups and workshops experimented with role plays in preparation for draft board appearances and civil rights activities.

The Fellowship of Reconciliation (FOR) formed the Nonviolent Action Committee with A.J. Muste, John Swomley, and James Farmer in 1942. Their teams provided leadership on racism and militarism. CORE grew out of this FOR committee. From 1947 to 1954 Bayard Rustin and George Houser conducted month long training and action projects with groups from 15 to 25 who were college age or older. Their purpose was to eliminate segregation and discrimination in the Washington, D.C., area. CORE's training included lectures on nonviolence, role plays, sociodrama, group decision making, action, and evaluation. Participants developed their own "community" through working together. They met with community leaders, negotiated settlements, learned publicity techniques, and led direct action projects. CORE's concept of training was constant interaction of analysis, training, and action.

During the Montgomery bus boycott (1956), the Southern Christian Leadership Conference (SCLC) took the religious tradition of mass meetings and used them for political education and action. Through singing, preaching, teaching, and prayer, people developed solidarity, identity, emotional commitment, and the strength for a grueling boycott. Weekly (later semi-weekly) mass meetings were held in black churches with pep talks on nonviolence. In Birmingham (1963) nonviolent training emphasized role plays, lectures, and making a commitment to nonviolence by signing a pledge card. Martin Luther King, Jr., lectured nightly at the mass meetings on nonviolence.

There was a close relationship between the peace and civil rights move-

In the US nonviolence training began with the civil rights movement.

CIVIL RIGHTS TRAINING WORKSHOP

James Lawson, Southern FOR staff, developed in 1957 the following training session used throughout the South with groups ranging in size from 10 to 300 people on campuses and in communities on two successive days. These workshops laid the groundwork for the large scale civil rights direct action civil disobedience movement which began with the sit-ins on February 1, 1960.

(1) History of nonviolence with Gandhi, Luthulhi in South Africa, Dolci, World War II, and the U.S. scene starting with religious liberty, the Freedom Rides, CORE and other civil rights activities.

(2) Theology of nonviolence from the old to the new testaments.

(3) Methods of nonviolence.

(4) Role playing.

(5) Discussion of Montgomery bus boycott with the FOR "comic book."

(6) Participants were expected to do some nonviolent experimentation in their lives overnight.

(7) Reporting on what they did and learned in their nonviolent experiments.

(8) Attempt to solicit commitment to SCLC.

(9) Nonviolent strategy for change from case studies.

(10) Begin planning a potential local campaign or project.

(11) Develop an on-going organization.

Carl Zietlow, *A Reflective History of Training for Nonviolent Action in the Civil Rights and Peace Movements 1942-1972.*

ments. They had common philosophical roots, trainers, and techniques. In 1962 the Student Nonviolent Coordinating Committee (SNCC) and the New York Society of Friends held the Nyack Consultation on Training for Nonviolent Action where 25 peace and civil rights activists planned extensive training programs. Mississippi Freedom Summer training in Oxford, Ohio, was conducted by peace trainers and financed by the National Council of Churches for the civil rights movement. Many young people came from the universities where free speech and university reform movements were the strongest. A number of Students for a Democratic Society (SDS) leaders had already been active in SNCC. These same students started organizing teach-ins against the Indochina War. Women, outraged about the overt sexism in SNCC, started women's caucuses in SDS chapters, beginning the early stages of the women's movement.

Tactical nonviolence training for actions became prevalent during the mid 1960's in the civil rights and late 1960's in the Indochina War movements in preparation for mass campaigns and demonstrations. Lectures, discussions and role plays were the basic components. In the Indochina War movement the commitment and philosophy of nonviolence became secondary to its tactical adherence. Typical three hour training sessions included orientation, role plays, quick decisions, and situation analysis. The majority of sessions were conducted to train marshals (known as peacekeepers today) for rallies and marches, not participants. These trainers became specialists. They no longer served the dual role of organizer and trainer. Organizers increasingly relied on training staffs.

By 1971 it became evident that trainers and organizers needed to work more closely together. Jerry Coffin, on leave from WRL to the Mayday Tribe staff, wrote the *Mayday Tactical Manual*. Carl Zietlow and Brian Jaffee wrote *Training Manual for Nonviolent Direct Action for Spring Actions*. Participants, as part of affinity groups, were being trained regionally at training centers for the People's Lobby and the Mayday Actions. Total arrests for those two weeks of activities reached about 15,000 in Washington, D.C., alone.

The United Farm Workers movement developed (in 1965) in a very similar way to the civil rights movement. Workers were trained at large meetings where all who joined the strike took a nonviolent pledge. Cesar Chavez, who like King was a charismatic leader, lectured long and hard on nonviolence. The unique contribution to nonviolent training technique by the Farm Workers movement was the El Teatro Campesino. They performed during every mass meeting training session from 1966 with actors who were also farm workers. They performed role plays on stage about conflict situations workers could expect to encounter on the picket line. Then the audience determined through lively discussion, impromptu role plays, and evaluation, possible solutions. Discipline was required and considered essential to the success of the movement.

During the late 1960's and early 1970's, training centers with permanent staffs were founded (e.g., Chicago Nonviolent Training Center, Institute for the Study of Nonviolence in California, Quaker Project on Community Conflict in New York, Martin Luther King, Jr. School of Social Change in Chester, Pennsylvania, and Movement for a New Society in Philadelphia). A network of trainers grew. National and international trainers' conferences were held through the 1970's with new techniques being explored for decision making and group process.

Nonviolence training was an integral part of the anti-nuclear movement from the beginning of its mass activist phase in the late 1970's. Training sessions provided preparation for civil disobedience, usually a blockade or occupation at a nuclear power plant. For the larger actions handbooks were written containing logistical, political, legal, and philosophical information. Training sessions eventually grew from three to eight hours. Though the "tactical versus philosophical" nonviolence discussion surfaced almost immediately, philosophical nonviolence continued to be presented during most sessions across the country. Participants were trained for affinity group decision making and action with role plays, quick decisions, hassle lines, and evaluation. During the 1977 Seabrook occupation, affinity groups learned to operate collectively in stressful conditions, relying on decision making techniques learned during training sessions.

The relationship between the anti-nuclear movement and the peace movement has been close, just as the civil rights and peace movements were close. The New England American Friends Service Committee provided the first trainers for the 1976 Seabrook occupation. As the anti-nuclear movement grew,

ANTI-NUCLEAR TRAINING SESSION

Typical Training Session for civil disobedience action at a nuclear power plant. April, 1979 SHAD Alliance for Shoreham Occupation. 6½ hours.

(1) Introductions	5-10 minutes
(2) Explanation on the Training Session	5-10 minutes
(3) History of SHAD, Shoreham and Seabrook	10 minutes
(4) Nonviolence	45 minutes
(5) "Active Nonviolence" Slide Show	30 minutes
(6) Sexism, Racism, Classism	20 minutes
(7) Consensus	20 minutes
LUNCH 40 minutes	
(8) Consensus Exercise	20 minutes
(9) Nuclear Weapons/Nuclear Power	30 minutes
(10) Occupation Scenario	30 minutes
(11) Occupation Guidelines	5 minutes
(12) Legal	30 minutes
BREAK 10 minutes	
(13) Mass Arrest Role Play	25 minutes
(14) Fears & Feelings	20 minutes
(15) Affinity Groups Formation	30 minutes
(16) Evaluation	10 minutes

organizers and trainers came from the peace and environmental movements. During training sessions and in handbooks, links were made between the issues of nuclear power, nuclear weapons, sexism, and racism. Many antinuclear activists had been activists during the Indochina War. Even organizers' training programs conducted by Movement for a New Society (MNS) and the War Resisters League trained antinuclear activists as well as peace, religious, co-op, and community housing activists.

Exercises

Exercises used in nonviolence training usually fall into one of the following categories: process, group dynamics, sensitivity, vision/strategy, and tactics. Process exercises include introductions, evaluation, facilitation, and clarification. Group dynamics exercises include listening, participation level, group observation, and priority setting. Sensitivity exercises include energizing, cooperative and sharing games, confidence building, and trust development. Vision and strategy exercises include methods to pinpoint ultimate goals, analyze case histories, and develop long term strategy. Finally, tactic exercises include role plays, extended role plays, hassle line, quick decision, and situation analysis.

For the purpose of brevity, I will only focus on the tactic exercises. Extensive information on the other exercises is available from Martin Jelfs, *Manual for Action* (1977), and Coover, Deacon, Esser and Moore, *Resource Manual for a Living Revolution* (1977).

General Role Play

General Role Play is an impromptu acting out of a given situation in preparation for an anticipated event or to evaluate a past incident. The purpose is to analyze the dynamics of roles, emotional responses, strategy testing, and to develop interpersonal skills in anticipating and reacting to these situations.

Trainers should prepare for role plays by writing a scenario in advance (choosing a relevant anticipated action), and consider the values to be transmitted. The purpose of the role play should be determined. Describe the scene, characters, roles, and note any special instructions for a particular group. It is important not to reinforce stereotypes, and to create people and situations that are real. Then list questions that you think are pertinent to ask during the evalua-

The role play is an impromtu acting out of a situation in preparation for an anticipated event.

Street speaking role play by participants of 1980 WRL Organizers Program. Photo by Grace Hedemann.

tion discussion.

In presenting a role play, briefly describe what a role play is and how it works to the participants. Explain that it is not a test and no one is being judged. Emphasize that there is no correct response. Then present the scenario quickly, vividly, and clearly. Limit the number of questions and detailed answers. Let people use their imagination. Indicate the physical layout. Ask participants to volunteer for the various roles. Give special instructions for each role separately to ensure spontaneous reactions. Give participants a few minutes to plan their strategy or tactics. Trainers may at this point take individuals aside to whisper the special instructions within a role. Cut the role play at a natural break when it exhausts itself, when the major issues have been raised, or when participants have become over involved. Trainers should be observing the action carefully and be ready to recall incidents which might be omitted in the evaluation discussion.

The evaluation should be brisk and to the point. The group might want to move to another location for discussion, to allow everyone to unwind from the action. Initially allow spontaneous reactions from all the characters. Get the facts on what happened, who did what, and the response. Ask particular characters how they felt when a given incident took place. Probe for alternative solutions. Question conclusions as a relevant tactic. Question solutions in light of nonviolence philosophy. Participants should summarize results of the discussion.

Hassle Line

Hassle Line is a one-on-one verbal role play. In a short amount of time a hassle line will generate a lot of information. All particpants must take an active role. Have participants form two lines facing each other one-on-one. The scenario is presented with one line taking one role and the other line taking the second role (e.g., Wall Street worker and demonstrator discussing nuclear power investment). Give participants no more than one minute to get into their role. Start and freeze the action within three to five minutes. Reverse roles, and mix participants within a line. This procedure minimizes falling out of the role with the same partner. Give a minute to prepare for role and begin action. Evaluate the same as a role play.

Quick Decision

Quick Decision exercise presents a crisis situation to an individual or small group (3-4 people) which requires an immediate solution. The exercise encourages initiative and action, and tests good decision making process.

Trainers ask participants to break into groups of three or four. Explain the group's function and scenario. Set a two to three minutes time limit. Start and stop discussion with a stop watch. Do not listen to pleas, "Just one more minute!" Have participants remain with the group for discussion and evaluation. Trainers ask each group to report on their solution. Compare various solutions. Have each group describe the decision making process that led to the solution. Evaluate the process as well as the solution.

The hassle line is a one-on-one verbal role play.

Quick decision exercise presents a crisis situation to an individual or small group which requires an immediate solution.

Situation Analysis

Situation Analysis presents graphically a specific event with character, roles, location and physical surroundings. The exercise explores alternative tactics through discussion and diagram, and tests discipline during a crisis.

Trainers should place situation on a chart or blackboard. Explain the situation verbally. Give the group a few minutes to think about it. Ask how each of the participants in the situation would respond and why. Explore various reactions and alternatives. Trainers can throw in a new variable after discussion begins to assimilate pressures of a real situation. Encourage the group to role play a disagreement. Put a time limit on the decision making process. Then evaluate.

Controversies and Dangers

Despite the proven value of nonviolence training, there exists many differences of opinion, controversies, and important limitations that all trainers should be aware of. First, despite good intentions, training can dictate politics, become rigid, create an elite, and exclude working people from actions because more time is required to be trained. Some people feel that training is an inadequate substitution for experience. They even see training becoming a substitute for, or possibly an escape from action. Training can be done for the sake of it. As a result, training diverts time, energy and resources from the ultimate goal. Some people question whether training is facilitating action or teaching the "correct line" and thus eliminating spontaneity and creativity.

To minimize these pitfalls, the following guidelines should be helpful for good training. First, participants' input on agenda, facilitation and evaluation are vital. Second, always be clear that training is subordinate to organizing. Third, stress participants' aspirations and tailor sessions to the constituency. Fourth, consider the dynamics and the physical needs of the group. Fifth, train in teams. Sixth, exchange roles with organizers periodically. Do not always be the person in your group to do the training. Share the responsibility. Seventh, remember training is the most meaningful in anticipation of an immediate event, where situations of stress are more real. Training for some unspecified action, sometime in the future, against some unknown opponents, at an undetermined site, for who knows what reason, has little value.

Resources

Almost all materials written on nonviolence training history and exercises is out-of-print. However, the International Seminars on Training for Nonviolent Action (ISTNA) can xerox almost all resources listed in Michael Randle's **Bibliography on Training for Nonviolent Action** (1978), in addition to other materials. Write ISTNA (Box 515, Waltham, MA 02254) for the latest literature list and prices. Listed below are the resources I have found the most helpful.

Bibliography on Training for Nonviolent Action, Michael Randle (1978), $5, plus $1.50 shipping from ISTNA. Annotated bibliography on all aspects of nonviolent training.

Resource Manual for a Living Revolution, Coover, Moore, Esser, Deagan (1985), New Society Publishers, 4722 Baltimore Avenue, Philadelphia, PA 19143, 330 pp., $9.95. A comprehensive training manual.

International Seminar on Training for Nonviolent Action and **North American Seminar on Training and Organizing for Nonviolent Action** (1977). Packets produced following both conferences are available from ISTNA.

A Reflective History of Training for Nonviolent Action in the Civil Rights and Peace Movements 1942-1972, Carl Zietlow (1977), available from ISTNA. Excellent study and analysis.

Training for Nonviolent Action: Some History, Analysis, Reports of Surveys, Charles C. Walker, editor (1973), available from Charles Walker, Box 92, Cheyney, PA 19319. Good background.

Situation analysis explores alternative tactics through discussion and diagram.

Training can dictate politics, become rigid, and create an elite.

Training can become an escape from action.

Training should be subordinate to organizing.

Training for some unspecified action, sometime in the future, against unknown opponents, at an undetermined site, for who knows what reason, has little value.

PEACEKEEPING

By Grace Hedemann

The purpose of peacekeepers is to assist demonstrators, not police them.

Peacekeepers (previously known as marshals) are trained demonstrators who accept responsibility for the flow and tone of a demonstration. Peacekeepers are helpful for marches, rallies, vigils, even civil disobedience actions. Anytime a local group has an event, there should be participants prepared to dispense information and deal with unanticipated problems. Organizers cannot be everywhere at all times.

The attitude of a peacekeeper is very important. They reflect the organization to participants. Therefore, peacekeepers should be cheerful, helpful, and calm. Their purpose is to assist demonstrators, not police them. They need to be flexible, quick to anticipate explosive situations, and competent to defuse potential disruption. They should be prepared to locate organizers quickly when negotiations with police are required. They should be informed about the location and length of the demonstration as well as location of restrooms, phones, and emergency services. They should be prepared to refer media people to the organization's media coordinators for packets and schedule information.

Peacekeepers should be trained at least one day prior to the demonstration.

Peacekeeper Training Sessions

Peacekeepers should be trained at least one day prior to the demonstration to allow them time to relax, and review problem scenarios. Training sessions should be small (10-15 people) to allow everyone a chance to ask questions. If the demonstration requires more peacekeepers, have several trainers run sessions simultaneously. It is best if peacekeepers operate in teams from two to four people. They should train together to develop trust and a quick decision making process. Their specific role should be defined at the training session. For instance, stage security, moving or stationary peacekeeper, runner, negotiating team, or special trouble shooting team. To communicate between peacekeepers during events, use bullhorns, hand signals, runners, walkie-talkies or radio. Bullhorns, hand signals, and runners are the most reliable and economical for local groups.

Training sessions vary in length from 1½ to 3 hours. Use discussion, role plays, situation analysis, and quick decision exercises (see the Nonviolence Training chapter). The following is a typical peacekeeping training session (sessions will vary depending on the type of event you are training for):

peacekeeping introduction	15 minutes
demonstration scenario	15 minutes
team selection and roles	15 minutes
role play I	10 minutes
role play II	10 minutes
[break]	10 minutes
situation analysis	25 minutes
quick decisions	25 minutes
role play III	30 minutes
questions and evaluation	15 minutes.

Suggestions for Peacekeepers

A one page sheet with reminders such as the following could be reproduced and distributed to peacekeepers before a demonstration.

Heckling

• Try to engage hecklers in conversation in the rally situation. They may be frustrated, and can communicate only by heckling. In a march, the peacekeeper's main responsibility is toward the marchers. Keep marchers moving around hecklers.

- If you do talk with hecklers, discuss, do not argue; arguing only gets both parties uptight.
- Be polite. Smile. Nothing is more disarming.

Scuffles

- Tell others to stay away. Keep between the scuffle and the marchers. Keep the march moving. The peacekeeper's back should generally be toward the scufflers, while urging others not to join.
- Let the scuffle fizzle out. You do not need to play hero and try to interpose yourself.
- Do not touch or push people; most people resent such action.
- Do not run toward fights. Move quietly and quickly to a scuffle if you can help to isolate it.
- Stay calm. It is only a fight.

Arrests

If one of the marchers gets busted . . .

- Urge people to stay away from the scene.
- Do not try to block the police or their vans. Urge others not to; it will only provoke the police.
- Observe what happens: why the arrest; who is arrested; names and badge numbers of police. Or get others to observe, if you cannot. Be careful to keep some distance in observing.

Police

- Maintain contact between yourself and the police whenever possible.
- Inform police of your intentions, rather than asking permission.
- Be open to their legitimate concerns, such as traffic flow.

Disruptions Within the Demonstration

- Talk with disrupters if possible. If they are demonstrators, they may accept good arguments why the demonstration should be peaceful or have a certain tone.
- Do not let disrupters distract the rest of the demonstrators. Keep people's minds on the demonstration by encouraging them to keep moving, singing, chanting, or whatever is appropriate to the situation.

Suggested Role Plays

March

- Hecklers.
- Moving march lagging behind line in front; moving too quickly; passing heavily populated corner.
- Outsiders grab demonstrator's sign.
- Group of demonstrators begin chanting "off the pigs."
- Police stop march.
- Group of demonstrators decide to change route of march.

Rally

- Hecklers.
- Rally dispersal.
- Man faints.
- Disrupters demand to speak.
- Demonstrators demand to be allowed into press area.
- Media people disruptive by insisting on interviewing speakers and demonstrators during rally in front of stage.

Vigil or Picket Line

- Demonstrator joins picket line with a "Fuck the draft" sign.
- Police inform vigil they must be a moving picket line.
- Silent vigil disrupted by inquisitive passerby; hostile passerby.

Civil Disobedience Actions

- Untrained demonstrators want to join the CD.
- Demonstration supporters taunt police.
- Passerby wants to know what is going on; outraged passerby; sympathetic passerby.
- Police pull CDer by hair or use club under CDers neck to move them.
- Police horses step on demonstrators.

Suggested Quick Decisions

March

- Person approaches march saying they represent 40 people and asking how to join.
- Someone seizes a bullhorn and begins shouting provocative slogans.
- Someone faints during the march.

- Bricks are tossed over demonstration toward police.
- March is stalled, people are impatient and cold.
- During march five demonstrators attack an isolated policeman.
- Marchers harrass peacekeepers, calling them "pigs."

Rally

- Someone seizes a bullhorn and begins provocative slogans.
- During the rally, 15 people begin chanting "pig" to a group of nearby police. Several hundred people pick up the chant.
- During the rally, five demonstrators begin a fistfight.
- A small group breaks away from rally with the intent of breaking into a city administration building.

Vigil

- Silent vigil interrupted by media insisting on interviews.
- Police charge into a picket line without warning.

Civil Disobedience

- Police begin to club CDers.
- Affinity group breaks demonstration discipline by running toward police barricade.

Suggested Situation Analysis

March

- A large march of 1,000 is moving down the street. The demonstration has previously been warned that it will not be allowed to reach its goal. Suddenly tear gas is released at the front of the march; the gas drifts through the line of march, frightening people more than debilitating them, and panic begins to grip some people. What action can peacekeepers take?

Rally

- Diagram speakers' stage and peacekeepers placement. How can peacekeepers be placed to help insure that speakers will not be disrupted by individuals or small groups wishing to take over the platform?

Vigil

- Diagram an attack on a vigil. Indicate placement of peacekeepers, vigilers, police, passersby, attackers.

Civil Disobedience

- A legal rally and a civil disobedience action take place side by side. Diagram how peacekeepers keep groups separated, and yet create an atmosphere that is supportive of each group.

A note of special thanks to the Friends Peace Committee's Marshals Handbook *by Robert Levering, Chuck Noell, Lynne Shivers, Susan Terdiman, and George Willoughby. "Suggestions for Peacekeepers" and "Suggested Exercises" were taken primarily from that handbook.*

CONDUCTING A VIGIL

By Charles Walker

A vigil at its best is a delicately wrought instrument for communication. Its notable features are composure, watchfulness and persistence.

There are several styles, each with their own purpose. One emphasizes just being there. Relatives who gather at a mine entrance when disaster strikes don't organize themselves. They can do little except stay there. Another common form is the religious observance, often accompanied by special disciplines such as fasting, reading or staying awake for protracted times.

In others, persistence is the key. The vigil at Fort Detrick, the germ warfare research center in Maryland, lasted for 22 months. For one full year the vigil was kept every day from 7 am to 5 pm, not missing an hour. The Times Square vigil against the Vietnam War occurred every Saturday from 1964 through 1973. In 1960 a thousand Quakers stood in silence for two days around the Pentagon. This vigil emphasized inward reflection, composure and maximum impact on those who saw it.

Individual vigils reflect the style of the person doing them, usually emphasizing

The features of vigils are composure, watchfulness and persistence.

Vigil in support of draft resister Bob Eaton, August 1969, at the WRI Triennial in Haverford, PA. Photo by Theodore Hetzel.

the opportunity to talk with those who show interest. Silence may be appropriate if the vigil is protracted or well publicized. Otherwise, talking seems more useful than silence. Perhaps one of the most effective single person vigils was conducted outside the White House protesting the Vietnam War. President Nixon had become so irritated at the vigiler's presence that he ordered his aides to get rid of the protester.

The following suggestions are offered for groups numbering from a few people to a few hundred, for a time lasting several hours or several days. They are not "rules" but suggestions that can be adapted to the group, time and occasion.

- Establish the pattern, possibly a line or circle, where the vigil can be readily seen, and not easily disrupted by passersby. But be careful not to block entrances, sidewalks, or passageways.

- Stand far enough apart to extend the line as much as practicable (e.g., an arm's length or two apart). This increases the visual impact of the group, and minimizes temptations to chat and socialize.

- Try to maintain silence and composure while on vigil. Those who talk with each other on line will be perceived by observers as more interested in each other than in communicating their message.

- If a passerby wants to talk, suggest that the two of you go aside to do so, while the vigil continues uninterrupted.

Candlelight vigil at beginning of 1976 Continental Walk, Ukiah, California. Photo by Janet Bunje.

Answer brief questions on the spot.

- Leafletters should be separated from the vigil line.

- To talk, smoke or rest, leave the line and go to one side. Choose a special spot where coats, gear and other items can be left, and kept under observation. Otherwise, the clutter around a vigil of several hours can assume distracting, even amusing, proportions.

- A vigil intently kept can become very tiring. Individuals may withdraw for a time. Possibly at half hour intervals the whole line can walk around in some orderly fashion, such as an oval, for a few minutes. Do this more often in cold or rainy weather. This should not be considered as a "break" in the vigil but as part of it.

- Monitors should avoid scurrying about, or giving loud instructions to distant parts of the line. If geography permits, stay behind the line. Minimize the need to give instructions by holding advance briefings or giving an explanation sheet to participants.

- Those at each end of the line can do much to set the tone, by their demeanor and by faithfully maintaining the spirit of the vigil. They are usually the first to be seen, and instantly communicate something at the group. Example is by far the best way for participants to help each other remember and maintain their purpose.

- The silent line should not be seen as an imposed structure to present a certain image, but as a design providing a wide range of opportunities for the participants. Some like to concentrate on eye contact with those who pass by, in cars or on the sidewalk. Others will consider it a religious observance. Yet others will think or reflect, or just stand there.

- Use signs sparingly.

- For particularly long vigils, either individuals or the group may wish to keep a diary of thoughts, conversations, and follow-up opportunities. This material can later be used for reports, etc.

- Large vigils require careful organization and planning. The larger the vigil, the more difficult it is to start. Avoid herding techniques that sometimes result when situations go awry. In briefing sessions, ask participants to help get things underway with patience and good humor.

- Concentrate on the *quality* of the vigil. Numbers help but are not decisive.

Picketing

Vigiling and picketing are in many ways similar, e.g., they both usually involve small numbers of people, they operate in a line, and can be quickly organized. However, there are some distinct differences. Picketing is rarely silent, usually involving chanting or singing. Pickets are frequently moving, and sometimes have a "picket captain" to ensure the line doesn't become sloppy and to coordinate the chanting. The number of signs at picketing events is maximized.

Hiroshima Day picket in Honolulu, 1958. Photo by Honolulu Advertiser.

Picketing is rarely silent, usually involves chanting or singing, and is frequently moving.

WAR TAX RESISTANCE

By Ed Hedemann

> If a thousand people were not to pay their tax bill this year, that would not be a violent and bloody measure as it would be to pay them and enable the State to commit violence and shed innocent blood."
>
> —Henry David Thoreau

THOREAU

U.S.   5 cents

A. J. Muste once pointed out that "the two decisive powers of the government with respect to war are the power to conscript and the power to tax." To refuse to join the military or to work for the military industry and yet to pay Federal taxes is still contributing to war and preparation for war.

All governments basically rest on the assumption that people will obey. Governments rely on force from time to time to instill a degree of fear, the most powerful weapon of control with the general public. A whole army cannot budge a noncooperating citizenry. Senator Bellmon of Oklahoma quoted an IRS official as having said that "If the taxpayers of this country ever discover that the IRS operates on 90% bluff, the entire system will collapse."

At least as important as minimizing their participation in the war-making machinery, tax resisters seek to *confront* the government with their non-payment and *redistribute* the money to non-military groups. In this way, war tax resistance can have a three-fold impact of non-cooperation, protest, and direct action.

Historically, war tax resistance has been around ever since taxes were collected for wars. American war tax resistance began with Quaker and Mennonite opposition to the French and Indian War in 1755. Henry David Thoreau's opposition to the Mexican War resulted in his being jailed for non-payment of taxes and his subsequent essay, "On the Duty of Civil Disobedience." Modern American war tax resistance began with the huge increase in military spending in World War II. War tax resistance peaked during the Vietnam War when an esti-mated 20,000 people stopped paying part or all of their income tax and at least 200,000 stopped paying their telephone tax.

Taxes

There are all kinds of taxes. Which ones do war tax resisters resist? Since virtually all war and military spending emanates from Washington, DC, money collected by the *Federal* government is to be resisted—but not *all* of it.

Each year, the Administration tries to make military spending appear to be a small part of the budget—far outweighed by money to human needs—submitted to Congress. The President's proposals are put into the form of a *Unified Budget,* which combines *Federal Funds* (money Congress and the President have control over) and *Trust Funds* (money for Social Security, airports, and highways, which Congress and the President do not have control over). Trust Funds are used to swell the "human" side of the budget, making the percentage given to the military look smaller. In reality, Congress has little control over the Trust Funds and just acts as a holding agent for them.

Federal Funds, which pay for wars and the military, get money from individual income taxes, corporate income taxes, excise taxes, customs, estate, gift taxes, etc. In addition, years in which there are deficits, Congress borrows heavily through Savings (previously known as "War") Bonds, and from various retirement and trust funds. Because it is the largest, the most important of all these sources is the *individual in-*

come tax. For purely symbolic value, the Federal *excise tax on telephone service* is also important because it has been used as a "war tax" from World War I to the Vietnam War. The rest of the taxes (e.g., corporate income, alcohol excise, and tobacco excise) are more difficult to resist.

For the past several years, military spending has varied between 35% and 45% of Federal Funds. In addition, Interest on the National Debt (almost entirely created by deficit spending due to wars and enormous military budgets) and Veterans benefits together amount to another 20% of Federal Funds. This means spending for current military and past wars has varied the past few years from 50 to 65% of Federal Funds.

How To Resist

The Telephone Tax. Your monthly telephone bill contains a Federal excise tax (currently at 3%, but has varied from 1% to 10% over the past twenty years), which contributes to the Federal Funds portion of the US Budget. To refuse payment, simply subtract the tax from your bill (note that the tax often appears in two places in your bill: on the local portion and on the long distance portion) and enclose a letter to the telephone company with your payment, explaining that you are paying the full bill less the Federal tax because of your opposition to military spending. The telephone company will *not* cut off your phone service (since it is illegal to do so for nonpayment of the tax), but simply forward the fact of your nonpayment to the Internal Revenue Service.

The Individual Income Tax. If you "owe" the IRS money on April 15, there are several ways to refuse payment. First, you must decide how much you want to refuse: a token amount (e.g., $10), the amount which goes to current military spending (about 40%), the amount which goes to current military plus past military spending (about 60%), or all of the tax claimed by the IRS. The logic behind not paying *any* is simply that any money sent to the Government will go mostly towards past and present military spending. You cannot earmark your money, asking that it be spent only on the "good bits." People who divert their resisted taxes directly to social programs have a greater positive effect than if they allowed the Government to get the money.

To refuse payment, you can

- fill out the form as usual and simply enclose a letter instead of a check; the advantage of this method (over many of the ones below) is that it avoids the $500 "frivolous" penalty

- fill out your 1040 form claiming a "war tax" credit or deduction, thus reducing or eliminating the amount due; the advantage of taking the deduction (over the credit) is that it allows you appeal rights within the "audit division" of the IRS before going into the "collection division;" however, both these methods may subject you to the $500 "frivolous" penalty

- sign a blank return and claim the Fifth Amendment on every line; this also may subject you to the "frivolous" penalty

- send a letter of explanation instead

Spending for current military and past wars has varied from 50 to 60% of Federal Funds during the past few years.

People who divert their resisted taxes directly to social programs have a greater positive effect than if they allowed the government to get the money.

Bergstrom AFB, Austin, Texas, April 17, 1972. Photo by Grace Hedemann.

The usual way to circumvent withholding is to claim sufficient "allowances" on your W-4 form.

Though it is not inevitable that the IRS will collect resisted taxes, you should always expect that possibility.

Your bank account and salary are the most likely targets for an IRS collection.

of filing; this method will probably result in your being charged with "failure to file"

- ignore 'em altogether.

For more details, consult the *Guide To War Tax Resistance.*

Withholding. Most people do not have the opportunity to refuse payment on April 15 because their money has been withheld by their employer each pay period. Being self-employed or doing certain types of labor (e.g., domestic work) does not require withholding. Some people have set up "employment agencies," selling their labor to employers. In this case, it is the "employment agency" which is required to withhold. However, the usual way war tax resisters use to circumvent withholding is to claim a sufficient number of "allowances" on their W-4 forms to reduce their withholding. "Allowances" not only include dependents but can also refer to estimated deductions, credits, etc. Your employer does not need to know how you determined the number of allowances, just the total. However, the IRS has asked employers to notify them if an employee claims more than 14 allowances or if the W-4 form seems suspicious. If the employee owed no taxes the previous year, then it might be possible to claim "exempt" from withholding on the W-4 form. For more information on withholding, consult the *Guide to War Tax Resistance.*

Consequences

There is no guarantee that the Government will respond to your tax resistance, but you should expect one. Generally, the IRS will send a series of notices, and make telephone calls or visits to the resister. These communications will indicate a "deficiency" in taxes due plus interest and a penalty of some sort. In 1983 the IRS began levying a new penalty—the "frivolous" fine. This penalty (which is $500) has nothing to do with whether a person is resisting taxes, but is added if a person "alters" their 1040 form (e.g., writing in a "war tax deduction").

Depending on the amount due, the persistence and politics of the IRS agent, the resister's personal situation, and the phase of the moon, the IRS may or may not proceed any further. The notices are part of the "90% bluff" system. Most people pay as a result of the threatening nature of these communications.

If the IRS proceeds further, it usually looks for a bank account near where the resister lives or works. An account in another city or state, and caution to whom you write checks, often prevents discovery of such an account. The IRS may also levy your salary. To avoid this you should change jobs, be self-employed, get paid in advance, or have a sympathetic employer willing to stand up to the IRS.

If the IRS still has not succeeded, that may be the end of it. However, in a handful of cases the IRS has been known to seize property (e.g., TV, bicycle, car, or even a house), auction it off, and return the money to the resister less the tax (as well as interest and penalties). In a very few cases, resisters have been taken to court and jailed a few weeks or months for refusing to reveal sources of assets in court, etc. There is a statute of limitations which says that the IRS must collect the taxes within a certain period of time (usually six years) or else give up.

At any point if the stakes become too high for the resister, she or he can "bail out" and pay the taxes for the year in question. That will usually end the IRS harassment.

Demonstrations

Tax resistance is usually a very personal act, which sometimes takes a great deal of courage, unless there exists support from a community of resisters.

If tax resisters band together for a nonviolent direct action project, tax resistance becomes more effective and political. Such projects often require a lot of imagination because the numbers of resisters and sympathizers are small.

Listed below are a few ideas which have been used in the past on such days as April 15:

- leaflet in front of the entrance of the IRS, Federal Building, or Post Office (for variation, try stapling a "tea bag" on each leaflet—these leaflets won't be thrown away)
- leaflet inside the building where the

IRS is counseling taxpayers—this "ups the ante" and often makes your action more dramatic

- set up a war tax resistance counseling table inside the building
- conduct a vigil with posters and leaflets
- stage a guerrilla theater skit
- have a rally—speakers, music, donate resisted taxes to a community group
- place war tax resistance literature on IRS shelves along side the regular IRS forms
- rubber stamp IRS literature with DON'T PAY," etc.
- distribute helium-filled balloons which read "Don't Pay War Taxes" to people entering the building
- hang a banner stating "Don't Pay Death Taxes" on the building
- paste up posters or other literature on the building.

When writing literature for distribution on the streets, it is often very effective to contrast how much is being spent on the military with what the needs are in your community or the country. For example, one Navy A6-E fighter plane is equal to the aid not given to a fully equipped fire company in New York City. Also, you might mention how much money leaves your community to the Federal government in the form of individual income taxes to how much comes back in the form of services and jobs (usually a deficit). In addition, point out that it's not welfare (about 5% of the Budget) which causes taxes to be so high, but military spending.

Leafletting *inside* the IRS on April 15 not only provides an excellent opportunity to talk with people but presents a strong contrast with the smooth tax collecting machinery of the IRS.

If the IRS seizes property for taxes, turn their auction into a demonstration.

New York City peace march, 1971. Photo by Diana Davies.

"Alternative funds" are useful vehicles to redistribute tax-resisted money to community groups, as well as to provide a security system for tax resisters who suffer an IRS seizure.

If the IRS does seize some property of a tax resister and plans to auction it off, take advantage of the opportunity. Organize a counter-auction, hold a demonstration, submit creative bids, alert the media, make a fundraising party out of it.

The Peace Tax Fund

Another vehicle for education about misplaced economic priorities is organizing around the Peace Tax Fund (PTF) bill in Congress.

The National Campaign for a Peace Tax Fund (2121 Decatur NW, Washington DC 20008) is a national lobby which has succeeded in introducing a bill in both the House and Senate to set up such a fund.

Though not a form of tax resistance, the basic purpose of the Fund would be to reroute the portion of a conscientious objector's tax money equal (in percentage) to what is spent by the Department of Defense. The money would be used for research and peaceful methods of settling international disputes, disarmament efforts, etc.

Resources

In 1982 a coalition of groups working on war tax resistance formed as the National War Tax Resistance Coordinating Committee (NWTRCC). If your group wants to affiliate, contact the office at NWTRCC, PO Box 2236, E. Patchogue, NY 11772. Listed below are some of the key resources for war tax resisters.

Guide to War Tax Resistance, 124 pages, published in 1986 by the War Resisters League. The most comprehensive and up-to-date sourcebook on war tax resistance. Contains detailed chapters on how to resist, consequences, the Federal budget, stories of war tax resisters, etc.

War Tax Manual for Counselors and Lawyers, 240+ pages, published in 1985 by NWTRCC. As it says, it's for counselors and lawyers; has an extensive legal section including legal citations.

Handbook on Nonpayment of War Taxes, 55 pages, published in 1981 by the Peacemakers (PO Box 627, Garberville, CA 95440). This is an updated version of the first war tax resistance handbook. Contains lots of personal histories.

People Pay for Peace, 108 pages, written by William Durland and published in 1984 by the Center on Law and Pacifism (c/o Pendle Hill, Wallingford, PA 19086). Good on religious basis of and legal arguments for war tax resistance.

Network News is published every month or two by NWTRCC. It is the best source for the latest in war tax resistance: changes in the tax law, what's happening to resisters, organizing ideas, new resources, etc.

ORGANIZING A BOYCOTT

The boycott is a type of direct action which can take a number of different forms: refusal to buy a certain product or shop in a certain store, discontinuation of social relations with a particular person or institution (ostracism), or selective refusal of workers to handle particular items.

The most familiar boycotts in recent American history have been the 1956 bus boycott by Montgomery blacks, the lettuce and grape boycotts by the United Farm Workers, the J.P. Stevens boycott of textile goods, the boycott of ITT's Wonder Bread and Dow Chemical's Saran Wrap during the Vietnam War, and the Nestlé boycott in the early 1980's. Though the term boycott originated in 1880 when used by Irish peasants against Captain Boycott, its practice goes back through recorded history.

The focus of this chapter will be on organizing a consumer boycott. For more on the history and different usages of the boycott, see *The Politics of Nonviolent Action* by Gene Sharp.

wise chances of success will be significantly diminished. One of the difficulties of the J.P. Stevens boycott was that few of their products were labeled "J.P. Stevens." A boycott of an exotic or not very common item, such as wild rice, might make the economic impact negligible.

The boycott should be as narrowly defined as possible. The shotgun approach of boycotting a lot of different products promotes confusion as to what is being boycotted and makes potential participants feel overwhelmed. It is far better to focus on one item. That is why the UFW carefully chose grapes as their first item. Then when that boycott succeeded they moved on to lettuce. However, they ran into difficulty during their lettuce phase, when the grape contracts ran out and the growers did not re-sign. So both lettuce and grapes became part of the boycott.

The basic goals of a boycott are to educate people about the injustice which stimulated the boycott, and in some small way to have an economic impact on the corporation involved.

The Boycott Strategy

Deciding on the form or object of the boycott is perhaps the most critical step in the whole effort; so it must be planned carefully. The basic strategy for a consumer boycott is to find a key company involved in the injustice you are struggling against or a product which is a convenient symbol of an oppression (e.g., the British salt monopoly in India during its struggle for independence). This company must have a readily accessible and identifiable consumer product. This product should be one that consumers can easily forego (e.g., grapes) or find a substitute (e.g., Wonder Bread), other-

Involving Other Groups

Depending on the nature of the boycott, key constituencies to consider approaching are religious groups, student groups, women's organizations, civil rights and other social justice organizations, local unions, and peace groups. Possible steps for the involvement of these groups are as follows:

- send the basic boycott material
- contact the organization and ask for their endorsement and support
- show a film or slide show, if any, to a membership meeting
- seek resolutions of support; send

Leaflet key stores on a regular basis.

Solicit endorsement from community leaders, organizations, and others in an effort to educate about the boycott as well as develop support.

Visit the retailer with a delegation of representatives from the community.

copies to retailers and municipal office holders

- get volunteers to distribute leaflets in neighborhoods, sporting events, bus and train stations, shopping centers, and other community areas
- form delegations of religious, civil rights, community, and labor representatives to meet with local elected officials
- attend city council meetings and introduce resolutions in support of the boycott
- inform the local paper about the resolution to be introduced and background information
- visit stores with leaders of the various constituencies
- call each organization endorsing the consumer boycott and ask them to set up visits and recruit volunteers for leafletting one day a month
- have supporters mail or hand deliver pledge cards to store manager
- set up regular days for leafletting (be sure to cover Saturday and shopping nights)
- create events interesting to the press (e.g., rallies or "human billboards")

- each organization which has pledged to help should set up "visit committees" to visit stores, without appointment, and speak with the manager
- organizations should recruit others to phone the store
- meet with head of store on a regular basis to discover if there's been any change in policy (at the same time survey quantity of the boycotted item in stock to see if the store is buying more or less).

Leafletting

Leafletting retail stores is an important tactic in any consumer boycott, so care should be taken to make it as effective as possible. Unless you have an abundance of volunteers to leaflet, key stores need to be selected for leafletting on a *regular basis* during peak shopping hours. Energies and spirits can be dissipated rapidly if a "shotgun" approach is taken. Concentrate on one store; win it; then move on to the next. If your campaign is able to cover more than one store at a time, have people leaflet simultaneously.

Before beginning the leafletting, make sure the store is still stocking the boycotted product. Be sure all leafletters are familiar with the literature and issues. Keep the number of leafletters down to two per entrance. Ask shoppers to take leaflets into the store with them. If they stop to talk, ask them to hand the leaflet to the manager. Don't clog entrances or get into heated arguments which inhibit leafletting.

Visiting the Retailer

Read all the available boycott literature in advance. Make sure the store is still selling the item, and how much is being stocked. Set up an appointment with the manager. Meet an hour before to prepare who is to say what. Ask the retailer to voluntarily discontinue selling the product. Tell the retailer that the boycott is directed to the conscience of the consuming public. Remind the retailer that you and your organization will be distributing leaflets identifying the store as well as others which carry the product. Give the retailer an idea of the campaign's scope (e.g., rallies, press releases, articles, interviews). Don't suggest names of substitute products, since retailers probably know these products better than you.

The Secondary Boycott

If your organization is boycotting a store because it is selling the objectionable product, that's a secondary boycott. It is illegal for unions covered by the National Labor Relations Act to engage in secondary boycotts. The legality for other organizations depends on state law. So before proceeding, check to see what you are up against. Also, a secondary boycott is harder to pull off than one against a product, simply because it is harder for consumers to avoid a whole store as opposed to one item.

Other Tactics

During the boycott of Wonder Bread (made by ITT, which also produced antipersonnel bombs during the Vietnam War), a team of women went into a grocery store on Long Island and taped boycott leaflets all around the bread shelves. In addition, they wrapped loaves of Wonder Bread in the leaflets. By closing time every loaf of bread had been sold except Wonder Bread. The Wonder Bread pile was untouched.

Consider supplementing the leafletting with a picket or rally. Stenciling the sidewalk or postering near the store may be useful in publicizing the boycott when no one is leafletting. But be careful that the stenciling or postering does not project the image of vandalism. At an advanced stage of the campaign, civil disobedience might be included. If there appears to be a stalemate in the boycott, perhaps trucks which carry the product could be blockaded. This would not be in place of the leafletting, but in addition to it.

For further suggestions on actions you can take, see other sections of this *Manual*, in particular, the chapter on "Campaign Organizing."

This chapter was prepared, in part, from material in "A Guide for Local J.P. Stevens Consumer Boycott Committees," and the WRL action outline, "Wonder Bread Boycott," by Jerry Coffin.

STUDENT STRIKES

The purpose of a student strike is to stop the functioning of the school until a set of demands are met or to punctuate the views of the student body. As with any strike, participation by a significant proportion of the students is necessary to have a visible effect and to prevent rapid demoralization. If a strike involves a minimal number of students, the risks are high for those participating: grades reduced, possible suspension, or expulsion. Further, because the potential for chaos is great, discipline of participants must be high.

So obviously, a student strike should be called as a last resort. The majority of students should already be in support of the demands.

Demands

Common to most schools are issues of academic and personal freedom. A popular but controversial teacher is fired, political activity is restricted, the student paper is censored, political rallies are forbidden, certain courses are not taught, are all examples of academic issues which have caused strikes in the past. Personal freedom issues have included dress codes (particularly, in high schools), dormitory curfews and other restrictions.

The famous 1964 Free Speech Movement at the University of California campus in Berkeley included an effective strike. The issue which sparked the strike and the movement was the right to set up tables, collect money, and generally organize on campus for "off-campus" causes. The 1968 Columbia University strike and demonstrations revolved around the University's intention to build a gym in a Black part of the city—displacing the current residents.

Sometimes student strikes are a result of issues which originate outside the campus community. For example, in 1970 there were strikes all over the country because of the US invasion of Cambodia, the murders at Kent State and Jackson State, and the repression of the Black Panthers. The spring of 1972 saw a lot of strike activity in response to the "air war." Demands in such cases frequently revolve around ending university complicity with, say, the military. Such complicity is commonly in the form of research grants from the Department of Defense, stocks in military industries, ROTC, access to the university by military or industry recruiters, members of the board of regents who serve on boards of military industries, etc.

Demands may range anywhere from seeking a hearing on grievances, to ending complicity with a particular wrong doing, or reversal of some restrictive rules.

Even though a strike may originate from some minor incident, the demands should be made political, wherever possible. Get to the root causes of the grievances. This helps educate the campus community as to the connections and broader issues involved.

A radical sociology teacher is fired by the Board of Regents, ostensibly because she has not published the requisite number of articles, yearly. The teacher, who is considered one of the best by students and faculty alike, suspects it is her biting criticisms of the patriarchal university system, the US involvement in El Salvador, etc. In such a case, the list of strike demands *might include* the following:

- re-instatement of the teacher, plus tenure
- elimination of the "publish or perish" requirement, particularly for instructors who are good teachers
- establishment of a new course or program of study on militarism and patriarchy in the US
- restriction of the Board of Regents power to that of fund raising
- affirmative hiring policy to place more

A student strike should be called as a last resort.

Even though a strike may originate from some minor incident, the demands should be made political.

women and minorities on the faculty, in the administration, and on the Board of Regents

- a greater role for faculty and students in university decision-making
- official university condemnation of US involvement in El Salvador
- reducing the complicity of the University with the military-industrial complex by divesture of all military stocks and bonds, eliminating ROTC, and terminating all military grants and contracts.

The basic plan is to shut down the normal functioning of the school, and open up a "liberated" campus. The administration plan could involve a combination of the following responses: ignore the strikers in hopes it will blow over; crack down on the organizers to scare the majority back to classes; offer a meaningless compromise or accept some of the minor demands; wait until a break in the school year or even call a recess in hopes the students will leave, thereby diffusing the strike.

Preparation

Every student strike goes through an immediate period of militancy and high participation, followed by a "letdown" phase when participation drops off as students go back to classes, vacation, or home.

To keep this "letdown" phase from demoralizing the organizers into thinking the strike has fallen apart, a good organizational structure must be established early. This structure should be based on a network of politically educated small groups in dorms and other places throughout the student community. A coordinating office and carefully planned series of events should be set up to maintain morale and build support.

One of the first steps is to call a strike meeting. The meeting should be widely advertised, open, and maximize participation. Open the meeting with reports on everything which led up to the meeting followed by people who wish to speak. Limit the length of time for each speaker so as many people as possible can speak, but not to the point where people begin to drift off. Then take a strike vote.

After the vote, set a strike date that is soon, yet gives you enough time for political education. Develop a list of demands with which the campus will be leafletted. Make policy decisions on trashing, the use of force on nonstriking students, attitude toward faculty and other school personnel, response toward police, etc. Set up strike committees that involve as many people as possible. The more people who have specific responsibilities and feel a part of the strike, the more likely it will succeed.

Organizing

Phase One—The Strike

Set up frequent and regular strike meetings to evaluate progress and administration responses. Plaster the campus with the strike call. On the day of the strike have the entire strike force out at all entrances, key gathering points, and major lecture halls with strike placards, leaflets, etc.

Any classes that meet after the strike date must be addressed by a strike representative. This means entering classrooms without permission and talking about the strike to scab students.

The strike sets the stage for campus liberation and ongoing community political work. But if students do not stay on campus, you have no political cadre. Do not allow the administration to close down the campus. If they close it, you reopen it as a liberated campus.

Phase Two—Campus Is Liberated

On the first day of the strike begin getting student and faculty signatures on a referendum petition demanding the opening of the campus for anti-war and other work appropriate to the demands. Demand that the administration turn over the campus and campus facilities to the strike committee for use as a liberated campus.

If the administration refuses to turn over the campus, decide which buildings are essential to your work and liberate them for your use. Be sure you have the people to hold the buildings against possible court injunctions (this means people willing to face arrest) and the use of police. If you are forced out of a building, be prepared to remount a liberation effort.

In the event the campus is closed after, or at the threat of, the strike, be prepared to demand it be opened for student use. The liberation of the campus is not an end in itself. The campus is being liberated for use as a center for ongoing political work in the larger community.

Make sure you have prepared the logistical support for the liberated campus.

The basic plan is to shut down the normal functioning of the school, and open up a "liberated" campus.

A good organizational structure must be established early.

Begin a strike after an open meeting and a strike vote.

Food must be made available and a system set up for its procurement, preparation and distribution. Mimeo facilities, phones, office space, meeting rooms, housing all need to be secured.

Coordination

If the student government or some other existing group is not appropriate or able to coordinate the strike and negotiate with the administration, a strike committee needs to be organized. Such a committee must be representative of all the strike task forces: fund raising, publicity, communications, leafletting, materials preparation, picketing, speakers, strike newsletter, legal, security, education, community liaison, and so forth.

Since the strike committee will likely be a large group and since the daily meetings need to be short, a smaller committee must be formed to free the larger group of collecting information, preparing agendas, and other massive amounts of detail that adds up to a lot of time taken from the major political discussion.

The two key task forces are coordination and communication. You must be able to turn out posters and leaflets rapidly. And you must be prepared to deal with rumors effectively. Your office must be equipped with phones. These phones must be staffed around the clock. A communications network needs to be established that can rapidly alert people in a crisis.

A daily (or more often) strike bulletin is essential. All who agree with the basic demands should be allowed access to airing her or his views in the bulletin. Set aside a room for making posters. Stock it with poster board, markers, paint, a silk screen and so forth. Get sympathetic art students to donate their skills. Print strike T-shirts.

A well-run strike is likely to get the establishment media to descend on campus. The administration, being very media sensitive, will probably portray strike organizers as violence-prone lunatics. Be very careful about clearing any press releases sent out and what is said to the media. Often, the media will exaggerate any disruption in order to make it more "newsworthy." *Always* focus on the political aspects of the strike.

Trashing and any physical damage should be avoided, not only because of adverse media play but because you are trying to convert or liberate the campus, not destroy it. So training for peacekeepers should be organized. These people would be used in mass demonstrations and at picket lines. There is nothing the administration would like better than to have a good excuse to call in the police or at least tarnish the image of the strike organizers. If there are a lot of tensions during the strike, your organizing offices may be trashed. So peacekeepers may be needed to work on patrols around the clock.

An important element to the success of any student strike is the support of the surrounding community: campus workers as well as workers from the community who do not work on campus, poor people, minorities, shopkeepers, the middle class, GIs and others. Approach these constituencies on how the issues of the strike affect them and how they can help.

In addition to the strike education and publicity efforts, other types of activities might be phased in. For example, demonstrations against the ROTC, street marches, sit-ins at the offices of key administration or government officials, and mass meetings in the community.

This chapter was assembled from "ON STRIKE!—A Working Outline for Campus Organizing" written in 1970 by Jerry Coffin, and the "Student Strikes" section of the O.M. Collective's Organizer's Manual.

A daily (or more often) strike bulletin is essential.

An important element to the success of any student strike is the support of the surrounding community.

Working with the Establishment

LAW, LAWYERS, AND COURTS

By Lauri Lowell

Political organizing challenges the existing power relationships in our society and the world through public statements and actions which express opposition to the status quo and offer working alternatives. The purpose of the law is to maintain the structure and power balance in society. Therefore, organizers inevitably will have to deal with the legal system in the course of an organizing campaign. In particular, civil disobedience by its very nature involves having to deal with the legal system more than most other forms of organizing. So what follows are the key considerations for those who need to prepare for arrests.

Legal Considerations in a Demonstration

Whether a demonstration is planned in two meetings or twenty, "legal issues" should be an item on the agenda. It may involve straightforward issues like getting rally and parade permits from City Hall or the police department, and arranging for a few legal observers to be on hand. If civil disobedience is planned, however, or if you think there might be problems which would lead to an unplanned arrest situation, then there are many issues to deal with.

Responsibility. First and foremost is the issue of responsibility. If the legal consequences of an action—including all the time-consuming and tedious follow-up work—are handled responsibly by the demonstrators, it can make the difference between an action that leaves a bitter residue of hard feelings and confusion

and one that seems to evolve into greater empowerment and political understanding. All too often, newly active demonstrators assume that the organizers or the legal supporters are going to take care of their cases for them. When cases drag on for days, weeks, even years, defendants lose interest; they move on to new projects, other concerns. *The legal follow-up is part of the action.* This needs to be truly understood and taken into account when organizing a demonstration of any kind.

Legal Support. Have good working relations with a sympathetic and trustworthy lawyer (see "Resource List" on how to find one). Determine the role of the lawyer early on. Be clear about decision-making power and structures, fees (if any), your expectations as to time, doing legal research, etc. You may want a team of legal people prepared to observe the action and offer support afterwards during processing and court proceedings. Attorneys may want to observe or participate in nonviolence training, in order to better understand the nature of the organization and action.

Charges and Penalties. This should be researched before the action. All demonstrators should be advised of what the possible charges and penalties are. Generally, they include disorderly conduct, resisting arrest, trespass, obstructing government administration, failure to obey an order of a police officer, destruction of property, assault, and others. There may be municipal, state or federal laws involved, depending on where you are demonstrating. Penalties may be slight (e.g., for first offender violations) or severe (e.g., for obstructing registra-

The purpose of the law is to maintain the structure and power balance in society.

Though court cases from demonstrations may drag on for some time, the legal follow-up is part of the action and should not be ignored.

Research all possible charges and penalties before the action.

tion, which is a felony). Generally, however, demonstrators get a suspended sentence, a few days, or at most 10 days to a month, and/or fines of $25 to $100. This really varies widely from place to place, depending on the political climate and what it is you did. Check the history of civil disobedience in your area; talk to other political groups about their experiences with the police and the courts.

Pro Se. A defendant has the right to be represented by counsel at her/his arraignment, where pleas are entered (but not during booking); defendants also have the right to represent themselves, which is called *pro se* (from the Latin, *for oneself*). Going pro se has the advantage of giving the protester the opportunity to communicate directly with judge and/or jury, question witnesses and state the moral and political reasons for what s/he did, whenever s/he gets a chance to speak. Often pro se defendants manage to get around court restrictions because they are presumed to be unfamiliar with legal process and the judge is concerned that they understand what is happening and not accidentally waive any rights. (A number of peace and anti-nuclear activists have become excellent lay advocates in their own and others behalf.) They may be able to say and do things that aren't otherwise allowed. It can be an empowering experience consistent with the empowerment of the civil disobedience action itself. A practical consideration is that in a large action, a limited number of lawyers would be available to represent defendants.

Drawbacks are that pro se defendants might botch things up a bit, not realizing what is going on. They may fail to object, for example, or unwittingly waive certain rights. Many pro se defendants have an attorney advising them in order to safeguard their rights and help them to proceed in court. Consult the excellent pro se manuals listed in the "Resource List."

Noncooperation. Noncooperation is a way of refusing to assist with one's own incarceration. A broad range of actions may be considered noncooperation, from refusing to comply with simple but humiliating demands, such as submitting to a strip search, to refusal to eat.

Many demonstrators choose to go limp at the time of arrest as a form of peaceful resistance. This involves physical discomfort and may impede one's ability to communicate with the arresting officer. Physical noncooperation may be sustained throughout booking, during court appearances and in jail. One risks being entirely misunderstood, however, and should be prepared to explain one's actions sincerely and intelligently.

Refusal to cooperate with court proceedings—not giving one's name or other requested information, refusing to talk, stand, enter a plea, etc.—may bring severe penalties. Some demonstrators choose to give their names, acting with the openness and confidence that characterizes the action; others choose to resist a system that keeps criminal records and punishes organizers and second offenders

Jim Peck, Ben Spock, and others being booked after "Stop the Draft Week" arrest in New York City, 1967. Photo by Diana Davies.

more harshly.

Noncooperation must be approached with conviction and understanding. It can be a powerful and spontaneous response to harsh or unjust treatment. One needs to be flexible and know when continued noncooperation serves no further purpose. Noncooperators can expect to be intimidated and threatened by authorities. It is difficult and rewarding, frustrating and empowering.

Bail. Bail is the most graphic example of the economic discrimination which pervades the criminal justice system. If you have the money, you can go free (assuming other criteria are met); if not, you can sit it out in jail. Bail solidarity is the attempt by as many demonstrators as possible to refuse to pay bail or accept personal recognizance unless it is offered to everyone, including organizers, repeat offenders, out of state residents, and noncooperators.

Communication among the entire group is difficult once processing has begun, so it may be best to maintain bail solidarity with those whom one is in contact during processing. Some protesters may choose to pay bail if, for personal, medical, work or other reasons, they need to be released. Others refuse bail and personal recognizance because both are conditioned upon a promise to return for trial, which implies acceptance of the authority of the criminal justice system to arbitrate guilt or innocence.

Pleas, Trials and Defenses. Defendants may plead guilty, not guilty, nolo contendere (no contest, which means one does not contest the facts), stand mute, or make a "creative" plea. Pleading not guilty will result in a trial date being set. A guilty plea will result in immediate sentencing, unless a special hearing for that purpose is set. No contest may be taken as either guilty or not guilty. A "creative" plea or standing mute is generally entered as not guilty.

Defendants have numerous options for their defenses at trial. They can present a legal defense, showing that the government has failed to prove beyond a reasonable doubt that they did what the complaint alleges. A more political defense could cite the Constitution as justification for what was done, relying on the First Amendment freedoms, for example. Or a defendant could invoke the doctrines of necessity or competing harms. These doctrines state that the action of defendant was warranted to prevent or call attention to a more serious harm. For example, trespass at the Rocky Flats Nuclear Weapons Facility was nec-

I SHARE YOUR CONCERN, GOVERNOR but as a rule we don't give life sentences for tresspassing...

Peg Averill

essary to prevent further production of nuclear warheads, which are designed to destroy life. Surely that is a greater harm than the harm of entering onto restricted property. Defendants have cited international law in their defense. Others make an "offensive" defense, seeking to put the government or offending institution on trial. These defenses work to a greater or lesser degree and are employed primarily for their political impact, not for their efficacy in getting the defendant acquitted, although one can always hope.

Sentencing. At this stage, the defendant has the absolute right to address the court on any issue related to the offense and on any matter which might influence sentencing. Whereas political and moral issues are generally ruled irrelevant during the course of the trial, there is more discretion in presenting them here. The judge will consider a number of factors in sentencing: the defendant's history of civil disobedience, the seriousness of the offense, whether some sort of public service would make more sense than punishment, his or her *own* feelings about the political situation which the action was about (though it's a rare judge who will admit to considering his/her subjective feelings), etc. Defendant may receive a fine, jail time, or a suspended sentence, which means the sentence is not executed unless the condition of the suspension is violated (such as committing the same offense within a particular time period).

Politics of the Legal System

Legal scholars and social apologists

Noncooperation must be approached with conviction and understanding.

Bail is the most graphic example of economic discrimination which pervades the criminal justice system.

Defendants may plead guilty, not guilty, nolo contendere, stand mute, or make a "creative" plea.

The crisis in the legal system lies in the class-biased, racist, and sexist character of social relationships and in the court structure which maintains these relationships.

What happens in court can be anything but solemn and predictable when people take the system into their own hands and demand that it respond to their needs.

No far-reaching transformations of power will ever be achieved in court.

would have us believe that the legal system is a neutral one which arbitrates disputes fairly among conflicting parties. Throughout history, however, unionists, suffragists, civil rights workers, communists, socialists, and anarchists, poor people, nonwhites, lesbians and gay men, and peace and anti-nuclear activists—all have found this not to be the case. In an essay entitled, "Law Against the People," (in an excellent volume of the same title, published in 1971, see "Resource List"), Robert Lefcourt describes the nature of the law:

> *It is not only that the legal apparatus is time-consuming and expensive; that unjust laws remain unchanged; that the Supreme Court has long refused to consider such "political" questions as the continuing wars in Southeast Asia and the exclusion of nonwhites, young and poor people from most juries; and that the legal system has failed to meet the expectations of certain segments of society. The legal system is bankrupt, and cannot resolve the contradictions which, like air pollution, have grown visibly more threatening to society but whose resolution still is not given high priority.* (p. 21)

Lefcourt goes on to say that the crisis in the legal system "lies in the class-biased and racist character of social relationships and in the court structures which maintain these relationships." (I would add 'sexist.')

The courtroom is designed to be a solemn, formal, highly ritualized forum whose complex rules and protocol can be mind-boggling and intimidating to the uninitiated. The language of the law—"legalese," as it is termed—has evolved over hundreds of years and was never meant to make the vagaries of justice transparent to the lay person. Legal per-

sonnel—judges, lawyers, prosecuters—are highly educated, fairly well-to-do professionals whose interests generally lie with the corporate and governmental elite whom they serve.

Political activists have been known to get into court and shake things up quite a bit. What *actually* happens in court can be anything but solemn and predictable when people take the system into their own hands and demand that it respond to their needs. This can be enlightening for court personnel, including clerks and reporters, as well as for the defendants themselves. For some, simply discovering that the judicial proceedings are not *fair* is a shocking and radicalizing experience. Many activists have come of age during their trials for simple trespass or disorderly conduct: they see connections to deeper political issues. Having been in court themselves, they may become more sensitive to the abuse and injustice faced by welfare mothers, tenants, blacks and Latins, and unemployed youth in criminal, housing and family courts.

Organizers need to develop sensitivity and awareness around the issue of class and race privilege as it relates to how nonviolent activists are treated in court. People who commit civil disobedience have tended to be fairly well educated, middle class and white. The courts generally regard them as a cut above the "common criminal" and treat them better. Protesters still get a hard time at the hands of the police, guards, prosecuters and judges and sometimes get stiff penalties. But frequently concessions are made and rules are relaxed. Sometimes people picked up for street crimes wait while dozens of protesters are processed ahead of them. An awareness of this situation is the first step towards breaking through the barriers between consciously political people and everyone else who moves through the criminal justice system.

No far-reaching transformations of power will ever be achieved in court. Rather, progressive court decisions will always reflect transformations that have been won through political organizing, education and consciousness-raising. Law reform has its place within the contest and confines of a broad-based political movement. It comes only after a social and political climate had been created so that the courts have to adjust the legal standards to fit the newly created social reality, a reality won in the streets, schools and factories.

Peg Averill

Controversies

The role of the law and lawyers is a controversial issue within the nonviolent movement, touching on questions of political expediency, cooptation, non-cooperation, elitism and professionalism, and the use of the courts as public forums for social change. These questions are important and complex and have to be considered by each organizing group as the need arises. (Consult the "Resource List" for in-depth discussions of these issues.)

The core of the problem is that all too often the political issue that sparked the demonstration gets lost in the morass of legal proceedings. In recent years, for example, peace and anti-nuclear activists have tried to use their CD trials to get matters of nuclear armaments or plant safety into the public eye. However, existing law says that testimony on low-level radiation and health hazards or international war preparations is not admissible in defense of an occupation or sit-in. It is not relevant or material to the offense, it is said. Nevertheless, defense teams try to get the testimony in. Assuming the press covers the trial at all, the public hears, not the actual scientific and medical data, but rather that the health or war issue has been raised and proofs offered by the defendants, only to have them excluded by the judge.

Important questions of political strategy are involved here because legal battles take lots of time, money and energy. Are they worth it? Continuing with the example of an anti-nuclear protest, should an organization put effort into trying to get a defense of necessity or competing harms allowed in their jurisdiction so that they can prove the facts of nuclear danger in court? Should they do whatever is necessary to get off and get on with their organizing? Would they do better putting energy into direct public education programs, such as slide shows, speaking tours, street theater, pamphlet distribution, etc.? Is a trial necessary to get sufficient public interest so that people will pay any attention to a public education program?

A legal case involves research, motion preparation, factual presentation and affidavits, depositions and interrogatories, court appearances, possibly jury selection, trial preparation, perhaps appeal. Will this lengthy, arduous, and expensive process "burn out" the most committed organizers, thus leaving future organizing to less experienced people? What does this do to an organization?

Finally, does proving something in court reinforce a bankrupt political system, thus undercutting our broader, long-range goals? Or is the interim goal of, say, raising consciousness about nuclear power and weapons so pressing and immediate that we must use whatever forums are available to us to reach people?

Resource List

"Civil Disobedience and Legal Strategy," Scott Kennedy, **WIN** Magazine, June 28, 1979. A discussion of some of the controversial legal issues facing nonviolent activists when they engage in civil disobedience.

Conscience and the Law: A Court Guide for the Civilly Disobedient, William Durland, editor, 1980, 116 pp., Center on Law & Pacifism, $5, A comprehensive volume covering the politics and philosophy of civil disobedience, First Amendment issues, and the court process—pro se, legal research, arrest, trial, defenses, appeal and imprisonment; a good bibliography.

Law Against the People: Essays to Demystify Law, Order and the Courts, Robert Lefcourt, editor. 1971, 400 pp., $2.45 (Vintage). An anthology of radical views on law, with essays on black liberation,. economics and capitalism, women's servitude under the law, civil liberties, the Soledad Brothers, resistance, military law, socialist law and more by Florynce Kennedy, Haywood Burns, Stanley Aronowitz, George Jackson, Arthur Kinoy, Michael Tigar, William Kunstler and others.

The National No Nukes Trial Handbook, the Anti-Nuclear Legal Project. 1980, 50 pp. (available from People's Energy Project Clearinghouse, c/o Massachusetts Lawyers Guild, 120 Boylston St., Rm. 1011, Boston, MA 02116). An excellent do-it-yourself manual designed for pro se defendants which can easily be supplemented with local materials, with sections on preparing for an occupation, arrest, defense, trial preparation, jury selection, presenting your case, etc.

Civil Disobedience Training Handbooks, from the Wall Street Action,

Important questions of political strategy are involved because legal battles take lots of time, money and energy.

Does proving something in court reinforce a bankrupt political system, or is it just another forum for consciousness raising?

Blockade the Bombmakers, or other actions (available from the War Resisters League). These excellent handbooks discuss all the major issues in preparing and carrying out a major civil disobedience action, with sections on noncooperation, doing time and legal considerations.

How to find sympathetic counsel in your area:

Contact local chapters of the National Lawyers Guild or the American Civil Liberties Union, or write to their national offices for names of local attorneys:

NLG, 853 Broadway, New York, N.Y. 10003

ACLU, 132 W. 43 Street, New York, N.Y. 10036

ELECTORAL POLITICS

By Patrick Lacefield

The struggle for social change takes different forms depending on the tenor of the times and the strength of our movement. At one given point, the focus may be on mass demonstrations or direct action. At another time, low-key educational efforts at the grassroots community level may be preferable. None of these are mutually self-exclusive and in fact they often work together to build the growth of the movement. Regardless of all else, when a movement begins to reach a point of real power in the society, it acquires an additional focus: electoral politics.

Among the pacifist left, heavily influenced by a neo-anarchist analysis of state power, to advance electoral politics as an arena of struggle is somewhat akin to praising the Catholic Church as a model for organizational democracy. Electoral politics, the argument goes, is invariably co-optive and strengthens the position of the status quo by acquiescing to and participating in the system. Electoral politics is centered around personalities, not issues, and acts to demobilize progressive activists while delivering only the most incremental of the changes we yearn to see.

Although there is some truth to this perspective on electoral politics, it is skewered by a misreading of American political reality and the value progressive activists have to gain from experience in the electoral arena. The fact is that all positions of power—electorally or non-electorally achieved—are potentially corrupting. Radicals participate in the electoral arena not for reasons of personality nor with an end in mind merely of reform. We are for reforms, but as means toward an end. We support reforms which mobilize and empower the progressive constituencies with which we make common cause if we are to achieve a fundamental transformation of this society. If the electoral system appears an unfavorable arena for our efforts, it is less a reflection of the electoral system than the fact that the society as a whole (and thus *all* arenas) are less than fertile ground.

The franchise—the right to vote for all Americans—was no ruling class ploy handed down to co-opt and divert the Movement from more serious endeavors. This gain, hard-won at the cost of many lives down through the years, is widely judged to be the most effective democratic means of decision-making in a mass industrial society. Most Americans relate to politics through the ballot-box and electoral campaigns. Much as we may rightly bemoan this and argue that politics is much more—community meetings, mass action, street meetings, etc.—the reality remains. One ordinarily does not make the quantum leap in politics from abstention on election day to committing civil disobedience at the Pentagon the morning after. In fact the American electorate is becoming more white, more middle and upper class and much older—and ultimately more conservative—as more and more Black, Hispanic, young and working people are demobilized and fail to participate in electoral politics. This abdicates power to the conservative and rectionary elements since our non-electoral efforts are insufficient on most occasions to affect significantly the course of events.

At every point in which non-electoral

When a movement begins to reach a point of real power in society, it acquires an additional focus: electoral politics.

Among the pacifist left, to advance electoral politics as an arena of struggle is somewhat akin to praising the Catholic Church as a model for organizational democracy.

The right to vote was no ruling class ploy handed down to co-opt and divert the movement from more serious endeavors.

"Before I teach the working class how to aim their bullets, they have to learn how to aim their ballots."

—Eugene Debs

Working in the electoral arena provides activists with valuable skills of fundraising, mobilizing volunteers, coalition politics, and experience in political organization.

In electoral work, you are forced to take to heart the old radical edict to "stop talking just to ourselves."

(or extra-parliamentary, if you will) struggles move beyond protest to politics, they acquire an electoral arm. This was true in the abolitionist movement with the efforts to elect anti-slavery Whigs and Democrats and the eventual formation of the Republican Party as a party of abolition. It made itself known in the formation of the Populist Party and within the Democratic Party during the agrarian unrest of the late 19th century and likewise in the movement for women's suffrage. When the foundations for industrial unionism were laid with the formation of the CIO and the sit-down strikes in the Detroit auto plants, unions discovered their gains through direct action would go for naught if they didn't proceed on the political front to insure the election of friends and allies to positions of authority. The civil rights movement came to have an electoral expression which insured the passage of the Voting Rights Act and fair housing and equal employment opportunity statutes. The battle against the war in Vietnam echoed in the chambers of the Congress and was fought out on electoral battlegrounds all across the country, and in doing so provided for the involvement of millions in the peace movement in their communities.

"Before I teach the working class how to aim their bullets," American socialist leader Eugene Debs observed in the 1920's, "they have to learn how to aim their ballots." Radicals have been involved in electoral work from the beginnings of the Republic—often through one of the major parties (usually the Democratic) and sometimes through the formation of third parties and independent tickets. In Europe, where mass socialist, communist and social-democratic parties contend for power, one finds little credence in anti-electoral sentiments. These parties also engage in politics through mass demonstrations, strikes, and other extra-parliamentary means. In the United States, within the confines of an electoral system skewered to favor a two-party setup with a Presidential system and single-member districts, the deck is stacked against third-party success. The initial successes of the old Socialist Party notwithstanding, the history of third party endeavors has been largely a history of failure.

So, political analysis aside, why should radical activists involve themselves in electoral work? Three reasons immediately come to mind : 1) to gain experience in political organization and techniques, 2) to acquire a solid ground-

ing in coalition-building and coalition politics and 3) to provide an accessible educational forum for ideas and issues.

In any electoral contest, be it on the national, state, or local level, the most important ingredient is political organization. It matters little how attractive your candidate or (in the case of referendums) your issue is if you fail to communicate her/him/it to the public. One way is through the broadcast and print media, and working in press or ad roles in a campaign can give invaluable experience to carry over to extra-parliamentary endeavors. One can acquire a sense of how to work with the media and, through advertising and the production of materials, how to present your issues in a style and format accessible to the public-at-large.

Another important element in political organization is the acquisition of valuable skills such as fundraising and mobilizing volunteers, both vital to the seriousness of any endeavor—electoral or not. In electoral work, you are forced to take to heart the old radical edict to "stop talking just to ourselves." The art of communication and political mobilization is a tactic—used equally with success by Mayor Richard Daley's regime in Chicago and the powerful Socialist Party organization in Milwaukee in the 1910s. In electoral work, you gain an appreciation for such skills as advance work and scheduling for rallies, foot and phone canvassing to turn out your supporters, and the acquired knack for targetting certain areas and constituencies for particular emphases—opportunities unfortunately only rarely brought into play in our non-electoral work today.

If the 1960s and 1970s taught us anything, it was that coalition-building is the means for effecting progressive social change. No one group in and of itself—neither students nor trade unions, minorities nor women—has the resources and wherewithal to make progress alone. The essence of electoral work is—in large part—that difficult process of bringing together people and groups with clout around a common concern, though they may disagree on many issues.

Finally, campaigns—winning or losing—are opportunities for education within a political format to which people are accustomed. You might never gain an invitation to speak to, say, the Brookdale Women's Club or local Machinists lodge under ordinary circumstances, where as an election campaign legitimizes an appearance. Even a losing effort can lay the groundwork for an ongoing political organization around an issue or issues. It may raise consciousness among the electorate and establish your issue as one important enough to be dealt with, to take a stand on. Moreover, it can lay the basis for a successful bid further down the road.

It bears emphasizing that all elections do not center around individual candidates. The device of the referendum and initiative—a holdover from the Progressive Era of the 1910s—allows activists to contest the powers-that-be on issues ranging from nuclear power to progressive taxation, from peace conversion to economic development, from rent control to environmental strictures. These efforts provide the very best of opportunities to bring issues of concern before the public, build working relationships with their constituencies, and battle the vested interests in the public arena. Although progressives are nearly always outspent by those interests by margins sometimes as high as 50-1, notable victories have been recorded, including the spread of rent-control ordinances by an aroused tenants' movement coast-to-coast, and setbacks for nuclear power in Montana, Oregon, Missouri and New Hampshire.

The key point to be made is that our movement cannot afford to yield any arena of conflict to the status quo and the vested interests which form their bulwark. Politically, we have much to gain from participation in electoral politics both in terms of moving this country in the progressive direction and in gaining experience and organizational skills that are applicable elsewhere.

Organizing a Referendum

The oldest adage in politics—making a virtue of necessity as it were—is that "winning isn't everything." True, it isn't everything; "raising issues" through the electoral process is likewise worthwhile. Still, as with other non-electoral efforts, one has to mount a serious effort—a show of strength rather than a display of weakness.

Let's take your average example. Centertown is a city of some 40,000 people—with a state university of 10,000—embroiled in a dispute over tax exemptions given by the city to Antax Corporation. Antax, a viciously anti-union chemical firm, has been given carte blanche by the city to dispose of toxic wastes into the neighboring river—a source of drinking water as well as recreation for the surrounding county. This is over and above what are considered by many to be excessively generous tax giveaways to the firm to coax it into relocating. Efforts through the courts have failed to stop the exemptions or Antax's right to pollute. The city council upheld the city's position by a 5-to-2 count on a straight conservative-liberal split.

Fortunately, the town's by-laws allow for binding referenda on questions such as these. People for A Better Centertown, a citizen's group, is determined to carry the issue to the voters. They start by thoroughly researching the referenda law (number of signatures needed, deadlines, etc.), and outlining a petition campaign through street tabling, door-to-door canvassing and the like to meet the goal of 150 percent of the required number (to allow for invalid signatures).

Even before they've launched the petitioning, they have sought to broaden their base from the initial student/environmental axis to reach out to power centers in the community dissatisfied with the city's handling of Antax. The city councilpeople who voted "nay" are naturals, as are trade unions in the area given Antax's reputation. Hunters and fishermen and their organizations will be opposed to the ruination of the local river, as will boating enthusiasts. The tax giveaways to Antax should rub taxpayers in the city the wrong way. After all they are paying the exemption out of their own pockets and will probably be called upon to shell out at some future point for anti-pollution measures to boot. Without some support from these broader power centers, the referendum will carry the student precincts and that's about all.

This is not to say that students are unimportant. After all Antax and the local business interests, working under the banner of Citizens for Growth and Prosperity are prepared to spend $90,000 to defeat the referendum. Since you won't be able to come anywhere close to that figure, you'll rely on a strong door-to-door canvass operation, along with phone banking and a concerted effort to place lawn signs (reading "Vote YES on Proposition A") in people's front yards. Students, along with unemployed workers and housewives/househusbands, constitute a potentially rich reservoir of the staff time necessary for a good showing.

While your campaign may be outspent, it should be neither outresearched nor outstrategized. When the business

All elections do not center around individual candidates.

The movement cannot afford to yield any arena of conflict to the status quo and the vested interests.

While your campaign may be outspent, it should be neither outresearched nor outstrategized.

Billboard in western Massachusetts, encouraging vote on bilateral nuclear weapons moratorium, 1980.

In any referendum campaign, raising money will be an early priority.

An effort without brief, well-written and well-designed literature for "ordinary people" is destined to go down to an inglorious defeat.

The difference between success and failure may lie in your election day operation.

interests argue for Antax with a plea for jobs and prosperity, you must be able to respond in kind—not with an argument about why those issues are unimportant, but rather with an alternative to and a solid critique of the Antax scheme. By examining past voting patterns you will map out a strategy to allow the maximum impact for your limited resources by, say, turning out higher numbers of voters in the minority and student wards as opposed to the more affluent and conservative areas.

Raising money will be an early priority. Even if People for a Better Centertown is unable to match its opponent's TV blitz, money—and only money—will insure well-designed, professional materials crucial to your effort's credibility in the community. Mimeographed materials may be passable on the campus, but an effort without a brief well-written and well designed—but persuasive— literature for "ordinary people" is destined to go down to an inglorious defeat. Fundraising will also be crucial to advertising in the local paper (particularly important if the paper opposes you editorially) and on the radio (a much better buy for the money than television). Direct mail, if you so choose, is yet another option, though postal rates are making it more costly than radio on a per-voter basis.

Speaking of media, you're going to need a lot of free exposure to counter the opposition's ad blitz. Find several people with both credibility and experience to serve as spokespeople and nab another such individual to serve as press secretary and focus exclusively on wooing the Fourth Estate. Events people should be appointed to ferret out each and every community meeting—no matter how small—and offer them a speaker on this most important of topics. A debate with the opposition is the usual way to sell it.

So, the People for A Better Centertown have done all this: raised about $10,000, done their homework, targetted their resources, drawn in a broad network of opposition to Antax and run a crackerjack volunteer and canvassing operation. On election day, they will just sit back and await the returns, yes?

No.

In fact, the difference between success and failure may lie in their election day operation. If they're smart, they've had someone in charge of election day preparation from the very outset of the campaign. In addition to having poll watchers (particularly important in locales with a history of fraud) the campaign will have workers distributing literature to the voters as they enter the polling place and will have covered the town with their posters (on light poles, etc.) the night before. The phone canvass will have yielded a list of favorable voters who will be called and urged to turn out. In special target areas where a big turnout is desired sound trucks and massive street leafletting will be on the agenda. When the polls close, the long day's work comes to and end and the waiting game for returns begins. If you have played your cards right, you will probably not be embarrassed when the people speak through the returns. The contacts you make and the coalition you bring together could well be the basis for an ongoing single-issue or multi-issue organization which will live to fight another day.

Because this chapter is necessarily shorter than a full treatment the subject deserves, extended reading about the possiblities and techniques of electoral politics is heartily recommended. Among the hundreds of books on the market, the very best are

The People's Guide to Campaign Politics, Gary Robert Schwedes, People's Lobby Press (3456 W. Olympic Blvd., Los Angeles, CA 90019), 1976.

Winning Elections: A Handbook in Participatory Politics, Dick Simpson, Swallow Press (1139 S. Wabash Ave., Chicago, IL 60605), 1974.

Storefront Organizing, Sam Brown, Jr., Pyramid Paperbacks, 1972.

LOBBYING

The variety of legislation that passes through Congress probably in one way or another concerns every citizens group in the country. So, from time to time, organizations incorporate lobbying of appropriate federal, state, and local officials into their program of activities.

There are several ways people can attempt to influence legislation:

- substantial money, gifts, or bribes to elected officials
- favors—political and otherwise
- voting for or against a candidate every 2, 4, or 6 years
- demonstrations
- indirect contact through public statements (e.g., billboards, ads, media editorials, talk shows, letters to the editor)
- direct contact through letters, phone calls, visits and petitions.

The first two ways are beyond our means and ethics, the next three are covered elsewhere in this *Manual*, and the last one is the subject of this chapter.

The first step in any lobbying effort is to become knowledgeable about the issue, and understand the pros and cons. You need to be aware of changes and currents in your issue through access to good news sources. Also being on the mailing list of appropriate Washington-based lobby groups is essential.

Though one person lobbying has some positive effect it is far more important to develop an organized effort of many people. However, the lobbying will be more effective if it appears to be a spontaneous response by many individuals, than if it appears to be coming from a group.

This chapter was pulled together from material by the Friends Committee on National Legislation and the Coalition for a New Foreign and Military Policy.

Letters To Officials

Letters are important not only to try to change views and votes, but affirmative letters help encourage and reinforce the "correct" position of public officials, so that they are less likely to change those views under pressure.

Make your letters brief, clear, and to the point. Begin with a commendation on a past vote or speech, where possible. Support a courageous stand and encourage continued leadership.

Concentrate on one issue and focus on a specific legislative goal. Give reasons for your stand in your own words. The less your letter sounds like a form letter, the better. Cite documented facts, include newspaper clippings, and relevant personal experiences.

Most of the mail received by a Representative or Senator is opened and answered by a staff member. To improve your chance of having the elected official see it, ask a question that cannot be answered by a form letter. The more challenging it is the better chance it has of reaching someone with influence. Also, write a follow-up letter if you're not satisfied with the reply.

On popular issues when the mail volume is especially heavy (particularly to the President), staff members have been known to simply scan letters to see if they are pro or con, and then weigh the pros and cons separately, rather than take the time to count all the letters. So if you wish for your letter to count more, write on heavier paper.

Make your letter timely. Letters sent just prior to subcommittee hearings and key committee and full House or Senate votes are the most effective ways to draw your Congressperson's attention to the issue.

Type your letter if possible, be careful to spell names correctly, and include your return address *on the letter*, since

The first step in any lobbying effort is to become knowledgeable about your issue.

Lobbying will be more effective if it appears to be a spontaneous response by many individuals.

In letters to a Congressperson, ask questions that cannot be answered by a form letter.

Often the depth of conviction can be more persuasive than the words themselves in a personal visit to an elected official.

Petitions are virtually worthless in influencing an elected official.

Postcards and form letters are far less effective than personal letters.

envelopes are often discarded.

Ask to be placed on the mailing list for your Congressperson's newsletter. Most Members distribute newsletters and often send questionnaires soliciting their constituents' opinions.

Personal Visits

You can arrange a meeting with your Congressperson either in Washington or in a local or district office. Most Members are home on the weekends and are often available to meet with a delegation of constituents. Local meetings are usually easier to arrange than Washington visits and more members of your group can generally participate.

To set up a meeting, contact the local office staff or the Washington office. If you have time, send a formal letter requesting an appointment signed by those people comprising the delegation. The more constituents your delegation represents, the better. Be sure to confirm the appointment by phone, and select a spokesperson to make the opening remarks. The best times for Washington visits are before 10 am and after 3 pm Tuesday, Wednesday, and Thursday.

Be on time. Be positive. Be brief. Be fair, but critical if necessary. Try to begin with areas of agreement and commendation for stands of which you approve taken by the Member.

State your views clearly and forcefully. Often the depth of conviction behind the words can be more persuasive than the words themselves. Be specific about what you want your Congressperson to do. Leave a statement or some printed material which summarizes your position.

If the Congressperson is not available, talk to her or his assistant. These people are often very knowledgeable, and quite influential in helping form the Member's views. At least you will have a better opportunity to hear where the Member stands on particular issues as reflected by the assistant's comments.

Other Forms of Contact

Petitions are virtually worthless in influencing an elected official. Their value is primarily as an organizing and educational tool for those who are signing them.

Western Union Personal Opinion Messages allow 15 words and are delivered within 24 hours to the White House or Congress, and cost little. Mailgrams are delivered the next day and allow up to 100 words. Call the Western Union office. These are especially useful just before a vote.

Person-to-person calls, especially if you have had previous contact with the Member, sometimes get through. Try to speak directly to the Congressperson. If you can't, ask for the legislative aide who handles your issue. Again, these are most effective just before a vote. Phone 202-224-3121 and ask for the Member by name.

Postcards and form letters are far less effective than a personal letter.

Some Key Lobby Groups

Friends Committee on National Legislation, 245 Second Street, NE, Washington, DC 20002. *Washington Newsletter* is issued monthly. Broad range of foreign and domestic issues.

Coalition for a New Foreign and Military Policy, 712 G Street SE, Washington, DC 20003.

National Interreligious Service Board for Conscientious Objectors, Suite 600, 800 Eighteenth Street NW, Washington, DC 20006. *The Reporter.* Very good on draft and recruitment issues.

MEDIA

By Grace Hedemann

Working with the media is not glamorous. Find responsible, thorough, energetic, imaginative, objective, informed members of your organization to do the job. Media work should be an integral part of your activities. Those who work with the media in your group should take care to *reflect,* not dictate, the politics of the organization. This media guide outlines the options available to your organization for "hard news" and publicity coverage.

"Hard News"

"Hard news" is that which appears in daily or weekly newspapers, news magazines, and radio and television news programs. Often the distinction between hard news and publicity or feature stories is determined by general interest in a particular subject (nuclear power), urgency or excitement (crime), personalities (stars), strangeness (cults), and difference of opinion (protest). Another element is the urgency of the news presentation and the amount of information available.

Gimmicks to make information or events more attractive may be counterproductive. Very often the gimmick itself becomes the news, not the information which should be treated as news.

Setting Up a Media Operation

Select a media committee (or person) to develop press contacts, media strategy, and a timeline. Have committee members take responsibility for specific tasks. Make sure they are among the most informed members of your group.

They must know how to be concise and to make judgements quickly. They must be accessible to reporters. They should return phone calls promptly, be friendly, open and honest. They should not be ashamed to admit they do not know the answer to a question, but promise to get an answer quickly. They should use common sense and never tell a reporter anything they do not want to see in print. *Nothing is off the record.*

To develop a media list, contact other organizations in the area with similar perspectives for a copy of their list. Monitor radio, television, and newspapers to find those who should be on your list. Check the "Yellow Pages" for listings. Some metropolitan areas produce annual media directories. Call the media to find out the appropriate assignment editors, news editors, and talk show producers. Note the cultural editors for special events you might organize. Call during non-deadline hours.

Put the media list on index cards. Make special notations on each card about deadlines, frequency of publication or air time, previous coverage, type of coverage, editorial slant, names of producers and reporters, etc. Besides the obvious radio stations, daily newspapers, and television stations, keep index cards on wire services (local and national), weekly/neighborhood newspapers, newspaper columnists, some out-of-town newspapers, movement publications (local and national), college and high school newspapers, college radio stations, newsletters of churches, associations, labor unions, and so forth.

For quick duplicating, put all addresses on sheets of labels (usually 33 to a sheet). Keep the master copy, but be sure to revise it periodically. Some copy places can xerox your sheets onto pressure-sensitive labels. For major events when you want to make a lot of media

> Those who work with the media should take care to reflect, not dictate, the politics of the group.

> Very often the gimmick itself becomes the news, not the information which should be treated as news.

> Never tell a reporter anything you do not want to see in print.

phone calls in a hurry, having separate "phone sheets" will be handy. In the left hand column make a list of the media with phone numbers next to each one. Then several volunteers at the same time can make phone calls and keep notes.

Develop delivery routes for news releases. If time is of the essence, car delivery is the fastest. You need two people per route—one to drive and the other to deliver. Make a master copy of each route. If you decide to mail news releases, determine the amount of time it will take the post office to process the mail.

News Release

Legal size (8½ " × 14") or letter size (8½ " × 11") paper can be used for news releases. Always type and double space your releases. If two pages are needed for the release, *collate but do not staple* them together. Design an organizational masthead which features the logo, name and address of the organization. If there is one person who regularly deals with the media that person's name and phone numbers should be printed in the upper right hand corner of the release under a heading "For further information." If no one does this work regularly, then it is better to type this information on the release each time.

On the upper left side of the release, write the date. Underneath the date, write "For immediate release" to indicate to a newsperson they can write the story immediately. If this is not the case, indicate a release date and time "For release after 10 a.m., E.S.T., Monday, February 9, 1981." Gear release dates and times to media deadlines.

Following the release date is the headline which should summarize the story for the convenience of the reporter. This should be typed in upper case letters. For example, PREPARATION FOR MASSIVE WALL STREET CIVIL DISOBEDIENCE ENTERS FINAL STAGES. Beneath the headline should go the dateline (e.g., NEW YORK, October 29), only if the release is being issued in a city other than the one indicated on the masthead. On the bottom of the first page, type "MORE," if the release continues onto a second page. On the top of the second page, list the headline and page number. At the end of the release, type "-30-." If there are any attachments to the release, itemize them on the last page of the release itself; for example, "Attached:

Text of Letter to Chairman of the Board, New York Stock Exchange." It is often helpful to provide the full text of letters, statements, or pertinent documents so that a reporter is not dependent upon quotes within the release itself.

The first paragraph of the release must contain the basics: who, what, where, when, and why. The release should be designed so that paragraphs can be cut from the bottom, but still retain continuity. Releases should be written in journalistic style, with short declarative sentences. Each paragraph should consist of no more than two or three sentences. The release should be written objectively, so that it could be legitimately printed verbatim in the newspaper. Look at articles in good newspapers to develop a sense of writing news releases they would likely print with little editing.

Always describe your organization in the last paragraph. Opinions should appear as quotations of your members. If you discover typos on your final copy and do not have time to retype the release, do not correct them unless related to vital information. Corrections on the original copy, will make the release look like a high school English paper.

News Statement

The news statement is used to provide reporters with a statement by an organization or individual without additional comment or background. The structure is the same as the release. The headline could read, for example, STATEMENT BY CITIZENS HEARINGS FOR RADIATION VICTIMS. There should be an introduction, such as, "The following is a statement issued by the Citizens Hearings For Radiation Victims in response to...." The statement should follow, given in its entirety.

Media Packet

The media packet is a folder containing several items: the release, documents of interest pertinent to the release, possibly a photograph, fact sheets, button or poster. Packets are used for major news conferences, complex subjects, or rallies when the text of speeches and biographical information on speakers should be provided to reporters. Be selective with the materials. Do not put too

The first paragraph of the news release must contain the basics: who, what, where, when, and why.

Opinions should appear as quotations of your members.

The release should be designed so that paragraphs can be cut from the bottom, but still retain continuity.

much in the packet or nothing will be looked at closely.

News Conference

The news conference presents *major* information, and is an opportunity to respond immediately to questions from reporters and requests for further information. Use a room which is well lighted, centrally located for the press, and large enough. The room should be set up with a headtable facing chairs in arena style for reporters. The panel of speakers (no more than four) should sit at the table facing reporters. It is helpful to have a table top lectern for broadcast technicians to affix their microphones. Coffee for the newspeople and water for the speakers is recommended. Provide a media packet with formal statements and miscellaneous documents, such as biographical material on the speakers and, of course, a news release.

Announce the news conference a week prior to the event with a news release. The release should briefly state the subject of the news conference and the panel of speakers. Have the news release delivered to the crews (or shifts) that you want to attend. Call all reporters the day before the news conference to remind them it is taking place.

Limit the time of the news conference. Keep it short with minimal, if any, rhetoric. Statements should be two or three minutes apiece. Also, try to have only two spokespeople present statements. (The rest of the panel can respond to questions.) Remember, the heart of any news conference is the questions.

Print and broadcast media have different needs at a news conference. Be aware and be helpful (electrical outlets, special interviews, etc.). Record all the names of reporters and media present at the conference. Call reporters who could not attend and give a report.

Media Area for Major Events

The media area for a rally or demonstration will be determined by the size of the event, mobility of the event, and whether it is an inside or outside event. Remember the purpose of this area is to allow reporters maximum access to their story, but without disrupting the event. Try to anticipate the needs of the reporter.

For a large rally, estimate the number of reporters you expect to attend. Then designate that area with ropes or saw horses. Use large, neatly printed identification signs at the front right or left of the stage leading into the media area. Break the area into at least two sections: *interview area* removed from the stage, and *viewing area* on the side and in front of the stage. If the stage is elevated high enough, allow reporters access to the entire front stage area; otherwise it should be one side or the other. Reporters need to be able to photograph head on and hear all speeches clearly. If you have the money and the event is large enough, you can always build a special photographers' ramp 20 feet from the stage and approximately 4 feet by 20 feet in size. Let reporters know where the closest phones are located. Provide chairs and refreshments, if possible.

Have separate stairs to the stage for photographers and camera crews to take crowd shots. Arrange interviews for reporters, and coordinate one-at-a-time access to the stage for photographers. Have plenty of copies of the speakers' schedule on hand. Make sure those arranging interviews know whether a particular speaker wishes to be interviewed after s/he speaks. Always have a photographer from your group cover the event for stories in movement journals and for fundraising purposes.

Media credentials can be a problem for the movement organizer. The purpose of checking media passes is to verify reporters' access to a limited area. Set up a media table at the entrance to the media area. For large events it is best to have at least three people check IDs. Have one person check standard media credentials on laminated cards with reporters' name, photograph, and institution. Have two other people check non-credential reporters (e.g., movement publications, freelance reporters and photographers).

To minimize problems with credentials have non-credential reporters OKed by phone prior to the event. Then list their names on special sign-up sheets to be used at the media table. Have all media people sign-in on sheets. Issue media badges after credentials have been OKed to identify reporters for security people. Give out media packets at this time. Media committee members should wear special tags so reporters can identify them when they need assistance.

For a mobile demonstration, media assistance becomes more difficult. Media committee members should wear identification tags, carry clip boards with sign-in sheets, and carry media packets.

The news conference should only be for *major* announcements.

At a rally, break the press area into an interview area and a viewing area.

Media committee members should wear special tags so reporters can identify them when they need assistance.

Some of the media at the May 6, 1979, anti-nuclear rally in Washington, DC. Photo by Grace Hedemann.

During any major event, keep an articulate member of your group at a phone at all times.

Wire services are the most important media in any area.

Always send a separate news release to the ''Daybook'' of the wire services.

Committee members should know where the action will take place and arrange interviews when asked. Depending on the area being covered, have a minimum of two media coordinators. You may want to schedule a news conference on site prior to the demonstration, during the demonstration, or at the courthouse or jail. If civil disobedience will be part of the demonstration, give reporters police officials' names, phone numbers, and responsibilities in regard to the demonstration. Tell reporters the location of the jail and the courthouse, and the most direct route to get to them from the demonstration.

During any major event, keep an articulate member at a phone at *all* times. Media coordinators at the demonstration site should call updates into the office periodically. Many radio stations have small staffs and cannot send reporters to cover news events. They take their stories off the wires or call for a phone interview. Phone interviews are common during civil disobedience actions.

Wire and News Services

Associated Press (AP), United Press International (UPI), Reuters, Religious News Service, Zodiac, Liberation News Service, and others provide news stories, photographs, and audio feeds across the country and around the world to major print and broadcast media. Stories may be transmitted instantaneously, weekly or monthly.

Wire services tend to write very straight, very factual accounts of events with a minimum of flair. They are usually written so that a paper receiving the story can use the whole story, or half, or cut it off after just a paragraph or two, depending on the availability of space and the degree of interest to the subscriber. Many times AP and UPI send stories out in the form of photographs with a long caption.

Wire services are the most important media in any area. If you have limited resources and time, call AP and UPI. Send them a release as a follow up to a phone call, unless over a period of years your organization has developed a working relationship. There are two levels of wire services at AP and UPI. The ''A'' wire is the national service that reaches every subscriber in the country. The local or regional wire reaches subscribers in the area. As part of the local/regional wire, there is a service known as the Daybook. The Daybook lists all major news events to take place in the area. Subscribers check the Daybook every morning before assigning reporters stories for the day. Always send a separate news release to the Daybook, and follow up with a phone call to insure your event will be listed.

If possible, get to know wire editors at local newspapers and broadcast media. If your organization is affiliated with a national organization, let local wire editors know. They then will realize there are local people who would be interested in a particular subject or group. Also, to encourage your story getting on the ''A'' wire, have friendly reporters in cities outside your area call their local wire services requesting the story.

Publicity

Publicity is a term that covers all those

media activities that gain on-going coverage of an issue, or pre-publicity for an event. Listed below are ways a local group can gain publicity. In addition check nationally as well as locally for media organizations that will provide free or minimal fee assistance to social change groups. These organizations can conduct media workshops, develop a media strategy for your group, and even produce slick television public service announcements.

Public Service Announcement

Most organizations use public service announcements (PSAs) to announce upcoming events. They use the same format and time allowed commercial advertisers. PSAs can also be used as part of an issue campaign. Respected leaders from churches, community, labor, consumer, and environmental organizations should be part of a media committee to promote such a campaign.

Radio and TV stations are obligated by the Federal Communications Code to present all sides of controversial issues of public importance, and to correct any imbalance that paid advertising creates. This does not mean the broadcaster will automatically air any PSA that you bring them. It does provide an opening. The respected media committee, especially with an attorney, can be very helpful during face-to-face appointments with public service or community service directors. They can also be helpful filing a formal Federal Communicaton Commission complaint. The print media is not obligated to provide public service space or present balancing views on controversial issues. However, use the same arguments for either medium and emphasize ethics and responsibility, rather than legal obligation with print.

To approach PSAs in a relatively simple way, write a letter to broadcast public service directors describing the organization, its purposes, activities, and why it is important that the station use a PSA. Attach several PSAs. Type and double space the script. On the top left side, list the beginning date, kill date, and length of spot in seconds and words. PSAs on 7½ IPS, ½'' track tape on a 5'' reel in a box are welcomed, but the cost and technical skill required is greater. The advantage of script versus cassette depends on what the local stations prefer. Standard PSAs are 60 seconds (120-150 words), 30 seconds (60-75 words), 20 seconds (45-50 words), and 10 seconds (25-30 words). Send the PSAs at least two weeks prior to beginning date, and follow up with a phone call. Always accompany a tape reel with a written script.

Advertising

Design small ads for alternative publications. Accompany the ad with a cover letter explaining why it is important the ad be placed without charge and describe your organization. Allow six weeks lead time. Do follow up.

If your group decides to run paid advertising in the establishment media, consider the following two ways to raise money. First, ask a local businessperson, who is sympathetic, if they would pay for it. List their name or the name of the business at the bottom of the ad. Second, ask prominent community members to contribute to the cost of the ad and list their names on the ad.

Only pay for advertising after trying to get free space. Ask about special rates for non-profit organizations. All ads should have a coupon with the name, address and phone number of the organization. In addition allow space on the coupon for a donation, request for more information, name and address of respondent.

Mass transit advertising can be very economical, especially if the organization qualifies for non-profit rates. Ads usually run a month and require a minimum number of ads be placed. Check standard size before designing and printing them. Radio advertising during rush hour times can be very effective. Follow PSA format.

Community Bulletin Boards

The Community Bulletin Board is a service provided by daily and weekly newspapers and the broadcast media. Cultural and community affairs forums tend to be the type of events listed. There is no charge. Usually the number of words is limited. Depending on the institution, a standard news release or special format is required. Check out all these details with each publication and broadcaster. Note the appropriate editor, deadline, and format on an index card. Announcements usually must be received two weeks prior to publication. Follow up with a phone call, and clip the

Public service announcements, advertising, and community bulletin boards are additional ways to publicize your activities.

announcement when it runs. Then you will have a good idea which media is worth contacting for other events.

Letters to the editor can be one of the most effective ways to publicize your views, if used effectively by your group.

Letters To the Editor/ Editorial Replies

Keep a clipping file and monitor editorial remarks on the broadcast media. A good clipping file will reflect how events have been covered, give ideas about possible feature stories, and provide the editorial stance of an institution. Take advantage of this information by writing letters to the editor, and replying to broadcast editorials. Encourage members of the group to do the same. Keep clippings in a loose-leaf binder, filed by issue. Respond within three days of the original publication. Rotate letter writers. Review, and reply to national publications as well.

Keep your writing brief and clear. Use short words, short sentences, and short paragraphs. Keep the letter to one idea or issue. This is more effective and increases the chances of the letter being published. Clarity is more important than any other quality. Be positive, not defensive. Double check quotes, facts, and figures. Use good taste. Keep the letter to 100-150 words to minimize editing. These same principles apply to broadcast editorial replies. In addition speak lively and direct into the camera or microphone.

Local talk shows are excellent vehicles for your out-of-town speakers.

Feature Stories and Interviews

Feature stories and interviews are difficult to obtain, but well worth the effort if you succeed. Use your clip file to determine news trends. Develop a story idea that gives depth to fastbreaking news. Approach a friendly reporter about the idea. Give a number of reasons why the story is important and suggest people who could be interviewed. Inform syndicated radio features editors about in-depth story ideas as well.

Once a newspaper is sold on an interview or story, it will assign a reporter and photographer. They will either visit your organization's office or request you visit the paper. Either way it is helpful to prepare a biographical sketch and background material on the subject. Be prepared, responsive, and brief. Do not answer questions which you are not qualified to answer.

Radio and TV Talk Shows

Become familar with local TV and radio talk show programs. Note producers, type of program, time and frequency. Check newspaper listings or the media directory. Make an index card and xerox label on each program. Talk shows are interested in current events, issues, books, and personalities. Some shows specialize in one kind of feature (e.g., entertainment personalities). Local shows are always looking for good speakers, especially those from out-of-town. Be aware of program competition, especially when a well-known speaker is being suggested as a guest.

Get to know program producers personally. Introduce the organization and its activities in person, if possible. If not, write an introductory letter. Include a suggested guest biography and background material on the subject. Then follow up with a phone call. Hand deliver packet to the show's producer. Attempt to develop friendly relations with the producer. Put them on the organization's mailing list and keep them posted on out-of-town speakers and new projects.

Resources

Making the Media Responsive and Responsible, Grace Hane Hedemann, **The Nonviolent Activist,** July-August 1985.

Media Access Action Package, Media Access Project (1609 Connecticut Ave. NW, Washington, DC 20009), 1980.

Talking Back: Public Media Center's Guide To Broadcasting and the Fairness Doctrine for People Who Are Mad As Hell and Aren't Going To Take It Anymore, Jonathan Polansky and Michael Singsen, Public Media Center (466 Green St., San Francisco, CA 94133), 1983.

War, Peace and the News Media, available from War, Peace and the News Media, 1021 Main Building, Department of Journalism, NYU, New York, NY 10003, 1983.

Classroom To Newsroom: A Professional's Guide to Newspaper Reporting and Writing, Terry Murphy, Barnes and Noble, 1983.

Biographical Information

Peg Averill is a freelance artist and cartoonist whose works have been frequently reprinted by Liberation News Service, *WIN* Magazine, *The Nonviolent Activist,* the *Guardian,* and other movement publications. Many of the War Resisters League's posters feature her drawings. She was a founder of Art for People in Washington, DC, as well as a member of the WIN staff (1976–1978).

Chris Brandt began his work in theater as an organizer of street theater for the Aktion 3 Welt in Freiburg, Germany. For the past fourteen years he has worked with the Medicine Show Theatre Ensemble.

Leslie Cagan is a lesbian socialist-feminist activist who works with the national Mobilization for Survival. She has worked with People's Alliance, the Coalition for a Non-Nuclear World, the June 12 (1982) Rally Committee, and the April (1985) Actions Coalition.

David Catanzarite was on the staff of the War Resisters League/West in San Francisco. His primary function there was to develop benefits and other fundraising activities.

Mike Clark is co-director of Student/Teacher Organization to Prevent Nuclear War. Formerly, he was Assistant Director of the Riverside Church Disarmament Program, and he was on staff of the Interfaith Center on Corporate Responsibility.

Jerry Coffin was active in the civil rights and anti-war movements, and was a member of the WRL staff (1969–1973). Among his WRL staff duties was coordination of the local organizing program. Jerry was an organizer for the 1971 May Day actions in Washington, DC, the 1972 ITT demonstration in Manhattan, and the 1978 Moscow-Washington anti-nuclear actions. He has been a member of the WRL Executive Committee and was on the Board of the A.J. Muste Memorial Institute.

Lynne Shatzkin Coffin did anti-war organizing at Syracuse University, was an organizer for the May Day actions in Washington, DC, before joining the WRL staff in 1971. Her duties while on the WRL staff focused on various Indochina war projects and local organizing. She has been a member of the WRL Executive Committee and was on the Board of the A.J. Muste Memorial Institute.

Clay Colt is active with the New England War Resisters League and the anti-War Toys Campaign. He co-edited the 1987 WRL Calendar, "Films for Peace & Justice," and is trying to raise his two sons nonviolently.

Gail Daneker is the co-founder and Associate Director of the Campaign for Peace & Democracy/East and West. Formerly, she was on the staff of the Institute for Community Economics and was co-director of Environmentalists for Full Employment.

George Dear, until his death in June 1985, was an activist in the War Resisters League, Illinois Citizens for Better Care, Gray Panthers, and was staff person for the Midwest Committee for Military Counseling.

Ruth Dear is on the War Resisters League National Committee, active in the Pledge of Resistance, Gray Panthers, and local peace work.

Kate Donnelly is working with War Resisters League/New England on the Anti-War Toys Campaign, and has a movement button and bumper sticker business. She co-edited the 1987 WRL Calendar, "Films for Peace & Justice." She was an organizer for the Women's Pentagon Actions and the Women's Encampment.

William Douthard was a member of the WRL Executive Committee from 1973 until his untimely death in 1981. His organizing began in 1960 with the Congress of Racial Equality in Birmingham, Alabama, and then the Southern Christian Leadership Conference. He was also a national coordinator of the People's Coalition for Peace and Justice, and was on the Board of the A.J. Muste Memorial Institute.

Dan Ebener was Director of Interfaith Activities for the Fellowship of Reconciliation from 1979 to 1983. He also worked with the FOR local and regional organizing program. From 1976 until he joined the FOR staff he was in charge of the social ministry program of the Catholic Charities Archdiocese in Dubuque, Iowa.

Carol Ehrlich was a founding member of the Great Atlantic Radio Conspiracy and the magazine *Social Anarchism.* She now works with a variety of local feminist groups and is the editor of *Womyn's Express.*

Howard J. Ehrlich is a member of the Great Atlantic Radio Conspiracy and is the editor of *Social Anarchism.* He serves on the board of Nuclear Free America.

Meg Gage is Executive Director of the Peace Development Fund. Before that she was a high school teacher for ten years, and is currently on her local school committee. She is involved in numerous movement activities in western Massachusetts, which have included the Traprock Peace Center and the Clamshell Alliance. Meg is the mother of two children.

Ed Hedemann has been on the WRL staff since 1973. His primary duties have been working with local groups, disarmament, war tax resistance, draft and counter-recruitment, and organizing issues. He was an organizer for the Continental Walk for Disarmament and Social Justice, the 1978 Sit-in for Survival, among other projects. He edited the *Guide to War Tax Resistance.* Ed refused induction into the military in 1969, has been a tax resister since 1970, and was one of the founders of the Austin (Texas) WRL local group.

Grace Hane Hedemann served on the WRL national staff from 1973 to 1985. She coordinated the annual WRL Training Program for organizers and handled local organizing and media relations. Grace was media coordinator for the 1976 Continental Walk, 1978 Sit-in for Survival, and the 1979 Wall Street Action among other projects. She was a founder of Direct Action/Austin WRL in 1970. Currently, Grace is the Managing Editor of *The Report in the Americas,* a bimonthly magazine published by NACLA (The North American Congress on Latin America).

Valerie Heinonen is on staff of the Interfaith Center on Corporate Responsibility.

Randy Kehler was on staff of War Resisters League/West in San Francisco from 1967 until his imprisonment in 1970 for induction refusal. After two years in prison he spent nine years in rural Franklin County in western Massachusetts organizing around local energy, agricultural, economic, and disarmament issues. From 1981 to 1984 Randy was national coordinator for the Nuclear Freeze Campaign. He has since returned to rural western Massachusetts.

Patrick Lacefield was on the national field staff of the 1976 Fred Harris Presidential campaign. He was the founder of the Columbia (Missouri) FOR/WRL, and was the national organizer for the March 22, 1980, anti-draft march and rally in Washington, DC. Patrick is the author of *El Salvador and Central America in the New Cold War.* He has worked with the New York City Democratic Socialists of America, and Americans for Democratic Action.

Steve Ladd was on staff of War Resisters League/West from 1974 to 1982. In 1982 he became an organizer for the northern California Nuclear Weapons Freeze Campaign. He has worked with the UC Nuclear Weapons Labs Conversion Project, Nuclear Weapons Facilities Task Force, and Survival Summer. Before joining the WRL/West staff, he was a draft resister and helped organize the Berkeley Peace Brigade.

George Lakey was a founder of the Movement for a New Society. He is author of *Strategy for a Living Revolution,* co-author of *A Manual for Direct Action,* and co-author of *No Turning Back: Lesbian and Gay Liberation in the 80s.* George teaches peace and social change at Haverford College. He is the father of three children.

Lauri Lowell is a non-practicing member of the New York State Bar. She was the legal coordinator for the mass civil disobedience actions at Shoreham (1979) and Wall Street (1979). She was a member of the WIN Magazine collective from 1977 to 1980.

David McReynolds has been on the WRL staff since 1960 and has been a member of the Socialist Party, USA, even longer. He ran as the SP Presidential candidate in 1980, but lost. David's main functions on WRL staff are writing, speaking, and working with coalitions. The issues he works with are disarmament, foreign policy, and the international movement. He is chairperson of the War Resisters' International. David is the author of *We Have Been Invaded by the 21st Century.*

Helen Michalowski was a member of the WRL/West staff until 1981. Her primary program issues were feminism and nonviolence, counter-recruitment and the draft. She is co-editor of *Power of the People.*

Susan Pines was a member of the War Resisters League staff from 1980 to 1985. She was a primary organizer for the 1980 Women's Pentagon Action, the WRL Women and Militarism Conference (1981), the WRL Feminism Conference (1985), and the April Actions Coalition (1985). Currently she is on the WRL Executive Committee.

David Richards was a student at the Martin Luther King, Jr., School for Social Change.

Charles Walker is a long-time activist, nonviolence trainer, and writer of books and numerous articles on all aspects of nonviolent action. He worked for many years in India with the peace and human rights movements. In this country he has worked with civil rights, anti-Vietnam War, and antinuclear movements. Currently, he is the Director of the Gandhi Institute in Cheyney, PA.

Donna Warnock was the feminism and nonviolence program coordinator on the War Resisters League/West staff. She was the founder of Feminist Resources on Energy and Ecology in Syracuse. She is the co-author of *Nuclear Power and Civil Liberties: Can We Have Both?* Currently, she leads workshops in multiple cultural alliance building, and disarmament and feminism issues. Donna lives in Oakland, California.

Dorie Wilsnack is on the national staff at the Mobilization for Survival. Formerly she was fundraiser at War Resisters League/West and co-director of the Agape Foundation in San Francisco. She is on the Council of the War Resisters' International and the Executive Committee of WRL.

War Resisters League

Believing war to be a crime against humanity, the War Resisters League advocates Gandhian nonviolence to create a democratic society free of war, racism, sexism, and human exploitation. The radical pacifism of the League is an effort to use education and nonviolent actions to deal with the complex political, social, economic, and psychological causes of war.

Even where there seems to be "peace," quiet deaths from starvation, poverty and disease that strike down peasants in Latin America, sharecroppers in Mississippi, unemployed miners in Appalachia, and babies in Harlem are as real and deadly as battlefield deaths from bullets and bombs.

Feminist thinking has brought a better understanding of the connections between militarism and sexism. It is not surprising that in a society which equates masculinity with domination, wars should develop. The spirit and style of feminism offers a striking alternative to the military psychology of America which stresses competition and aggressive (even violent) behavior.

The War Resisters League views nonviolence as an experiment, which, because it is different seems radical, and yet is necessary for survival. Our job is developing ways of social change which bring justice without the injustice and tragedy of violence. Pacifists are not looking for power—but for ways of changing society so it is a better place for all. We believe in involving as many people as possible in decisions about their own lives. Nonviolence makes this possible.

War Resisters League Local Groups*

NATIONAL OFFICE
339 Lafayette Street
New York, NY 10012

WRL/West
85 Carl Street
San Francisco, CA 94117

WRL/Southeast
604 West Chapel Hill Street
Durham, NC 27701

WRL/New England
PO Box 1093
Norwich, CT 06360

CALIFORNIA

WRL/Southern California
c/o Janet Johnstone
541 N. Gower
Los Angeles, CA 90004

Santa Barbara WRL
PO Box 22042
Santa Barbara, CA 93121

San Francisco/Oakland WRL
85 Carl Street
San Francisco, CA 94117

WRL/Redwoods
215A South Main Street
Ukiah, CA 95482

Northcoast WRL
1740 Buttermilk
Sunny Brae, CA 95521

COLORADO

Foothills WRL
c/o Barbara Alire
3024 Ross Drive #A-4
Ft. Collins, CO 80521

GEORGIA

Atlanta WRL
382 Mell Avenue NE #2
Atlanta, GA 30307

ILLINOIS

Oak Park WRL
PO Box 3003
Oak Park, IL 60303

MICHIGAN

Detroit WRL
3937 Avery
Detroit, MI 48208

MISSOURI

St. Louis WRL
438 N. Skinker Blvd.
St. Louis, MO 63130

NEW JERSEY

Monmouth County WRL
17 Riverview Avenue
Long Branch, NJ 07740

NEW YORK

New York City WRL
339 Lafayette Street
New York, NY 10012

Long Island WRL
331 Terry Road
Hauppauge, NY 11788

PENNSYLVANIA

Philadelphia WTR/WRL
2208 South Street
Philadelphia, PA 19146

TEXAS

Dallas WRL
1507 A South Ervay
Dallas, TX 75215

Houston Nonviolent Action/WRL
850 Jaquet
Bellaire, TX 77401

Red River Peace Network/WRL
1022 West 5th Street
Austin, TX 78703

UTAH

Utah WRL
2774 Wardway Drive
Salt Lake City, UT 84124

VERMONT

Green Mountain WRL
PO Box 693
Wells, VT 05774

WASHINGTON

Registration & Draft Counseling Center/WRL
221 South G Street #B
Tacoma, WA 98405

WEST VIRGINIA

Morgantown WRL
PO Box 744
Morgantown, WV 26505

as of January 1986

Index